A Textbook of

Ḥadīth Studies

A Textbook of

Ḥadīth Studies

Authenticity, Compilation, Classification and Criticism of Ḥadīth

Mohammad Hashim Kamali

THE ISLAMIC FOUNDATION

Published by

The Islamic Foundation
Markfield Conference Centre
Ratby Lane, Markfield
Leicestershire, LE67 9SY, United Kingdom
E-mail: publications@islamic-foundation.com
Website: www.islamic-foundation.com

Quran House, P.O. Box 30611, Nairobi, Kenya

P.M.B. 3193, Kano, Nigeria

Distributed by
Kube Publishing Ltd.
Tel: +44 (01530) 249230, Fax: +44 (01530) 249656
E-mail: info@kubepublishing.com

2nd impression, 2009/1430 H

British Library Cataloguing-in-Publication Data

Kamali, Mohammad Hashim
A textbook of Hadith studies: authenticity, compilation, classification and criticism of Hadith
1. Hadith – Criticism, interpretation, etc.
I. Title II. Islamic Foundation (Great Britain)
297.1'2406

ISBN 978 0 86037 450 3 *casebound*
ISBN 978 0 86037 435 0 *paperback*

Printed and bound in Great Britain by
CPI Antony Rowe, Chippenham, Wiltshire

Cover/Book design & typeset: Nasir Cadir

بسم الله الرحمن الرحيم

Contents

About the Author

BORN in Afghanistan in 1944, Mohammad Hashim Kamali is currently Professor of Islamic law and jurisprudence and Dean of the International Institute of Islamic Thought and Civilization at the International Islamic University Malaysia, Kuala Lumpur. He studied law at Kabul University where he also served as Assistant Professor, and subsequently as Public Prosecutor with the Ministry of Justice. He completed his LL.M in comparative law, and Ph.D in Islamic law at the University of London, 1972 and 1976 respectively. Following a period of employment with the BBC World Service, Dr. Kamali served as Assistant Professor at the Institute of Islamic Studies, McGill University in Montreal, and later as a Research Associate with the Social Sciences and Humanities Research Council of Canada. He was a Visiting Professor at Capital University, Columbus, Ohio where he served as a member of the International Legal Education team in 1991. He was a Fellow of the Institute for Advanced Study Berlin, Germany, 2000-2001. He served as a member of the Constitutional Review Commission of Afghanistan, May-September 2003, during which period he was appointed as a member of its Executive Board and subsequently as its Interim Chairman. He is a Fellow of the International Institute of Islamic Thought, and is currently on the International Advisory Board of eight academic journals published in Malaysia, USA, Canada, Kuwait, India, and Pakistan. In May and June 2004 he served as a consultant on constitutional reforms in the Maldives. He is currently a *Sharīʿa* advisor with the Securities Commission of

Malaysia. Professor Kamali has participated in over 100 national and international conferences, published 13 books and over 80 academic articles. He delivered the Prominent Scholars Lecture Series No. 20 at the Islamic Research and Training Institute in Jeddah, Saudi Arabia, 1996. His books, *Principles of Islamic Jurisprudence* (Cambridge, and K.L., 1991 and 1998); *Freedom of Expression in Islam* (Cambridge, and K.L., 1997 and 1998) and *Islamic Commercial Law: An Analysis of Futures and Options* (Cambridge, and K.L., 2001) are used as reference books in leading English-speaking universities worldwide. He received the Ismāʿīl al-Faruqī Award for Academic Excellence twice, in 1995 and 1997, and he is listed in leading *Who's Who in the World.*

Preface

MOST of the existing works on Ḥadīth in the English language I have seen are preoccupied with historical developments concerning ḥadīth and the debate over its authenticity. One finds little on the traditional coverage of ḥadīth studies (*ʿulūm al-ḥadīth*) and the methodology that ḥadīth scholars have employed to verify the reliability of ḥadīth. There is a wealth of literature on ḥadīth methodology and sciences in the Arabic language. The picture here is almost the opposite in that nearly every Arabic work on ḥadīth can be expected to offer a substantial coverage of ḥadīth methodology and take little interest in the history of ḥadīth and the debate over its authenticity. Only in recent decades, Arab and Muslim writers generally, and those with a western experience in particular, have addressed issues that feature prominently in the 20th-century writings of western origin concerning the *Sunna* and ḥadīth. The present volume does not propose to delve into historical developments as the English reader of ḥadīth can obtain this in the existing works. I have instead focused on the jurisprudence of ḥadīth, if I may use the expression, and have tried to offer, in a textbook format, the traditional coverage of ḥadīth methodology. One predecessor to my work that comes to mind is Muhammad Zubayr Siddiqi's *Ḥadīth Literature* (1961) which has partially covered the subject but is still inclined somewhat to treat the historical aspects of ḥadīth studies. His book was written at a time when interest in the more technical aspects of ḥadīth literature might have been somewhat limited among the English readers of Islam. That situation has changed, particularly in view of the existence now of the demand for more specialised works that offer a fuller treatment of ḥadīth studies. The emergence in recent decades of Islamic universities and institutions in several Muslim countries, including Malaysia and Pakistan, which offer full courses on ḥadīth in the English language, has underscored the need for English textbooks on Islamic disciplines. The present volume is an attempt to provide a reasonably manageable text for intermediate to advanced level study of ḥadīth methodology and literature, commonly known as *ʿulūm al-ḥadīth*. The approach I have taken in writing this work is somewhat similar to that of my *Principles of Islamic Jurisprudence* which I wrote some fifteen years ago on *uṣūl al-fiqh*. This has been very well received in Malaysia and English-speaking universities worldwide. I hope that the present text on ḥadīth studies will also make a favourable impact on the academic community here in Malaysia and abroad.

Following its publication in Kuala Lumpur (2000), Dr. Asiah Yaacob, of the Department of Qur'ān and *Sunna*, International Islamic University Malaysia reviewed this book and made the following remarks:

> Professor Dr. Mohammad Hashim Kamali has quenched the thirst of those who yearn for such a work. The book covers all the salient features of ḥadīth studies and is presented in a challenging style.... One novel feature of the book is Kamali's reform proposal, which is appended together with the conclusion. Most of his concerns are genuine... it is an essential reference work. I am sure that students and teachers alike will benefit immensely from Kamali's scholarly Discourse.

I would like to record a note of appreciation to my colleagues and students at the faculty of law of the International Islamic University Malaysia for their input and contribution to this work. I have worked here since 1985 and was able over the years to concentrate on writing and research in a congenial working environment. Associate Professor Dr. Nik Ahmad Kamal, the present Dean of the Faculty of Law has been helpful and supportive. The staff of the IIUM main library have also kindly assisted me with my frequent enquiries and I wish to thank them for their help. And last but not least I take this opportunity to thank Professor Mohammad Kamal Hassan, the IIUM Rector, for his interest in my academic work and his unfailing support to advance the culture of enquiry and research at this University.

1. The reader may be reminded that an Introductory discussion on ḥadīth terminology (*muṣṭalaḥ al-ḥadīth*) including an explanation of basic terms can be found in chapter eight below.
2. The Arabic term, *uṣūl al-ḥadīth*, has been employed by some authors, yet despite its accuracy and the more consolidated view of the discipline that it conveys, it has not become a standard terminology, and it is not as frequently employed as *ʿulūm al-ḥadīth*.
3. We prefer to use the simple and more generic English term 'ḥadīth studies', and utilise both *ʿulūm al-ḥadīth* and *uṣūl al-ḥadīth* as its Arabic variants.

Mohammad Hashim Kamali
International Islamic University Malaysia
July 2004

Transliteration Table

Consonants. Arabic

initial: unexpressed medial and final:

ء	ʾ	د	d	ض	ḍ	ك	k
ب	b	ذ	dh	ط	ṭ	ل	l
ت	t	ر	r	ظ	ẓ	م	m
ث	th	ز	z	ع	ʿ	ن	n
ج	j	س	s	غ	gh	هـ	h
ح	ḥ	ش	sh	ف	f	و	w
خ	kh	ص	ṣ	ق	q	ي	y

Vowels, diphthongs, etc.

Short:	ــَ a	ــِ i	ــُ u
long:	ــَا ā	ــِي ī	ــُو ū
diphthongs:		ــَوْ aw	
		ــَيْ ay	

[01] Introduction

ḤADĪTH studies in the title of this book refer mainly to ḥadīth methodology and criteria that seek to verify accuracy of the text and authenticity of ḥadīth. My treatment of the ḥadīth and its methodology is somewhat selective and does not propose to cover all of the numerous areas of this discipline; it does, nevertheless, attempt to cover most of the important headings of ḥadīth studies, commonly known as *ʿulūm al-ḥadīth*. A great deal of what is presented in this book is concerned with the methods of enquiry and principles which the ḥadīth scholars have formulated for verifying the authenticity of ḥadīth and accuracy of its message. "Jurisprudence of ḥadīth" might be said to be an equally acceptable equivalent in English of *ʿulūm al-ḥadīth*, which is, however, not usually employed in the relevant literature.

One of the main objectives of methodology, whether in the sphere of ḥadīth or other disciplines of learning, is to develop objective and scientific standards of enquiry and research. The purpose is to ensure adequate safeguards against subjectivity and error that might compromise reliability of the results of that enquiry. Methodological guidelines are particularly important to areas of research that involve value judgement and personal preference of the researcher, and also commitment to certain hypotheses in research. Religion is one such area where development of objectivity and impartial methods are at once difficult and most valuable. Muslim jurists and *ʿulamāʾ* have developed elaborate methodologies for the authentification of ḥadīth with the purpose precisely to enhance the scope of scientific objectivity in their conclusions. This they have done in full awareness that in no other branch of Islamic learning has there been as much distortion and forgery as in ḥadīth.

Objective knowledge is that knowledge which is open to public verification, and this is held to be true, in the modern world, of imperical knowledge, which can be accessed and verified by the public. The Islamic perception of objectivity and objective knowledge tends to differ, however, in that access, experimentation and whether or not it is verifiable by most people are not the defining elements of objective knowledge, although they remain to be relevant. Objectivity in the Islamic context is measured by impartiality, universality and justice. Objective knowledge is thus knowledge that internalises these qualities. Impartiality, and justice in knowledge, as in many other domains of human achievements, are noble qualities and Islamic scholarship has been very much concerned with the cultivation and acquisition of these qualities. "Compared to many other civilizations," wrote Osman Bakar, "Islamic civilisation has been quite successful in manifesting these qualities in the different domains of knowledge."[1] In the area of comparative religion, for example, the degree of scientific objectivity attained by medieval Muslim scholarship, as demonstrated, for example, in al-Bīrūnī's tenth-century study of the Indian religion, is yet to be surpassed.[2] Bakar elaborated that an area of knowledge is not considered more objective, from the Islamic viewpoint, than any other simply because it is verifiable by a greater number of people. Objectivity in Islam is inseparable from the religious consciousness of *tawḥīd*. Being created in the image of God, man seeks to emulate the divine qualities of the Creator. To be objective is, in a sense, to emulate God. Man is capable of objectivity because of the endowment in his nature of the divine qualities of impartiality and justice. Thus, there is "an important conceptual relationship between scientific objectivity and religious consciousness."[3] The Islamic intellectual tradition recognises many levels of objective truth. Physical, mathematical and metaphysical truths are objective in nature. Objectivity is also possible in non-imperical knowledge, such as in the religious, philosophical and metaphysical knowledge, precisely because man is endowed with the higher faculties of intellectual discernment, impartiality and justice.

Personal motives, sectarian bias, political, scholastic and theological factors had been known, from very early times, to have prompted misguided individuals to fabricate ḥadīth in order to advance their particular and partisan objectives. We also note that the twentieth-century scholarship on ḥadīth that has originated in the works of some orientalists is no less controversial in its sweeping generalisations that tend to further undermine the credibility of ḥadīth.

Moved by an acute sense of responsibility and the desire to safeguard the *Sunna* of the Prophet, peace be on him, against prejudice and error, the *ʿulamāʾ* have undertaken painstaking efforts to verify the authenticity of ḥadīth. Their tireless travellings and interviews, on a massive scale, for that purpose enabled them not only to obtain information on ḥadīth, but also impressed upon them the difficulty of the challenge they faced over the endless possibilities of error in the accurate rendering of ḥadīth. The methodology of ḥadīth, or *uṣūl al-ḥadīth*, that was developed as a result plays a roughly similar role in relation to ḥadīth as that of the *uṣūl al-fiqh* in relation to *fiqh*. The principal objective of both the *uṣūl al-fiqh* and *uṣūl al-ḥadīth* was to provide a set of methodological guidelines that ensured propriety in the exercise, in the case of *uṣūl al-fiqh*, of legal reasoning and *ijtihād*, and in relation to ḥadīth, to ensure authenticity in the text and transmission of ḥadīth.

Uṣūl al-fiqh and *uṣūl al-ḥadīth* also overlap to some extent, with reference especially to the study of *Sunna* and ḥadīth, which is a common theme in both these disciplines. It is of interest to note that the origins of *uṣūl al-ḥadīth* are traced back to al-Shāfiʿī (150-205 AH), who is also known as the chief architect of *uṣūl al-fiqh*.[4] The solitary ḥadīth, or *al-khabar al-wāḥid*, was a major theme of al-Shāfiʿī's pioneering work on *uṣūl al-fiqh*, the *Risāla*, which has by common acknowledgement earned him the epithet, '*Nāṣir al-Sunna*', the champion of *Sunna*. Yet it seems that neither al-Shāfiʿī's initial work on ḥadīth, nor the methodology of *uṣūl al-fiqh* as a whole, were enough to finally tackle the problem over the authenticity of ḥadīth. The ḥadīth apparently represented a special case, and a separate methodology for it was needed to address issues that could not be adequately dealt with within the framework of *uṣūl al-fiqh*. We do not have, for instance, a separate methodological discipline such as *uṣūl al-Qurʾān*, and what we have by way of methodology in *uṣūl al-fiqh* that relates to the Qurʾān is deemed to be sufficient. There was no pressing need for any elaborate methodology concerning the Qur'ān, due evidently to the undisputed authenticity of the text of the Qur'ān. Had there been accurate documentation of ḥadīth, as there is of the Qur'ān, there would have been little reason for a separate discipline in the name of *uṣūl al-ḥadīth*, and *uṣūl al-fiqh* would have presumably been sufficient for what it offered by way of methodology on the *Sunna*.

It seems that methodology operates best at a level of generalisation which entails a certain disassociation with particularity and individualised detail. This is perhaps a weakness of methodology in reference especially to social sciences and religion. A total preoccupation with objectivity and scientific method may prove to be a weakness of methodology in these areas. One can imagine, for example, that one may apply the rules of *uṣūl al-ḥadīth* and disqualify a ḥadīth that may well be authentic. Conversely, it would also seem possible to authenticate a ḥadīth on grounds of methodology that may, upon specific inquiry and research, prove to be spurious. The advice of caution that this analysis conveys is that one should not expect imperviable results through the application of a certain methodology to ḥadīth. This is another way of saying, perhaps, that the development of even a separate and a fairly rich discipline of *ʿulūm al-ḥadīth* has not eliminated all doubt over the question of authenticity in ḥadīth. This may also explain perhaps as to why we find the methodological rules of *ʿulūm al-ḥadīth* to be laden with subsidiary and exceptional rules, which might have been designed to make up for the possible weaknesses of the methodology they were applying. Is this not reflected in the fact, for instance, that the *ʿulūm al-ḥadīth* consist of over fifty, and according to some estimates, close to a hundred separate branches of learning! Some *ʿulamā'* have attempted to refer to all of these under the consolidated term, *ʿIlm uṣūl al-ḥadīth*, or simply *uṣūl al-ḥadīth*, that is, the jurisprudence of ḥadīth. Sometimes *muṣṭalaḥ al-ḥadīth*, and *ʿIlm dirāyat al-ḥadīth* are used as equivalent terms. Yet many of the leading writers on the subject such as al-Ḥākim al-Nīsābūrī's (d. 405 H), *Maʿrifat ʿUlūm al-Ḥadīth*, and Abū ʿAmr ʿUthmān b. ʿAbd al-Raḥmān b. al-Ṣalāḥ's (d. 643 H) *ʿUlūm al-Ḥadīth* have retained in these terms the pluralist feature of the ḥadīth sciences. Some *ʿulamā'* of the later ages, such as Jalāl al-Dīn al-Suyūṭī (d. 911 H), have preferred the term *ʿilm dirāyat al-ḥadīth*. *Uṣūl al-ḥadīth* is concerned with reliability of the narrators of ḥadīth and the subject matter of their narration, and evaluates their strengths and weaknesses to determine the authenticity of a reported ḥadīth as being the true utterance of the Prophet. The upright character and retentiveness of the narrator and the authenticity at every link of the chain of *isnād* are the main focus of the scrutiny that is proposed by the methodology of *uṣūl al-ḥadīth*.

Unlike the *uṣūl al-fiqh,* which is consolidated well enough to be commonly recognised as the legal theory of the sources, the *ʿulūm al-ḥadīth* is itemised and diverse – as if the *ʿulamā'* have tried to combine the two conflicting needs of an objective methodology, which was provided, but then had to be sub-divided into as many divisions as pragmatism and concern for particularity might have dictated. This has, in my opinion, added to the resourcefulness of *ʿulūm al-ḥadīth*, although at the expense, perhaps, of some compromise on consolidation. My overview of the methodology of ḥadīth in the following pages will hopefully show that we are not really short of an adequate methodology for ḥadīth, but there may be uncertainties as to whether it was developed early enough in time and was actually employed in a holistic manner to deliver its desired results. The present study does not seek to address every aspect of the methodology of *ʿulūm al-ḥadīth*, but attempts instead to present its most important features.

I begin this presentation with the reception and delivery (*taḥammul wa adā'*) of ḥadīth, to be followed in the succeeding two sections by the compilation of ḥadīth and methods that were employed in the documentation of ḥadīth from early times. Section four expounds ḥadīth literature and introduces the major ḥadīth collections, which is followed in turn by a discussion of the biographies of ḥadīth transmitters (*ʿilm tārīkh al-ruwāt*), and then a section on ḥadīth terminology, or *muṣṭalaḥ al-ḥadīth*. Section seven addresses the subject of forgery in ḥadīth (*waḍʿal-ḥadīth*), which is followed, in the next section, by impugnment and validation (*al-jarḥ wa'l-taʿdīl*). This last is mainly concerned with ḥadīth criticism and methods that the *ʿulamā'* have applied to expose weaknesses in both the transmission and subject matter of ḥadīth. The discussion over the criticism of ḥadīth is then continued, in sections nine and ten, under the two separate headings of *ʿilal al-ḥadīth* (hidden defects of ḥadīth) and *tadlīs* (concealment). The fairly detailed discussion of these two themes that is attempted fits in well with the main purpose of this study, which is to provide some insight into how the *ʿulamāʾ* have developed their resources in order to preserve and safeguard the authenticity of ḥadīth. This is followed in the next four sections by *mukhtalif al-ḥadīth* (conflict in ḥadīth), *ʿilm gharīb al-ḥadīth* (unfamiliar expressions in ḥadīth), *al-nāsikh wa'l-mansūkh fi'l-ḥadīth* (the abrogator and abrogated in ḥadīth), and *ziyādāt al-thiqāt* (additions to ḥadīth by reliable narrators), respectively.

Sections fifteen to eighteen expound the various classifications of ḥadīth. The discussion here looks into classification of ḥadīth into the three categories of Sound (*Ṣaḥīḥ*), Fair (*Ḥasan*), and Weak (*Ḍaʿīf*), the criteria of this classification, and how it relates to other classifications of ḥadīth which are reviewed in the succeeding two sections. The next chapter addresses the subject of confirmation and follow-up (*al-Mutābiʿ wa'l-Shāhid*) especially of *aḥādīth* (pl. of ḥadīth) that are transmitted by a single narrator and in need therefore of confirmation in order to be accepted. This is followed in the succeeding section by the prerequisites of authenticity that must be met by every ḥadīth that constitutes a valid basis of judgement. The discussion here reviews qualifications of the narrators of ḥadīth, conditions that must be fulfilled by a valid chain of transmission (*isnād*) and those that must be met by the text (*matn*) of ḥadīth. The book ends with a conclusion and a review of modern reformist opinion on some new projects that need to be undertaken in order to purify the existing ḥadīth literature from doubtful and unwarranted accretions.

ʿUlūm al-ḥadīth is basically concerned with methods and principles that ascertain the conditions of transmission and text (*sanad wa matn*) of ḥadīth from the two perspectives of narration (*riwāya*) and meaning (*dirāya*). The former is concerned with ensuring authenticity at the source and accuracy in the transmission and reporting of ḥadīth so as to prevent distortion and error, deliberate or otherwise, in ḥadīth transmission. The *ʿilm al-dirāya* is chiefly concerned, on the other hand, with the accuracy of the text of ḥadīth by paying attention to all the nuances of the language and purpose of the text as well as any ruling it might contain. There is a greater scope in this part for the jurist and *faqīh* in regard to the deduction of the rules of *Sharīʿa* from the language of ḥadīth, whereas the *ʿilm al-riwāya* may be said to be the concern mainly of the traditionist, or *muḥaddith*. Yet these two aspects of the ḥadīth sciences cannot be meaningfully separated from one another. Both are equally important in gaining knowledge of the *Sunna* and the rules of *Sharīʿa* that it contains. Some of the branches of *ʿulūm al-ḥadīth* that are concerned mainly with the transmission (*riwāya*) and look more into the *isnād* are *ʿilm tārīkh al-ruwāt* (biographies), *ʿilm al-jarḥ wa'l-taʿdil* (impugnment and validation), confirmation and follow-up (*al-mutābiʿ wa'l-shāhid*) and branches that focus on the exact identification of the narrator. Four other branches of ḥadīth sciences that relate more closely to the text or *matn* of ḥadīth are *ʿilm gharīb al-ḥadīth* (unfamiliar expressions in ḥadīth), *ʿilm mukhtalif al-ḥadīth* (conflict in ḥadīth), additional segments in ḥadīth (*ziyādāt al-thiqāt*) and *ʿilm al-nāsikh wa'l-mansūkh* (abrogation in ḥadīth). Certain other branches of ḥadīth such as *ʿilal al-ḥadīth* and *tadlīs* (subtle defects in ḥadīth) may equally relate to transmission and text.

Most of the numerous branches of *ʿulūm al-ḥadīth* are basically concerned with the precise identification of the narrators of ḥadīth and draw attention to the endless possibilities of error that can occur in the *isnād* or the *matn* of ḥadīth. I do not propose to give a detailed account of all of these but merely to provide an inkling thereof and then move on to focus on our selected topics.

A branch of the ḥadīth studies is thus entitled as knowledge of the localities and domicile of ḥadīth narrators (*maʿrifat awṭān al-ruwāt wa buldānihim*) and stresses the theme that identifying the place of residence, village and town wherein the particular narrator has lived and the exact place where he received the ḥadīth from his immediate source enhances the reliability of *isnād*. The first two generations of narrators of ḥadīth, namely the Companions (*Ṣaḥāba*), and the Followers (*Tābiʿīn*), are each the subject of a separate branch of ḥadīth sciences, known as *maʿrifat al-ṣaḥāba*, and *maʿrifat al-tābiʿīn*, and a third branch focuses on the senior and junior figures, namely, *maʿrifat al-akābir min al-aṣāghir* in every generation. Some ḥadīth narrators are known by different names and this can give rise to error and confusion; hence a branch of ḥadīth sciences is devoted exclusively to the knowledge of those who are known by different names (*maʿrifat man dhukira bi-asmā' mukhtalifa*). This is not just a function of the fact that Arabic names often consist of long series of attributions to father, son, mother, etc., but also that pen-names, nicknames and appellations were sometimes used by those who might have known the individual narrator by any of his other attributes or names.[5]

Another branch of ḥadīth sciences, known as *maʿrifat al-mu'talif wa'l-mukhtalif min al-asmā' wa'l-ansāb* (knowledge of the look-alike but different names and genealogies) discusses names which are written similarly but pronounced differently. There are numerous names of this type, so much so that some have written individual works on the subject. Names such as Salām and Sallām, ʿUmāra and ʿImāra, Kurayz and Karīz, Safr and Safar, etc., are written similarly in the Arabic script and text which may or may not provide the vowelling and declensions of words; and most often they are not given, hence the possibility of confusion of one name or narrator for another.[6] Resembling this last branch of ḥadīth sciences, there is yet another branch of ḥadīth which addresses ḥadīth narrators that had identical names and could easily be confused with one another. There were, for example, no less than six ḥadīth narrators by the name Khalīl ibn Aḥmad, and four Aḥmad b. Jaʿfar b. Hamdān, all of whom lived in the same generation, and many other cases of this kind. These have been isolated and identified by reference to other indicators such as the father's name, locality, teachers and disciples of the narrator in question, etc. This branch of ḥadīth studies is known as *maʿrifat al-muttafiq wa'l-muftariq min al-asmāʿ wa'l-ansāb*, on which al-Khaṭīb al-Baghdādī has written a book bearing the title *Al-Muttafiq wa'l-Muftariq* (concordant and discordant). A still related area of ḥadīth studies is known as *maʿrifat al-mubhamāt* (knowledge of the obscure) and it is devoted to clarifying obscure references to individuals that occur in some *aḥādīth*. Phrases such as "a man asked the Prophet" or "a woman asked a question ..." are ambiguous, but the individuals involved have often been identified by the researchers.[7] Instances have also been noted in ḥadīth of names which are not as they might appear to be, and ḥadīth scholars have often supplied the explanation so as to prevent confusion. For example Abū Masʿūd al-Badrī ʿUqba b. ʿAmr is a Companion who has actually not witnessed nor participated in the Battle of Badr, as the name might suggest. Sulaymān b. Ṭarkhān al-Taymī is not a member of the Taym tribe although the name might suggest so. This kind of information on ḥadīth transmitters is studied in *maʿrifat al-ansāb al-latī bāṭinuhā ʿala khilāf ẓāhirihā* (knowledge of geneologies whose appearance is contrary to what they actually are).[8]

Although the genesis of *ʿulūm al-ḥadīth* can historically be traced to the Prophetic period, it is basically after that period, that is, after the demise of the Prophet, peace be upon him, when his followers began to verify, collect, and compile his sayings and reports of his activities. The purpose naturally was accurate recording, retention and transmission of the *Sunna* of the Prophet. It is quite normal in this pattern of development to expect that collection and documentation of ḥadīth preceded the development of methodology for its authentification. For rules of methodology and procedure often emerge long after the subject matter which they seek to regulate. The rudiments of the methodology of ḥadīth were initially practised by the Companions and Followers without any attempt on their part to articulate them, and it was scholars of the subsequent generations that formulated the methods of admissibility of ḥadīth transmission and criteria that were to be met by the transmitters. These early inroads in ḥadīth methodology were enriched through the cumulative efforts of generations of scholars until it became an independent field and discipline of Islamic learning.

The *ʿulamā'* paid more attention to the development of methodology and reliability of ḥadīth transmitters after the incidence of political turmoil (*fitna*) in the community. Ibn Shihāb al-Zuhrī's (d. 120 H) work provided wider scope for ḥadīth methodology and Imām al-Shāfiʿī (d. 205) paid more attention to it in his major works *Al-Risāla* and *Al-Umm*. But major developments in ḥadīth methodology took place in the third century and ʿAlī al-Madīnī (d. 233) was the first to write on the subject. But even so, writing on *uṣūl al-ḥadīth* was piecemeal and rudimentary during much of the third century. They were less than comprehensive and did not address all aspects of ḥadīth methodology. The main focus continued to be on documentation of ḥadīth while leading compilers of ḥadīth also addressed methodological issues such as Imām Muslim in the introductory section of his *Ṣaḥīḥ Muslim*, and al-Tirmidhī in the concluding part of his *Sunan al-Tirmidhī*. Al-Bukhārī and al-Nasā'ī wrote separate works each bearing the title *Kitāb al-Ḍuʿafā'* that discussed weak and unreliable transmitters. Ibn Saʿd's (d. 230 H) *Kitāb al-Ṭabaqāt al-Kubrā* provided much detail on biographies of ḥadīth transmitters and a more specialised work on this was later written by Abū Ḥātim b. Ḥibbān al-Bustī (d. 354) bearing the title *Kitāb al-Ṭabaqāt* in which he only discussed the most reliable transmitters (*al-thiqāt*). These works are known to have laid down basic methodological guidelines on reliable and spurious *ḥadīth*. The methodological contents of these works were later isolated, enhanced and consolidated in more specialised works by the *ʿulamā'* of the fourth century. Thus came the work of al-Qāḍī Abū Muḥammad al-Ḥasan al-Rāmhurmuzī (d. 360 H), *Al-Muḥdith al-Fāṣil Bayn al-Rāwī wa'l-Wāʿī*, which consolidated much of the development hitherto achieved in ḥadīth methodology, but it still fell short, as Ibn Ḥajar al-ʿAsqalānī (d. 852 H) later observed, of addressing all aspects of *uṣūl al-ḥadīth*. The main feature of this work was to bring together and consolidate aspects of *uṣūl al-ḥadīth* which were individually addressed before. The next landmark work was that of al-Ḥākim Abū ʿAbd Allāh al-Nīsābūrī (d. 405 H), *Maʿrifat ʿUlūm al-Ḥadīth* which was comprehensive and discussed some fifty branches of ḥadīth sciences, and yet according to Ibn Ḥajar al-ʿAsqalānī, it is poorly consolidated and less than all-inclusive. Then came the two works of al-Khaṭīb Abū Bakr al-Baghdādī (d. 463 H), entitled *Al-Kifāya fī Maʿrifat Uṣūl ʿIlm al-Riwāya*, and *Al-Jāmiʿ li-Ādāb al-Shaykh wa'l-Sāmiʿ* on the correct methods of ḥadīth narration, and then many more works to follow. Abū ʿAmr ʿUthmān b. ʿAbd al-Raḥmān al-Shahrazūrī's, also known as Ibn al-Ṣalāḥ (d. 643 H) *ʿUlūm al-Ḥadīth* has been widely acclaimed and has remained a work of reference on the subject.[9] ʿImād al-Dīn Ismāʿīl Ibn Kathīr's (d. 774 H) *Al-Bāʿith al-Ḥathīth ilā Maʿrifat ʿUlūm al-Ḥadīth* is another work of repute on the subject, which has in many ways supplemented and taken a step further the work of his predecessor, Ibn al-Ṣalāḥ. Some aspects of *uṣūl al-ḥadīth* that were of obvious importance to the subject, such as the science of impugnment and validation (*ʿilm al-jarḥ wa'l-taʿdīl*) were addressed at an early stage by leading figures such as Yaḥyā b. Maʿīn (d. 233 H) and Imām Aḥmad b. Ḥanbal (d. 241 H) and others, as will later be elaborated in the relevant parts of this work. Our study of *ʿulūm al-Ḥadīth* may thus begin with introductory information on the reception and delivery (*taḥammul wa adā'*) of ḥadīth as follows.

[02] Reception (*Taḥammul*) and Delivery (*Adā'*) of Ḥadīth

IT is reported that the Prophet used to speak to his audience clearly and elaborated or repeated his point whenever he doubted the reception and understanding of his audience. Sometimes he asked his Companions to repeat his message, or he asked them a question to alert them as to the accuracy of their reception. ʿĀ'isha al-Ṣiddīqa has been quoted to have said that "the Prophet, peace be on him, did not summarise his speech ... and he spoke in a way that if one were to count his words, they could be counted."[1] She has also been quoted to the effect that "whenever she did not hear anything (that the Prophet had said) she went back over it until she clarified and understood it."[2]

Anas Ibn Mālik has also been quoted to have said that "when the Prophet gave *salām* (greeting) to anyone he (often) said it three times and when he spoke a word he repeated it three times until it was understood."[3]

The Prophet did not, however, expatiate in speech and did not speak without need, but when he spoke, according to reports, he used the whole of his mouth rather than lips only. He would diversify his theme so as to keep the interest of his audience. He also conveyed his purpose sometimes through practical illustration. His Companions saw themselves as recipients of his teachings and carriers of his message. To this effect ʿAbd Allāh b. Masʿūd is quoted to have said that "when a man from among us was taught ten verses (*āyāt*) of the Qur'ān, he did not go further until he understood their meaning and manner of action upon them."[4] The Companions were also noted for their eagerness to be present in the Prophet's company and learn from him. ʿUmar b.

al-Khaṭṭāb thus went on record to say that "I and a neighbour of mine from Banū Ummaya b. Zayd used to take turns in attending sessions with the Messenger of God. He would attend one day and I the next and then we informed one another of the events of the day and any new revelation that might have been communicated."[5]

Ḥadīth scholars have specified certain conditions that must be met by anyone who receives and carries the ḥadīth and then delivers and transmits it to others. These conditions are basically concerned with the legal capacity of the receivers and transmitters of ḥadīth.

One who receives the ḥadīth must be a discerning person who has attained an age that enables him to listen to and retain the ḥadīth and convey it to others. The precise age is a subject of disagreement but the legal capacity of a receiver of ḥadīth is known to be different to legal capacity for purposes of civil and commercial transactions. A discerning child of seven, and according to some, five, years of age may not be capable of concluding a transaction or contract and yet may be able to comprehend what he hears and retain it or even transmit it to others. Many have specified that the child should be able to understand speech addressed to him and be able to give an answer. The child in question may write what he hears or may not and the *ʿulamā'* have not specified any particular age for purposes of writing.[6]

The Companions and others have thus accepted the ḥadīth transmitted by Maḥmūd b. al-Rabīʿ who said:[7]

> When I was a boy of five, I remember, the Prophet, peace be on him, took water from a bucket (used for drawing water out of a well) with his mouth and threw it on my face.

The question as to whether a disbeliever (*kāfir*) is qualified to be a recipient and carrier of ḥadīth is answered in the affirmative provided that he is a Muslim when he transmits the ḥadīth to others. A *kāfir* is thus qualified to receive ḥadīth but not to transmit it. To accept ḥadīth transmitted by a disbeliever would mean that Muslims are bound by his report that consequently becomes a part of their religion, which is unacceptable.

One who transmits ḥadīth must also be a person of just character (*ʿadl*). Possession of just character or *ʿadāla*, although often linked with observance of religious duties, avoidance of major sins, some particularly degrading minor sins or even profanities that are not necessarily sinful yet degrading, such as the company of corrupt persons, indulgence in demeaning jokes, etc. Yet *ʿadāla* is a holistic attribute of character which inspires confidence in the truth, uprightness and reliability of a person. This is a question of integrity, honesty and *taqwā* that people are often known either to have it or not.

And lastly the transmitter of ḥadīth must have a retentive memory (*al-ḍabṭ*) which means that he was alert and attentive when receiving the ḥadīth and retained it with due diligence as to its accuracy from the time of reception until delivery and transmission. A person of sound memory that is able, with or without the aid of writing, to ensure the integrity of ḥadīth against error, distortion and change is usually qualified as retentive (*ḍābiṭ*). The quality of retentiveness is also known by virtue of the fact that a person's speech is in agreement with the work of those who are known to be upright and retentive. An occasional discrepancy or disagreement is of no consequence provided that the general calibre and purpose of one's work is agreeable when compared to the works of recognised and reliable transmitters. If instances of conflict and discordance are frequent, the quality of *ḍabṭ* will be difficult to establish.[8]

Transmission of ḥadīth is consequently not accepted from a person who fails to fulfil the five conditions of *adā'* which are Islam, majority, sound intellect, just character and retentiveness – whereas there is basically one precondition of reception (*taḥammul*) which is intellectual discernment (*al-tamyīz*). We now turn to the methods of reception (*taḥammul*) and those of delivery (*adā'*) of ḥadīth which are separately discussed as follows.

Methods of Reception (*al-Akhdh wa'l-Taḥammul*)

The transmitter of ḥadīth is likely to have received the ḥadīth in any of the following ways which the ḥadīth scholars have identified in an order of decreasing scale of reliability. But before reviewing these methods, it should be noted that they were applicable in earlier times, that is before the documentation of ḥadīth in reliable collections by such scholars as al-Bukhārī and Muslim. The methods of receiving ḥadīth that are discussed below effectively ceased to apply after the compilation of *al-ṣiḥāḥ al-sitta*, the six sound collections of ḥadīth. Nowadays we simply receive the ḥadīth through the written records of ḥadīth by learned men who made the effort of verifying and recording the ḥadīth with diligence and care to ensure that they only recorded ḥadīth from transmitters whom they verified as upright and reliable. Ever since the availability of these highly acclaimed collections, scholars and students in search of ḥadīth simply locate the ḥadīth in these sources and refer to it, and they do not, on the whole, need to verify reliability of the chain of transmission and text of the ḥadīth, nor do they need normally to refer to the various other aspects of the ḥadīth methodology. But this facility was not available prior to the compilation of the major collections of ḥadīth. Because of the existence, in early times, of doubtful and fabricated matter into the general body of ḥadīth, transmitters of ḥadīth were required to specify as to how exactly did they receive it themselves. Was it through direct hearing (*al-samāʿ*), which is regarded to be the most reliable of all methods, or some other manner of reception? This information was necessary for the scholars of ḥadīth to enable them to evaluate the grades of reliability of the ḥadīth they were recording in their collections. The eight methods of reception that are known to ḥadīth methodology are as follows.

1. Direct hearing (*al-Samāʿ*): The recipient of ḥadīth according to this method has received the ḥadīth through direct hearing of the ḥadīth from a teacher, or a *shaykh*, who has recited it either from memory or from a written record. The teacher in this case is most likely to be someone in the generations following that of the Companions, simply because ḥadīth verification and transmission through accurate recitation and recording actually started after that time. When a Companion narrated ḥadīth from the Prophet, he or she was not normally faced with the question of how he or she actually received it from the Prophet. Although the question is not irrelevant and even the Companions have often indicated the occasion or context in which they heard the Prophet saying something or approving a particular act or conduct, since there were basically no intermediate links or contacts involved, questions were not asked as to the manner of *taḥammul* and *adā'* (reception and delivery) of ḥadīth. These methods were identified basically through the development of ḥadīth scholarship and emergence

of learned men of ḥadīth who taught ḥadīth to a circle of disciples and it was through this teaching that the disciples became qualified to transmit the ḥadīth down the line of *isnād*. The disciple who received the ḥadīth may have heard and written it down at the time of hearing, or wrote it afterwards. If he was the only one present, he would be likely to transmit the ḥadīth by the word *samiʿtu* (I heard so and so ...) or *ḥaddathanī* (so and so spoke to me), or *akhbaranī* or *anba'anī* (so and so informed me). Direct hearing when indicated by the use of these expressions ranks highest on the scale of reliability as it inspires confidence in the accuracy of the message that was received in the first place. If there were more people present, or when the disciple was in a group of other disciples, he would be in a position to use the plural form of these terms in each case by saying, for example, that 'we heard', 'it was reported to us', 'we were informed' (*samiʿnā*, *ḥaddathanā*, *akhbaranā*, *anba'anā*) and so forth. The ḥadīth scholars usually required the transmitter not to use the plural term if he heard it alone from his teacher and to specify carefully if the use of the plural term was justified, and also to mention those who heard it together with him.[9]

According to a variant opinion, the plural terms '*ḥaddathanā*' and '*akhbaranā*' are in a sense preferable to '*samiʿtu*' in that they convey a deliberate and purposeful address whereas '*samiʿtu*' does not integrate that sense of deliberate address by the teacher to the disciple. Be that as it may, direct hearing in the singular is still considered stronger. Sometimes familiarity and practice may take the place of some verbal expressions. Most of the reports from Ibn Jurayj, for instance, simply quote him by the expression '*qāla* Ibn Jurayj' (Ibn Jurayj said) as it was known of Ibn Jurayj that he did not narrate anything without directly hearing it himself in the first place.[10]

2. Recitation or Rehearsal (*al-Qirā'a ʿala'l-Shaykh*). The disciple in this case reads back to the *shaykh*, from memory or record, the ḥadīth which he has known from his *shaykh* or someone else, and wants the *shaykh* to verify its accuracy. This method, which is also known as *al-ʿarḍ*, requires that the reader comprehends what he reads and the *shaykh* is alert and awake so as to be able to spot any error or distortion in the rehearsal. The disciple who then transmits the ḥadīth is likely to

use a phrase such as 'I read to the *shaykh* who was listening' (*qara'tu ʿala'l-shaykh wa huwa yasmaʿu*) or if someone else from those present reports it, he may say 'this was read to the *shaykh* who was listening' (*quri'a ʿala'l-shaykh wa huwa yasmaʿu*) or such similar expressions that must, however, indicate the element of recitation or *qirā'a* therein to distinguish it from *al-samāʿ*.[11]

There is disagreement as to the relative strength of this method compared to direct hearing. According to an opinion which is attributed to Imām Abū Ḥanīfa, recitation is stronger than hearing as there is an element of repetition and endorsement therein. Imām Mālik has considered them to be equal and this is said to be the position generally of the scholars of Ḥijāz, and Kūfa including Imām al-Bukhārī. Having reviewed these variant views, Ibn al-Ṣalāḥ wrote that the correct position is that direct hearing still remains the stronger of the two methods.[12]

As for the actual terms used by the disciple, the clearest expression to convey *qirā'a* is "*qara'tu ʿalā fulān*" (I read this to so and so) or if by a third party to say "*quri'a ʿalā fulān wa anā asmaʿu*" (this was read to so and so and I heard it). The question as to whether the words '*ḥaddathanā*' and '*akhbaranā*' may be acceptable substitutes to rehearsal and recitation has received much attention. Some accept these as substitutes and others do not. There are also those who accept '*akhbaranā*' as a valid substitute but not '*ḥaddathanā*'. The *ʿulamā'* of ḥadīth do not accept either as valid substitutes. Then it is stated that '*akhbaranā*' may be accepted as a valid substitute if the recipients are actually in the plural. It is also noted, rightly perhaps, that no recitation or *qirā'a* can be valid, whatever the terms, without direct hearing by the teacher who actually paid attention when his disciple was reciting the ḥadīth to him.[13]

3. Permission (*al-Ijāza*). This is when the teacher or *shaykh* grants permission to one or more persons to transmit from him ḥadīth in a specified or unspecified context even without direct hearing or recitation. The *ʿulamā'* of ḥadīth are known to have employed this method with their disciples and the *ijāza* so granted was equivalent to a licence that they gave usually to persons they trusted. Of the various types of *ijāza* that are known to *uṣūl al-ḥadīth*, two types are

valid, and two have been rejected. The two valid forms of *ijāza* are firstly, permission granted to a specified person over something that is also specified; for instance, when a teacher or *shaykh* says to one of his distinguished disciples "I permit you to transmit from me the contents of this book, manuscript, or books," which are so specified. Secondly, where permission is granted by a teacher to his trusted disciple to transmit from him ḥadīth on a subject or subjects which the teacher has not specified. The Arabic particle '*ʿan*' (from) which frequently appears in the *isnād* of many prophetic reports of ḥadīth is taken to actually mean a grant of permission to the narrator by his immediate source, or *shaykh*.[14]

The two types of *ijāza* that are invalid are, firstly, of a specified subject matter to an unspecified person or persons, when the teacher says, for instance, that "I permit the Muslims or the people of Madīna in respect of such and such". Secondly, permission to unspecified persons concerning an unspecified subject matter. When the teacher says, for example, that "I permit anyone who wishes to report from me whatever I have said". These expressions are deemed to be too vague to qualify as *ijāza*. As a method, *ijāza* is known to have been granted by teachers of ḥadīth to their trusted disciples over ḥadīth or ḥadīths which are specified individually rather than by collection or volume.[15]

Ḥadīth scholars have debated the basic validity of *ijāza* and many in the Shāfiʿī school, including the Imām himself and Abū'l-Ḥasan al-Māwardī do not consider it as a valid method. It is thus said to be invalid to narrate a ḥadīth which has not been heard from the teacher and *shaykh*, who merely grants permission without actually pronouncing the subject matter of that permission. It is like the teacher telling his disciple that "I permit you to narrate from me what you have not heard," which should be avoided.[16] The general position on this, however, remains to be affirmative provided that there is adequate communication between the teacher and disciple. Some *ʿulamāʾ*, such as the Mālikī jurist Abū'l-Walīd al-Bājī, have gone so far as saying that there is general consensus (*ijmāʿ*) on the basic validity of *ijāza*.[17]

Certain other types of *ijāza* have also been held to be invalid and this includes *ijāza* granted to a child, and to a person who does not exist. This is because *ijāza* is in the nature of *wakāla* (agency) which requires that the *wakīl* be a competent person and a child does not qualify. Similarly, if a ḥadīth teacher addresses someone in such terms that "I grant you and your children and grandchildren that may come after you permission to narrate from me ..." since this type of *ijāza* concerns a person who is yet to be born the correct view here is that it is null and void. If *ijāza* is in the nature of *wakāla*, it is necessary that the *wakīl* is a living person and also competent to be a *wakīl*. No *ijāza* is therefore valid to a non-existing person. Imām Mālik is reported to have said that *ijāza* is not valid unless the person to whom it is granted is skilful and that the subject matter of *ijāza* is also clearly identified. To this Ibn al-Ṣalāḥ adds that the teacher should actually grant it in his words and not simply in writing. *Ijāza* in writing is still valid but weaker than the one that is accompanied by verbal pronouncement.[18]

4. Presentation (*al-Munāwala*). This is when the teacher/*shaykh* presents to his disciple his own manuscript and record of what he himself has originally received from his source and tells him that "these are what I have heard or received from so and so." This may be combined with permission (*ijāza*) for the disciple to transmit what the teacher gives him. The teacher may thus add "you may narrate it from me, or I grant you permission to narrate it from me." Sometimes it is the disciple who places in the hands of his *shaykh* a collection of what his *shaykh* has actually taught him and the *shaykh* verifies it to be correct, and returns it and grants him permission to narrate it. This is sometimes known as *ʿarḍ al-munāwala*. *Munāwala* that is accompanied by *ijāza* is regarded to be superior than the one where the teacher has not specified his permission, although both forms have in principle been validated.[19] Verification by the teacher is important and absence thereof vitiates the *munāwala*. Thus if a disciple approaches his teacher and shows him a book in two covers, saying that "this is based on your teaching and I seek your permission for me to narrate it," and the teacher then replies in the affirmative without actually verifying the contents of the work – this is not valid unless the disciple is a trusted and qualified person and the teacher acts from a position of confidence and trust.[20] Some *ʿulamā'* have also disputed the validity of a *munāwala* which is not accompanied by a grant of permission, or *ijāza*, saying that it remains doubtful and does not validate narration of

ḥadīth. Although *munāwala* without *ijāza* is regarded as a weak form of *munāwala*, the position still remains that it does provide a valid basis for narration of ḥadīth especially when there is a relationship of trust between the teacher and disciple.

5. Correspondence (*al-Mukātaba*). This is when the ḥadīth teacher writes the ḥadīth in his own handwriting, or asks someone else to write it, and then hands it over or sends it personally to his disciple with approval for the latter to transmit what the teacher wrote. This may or may not be accompanied with permission. The former variety is more reliable but the latter is also accepted. When there is permission and hand-over of written ḥadīth, it is equivalent to *munāwala*. It is also preferable that the written material is in the teacher's own handwriting, and if it is written by someone else the teacher should specify to the effect that his message was conveyed in so and so's handwriting. One often finds instances of *mukātaba* in the writings of ḥadīth scholars to the effect that "so and so wrote to me, or informed me ...". When this is said, it is most likely to be espoused with permission, even if the word permission or *ijāza* is not explicitly employed.

Critics have expressed reservations, however, in saying that the handwriting of one person sometimes resembles that of another and *mukātaba* should not therefore be seen as a reliable method of ḥadīth transmission. But this is considered to be a weak opinion and generally it is said that confusion due to close resemblance is not expected to be frequent. Some have even held, and rightly so, that *mukātaba* which is accompanied by permission is equivalent to *munāwala* that is accompanied by permission, and that it is one of the most reliable methods of reception and transmission of ḥadīth.[21]

6. Declaration (*al-Iʿlām*). This is when the teacher merely declares to his disciple that "this ḥadīth or collection thereof is what I have heard from so and so, or I received it from so and so" without saying anything as to grant of permission for the disciple to transmit it. But even so, it is said that permission of this nature is implied in the declaration and the disciple is consequently allowed to transmit it to others. He may not, however, transmit in the event where the teacher specifically asks him not to transmit it. Thus if the teacher declares to

his disciple what he has received from a valid source and then asks him in the meantime not to transmit it, he should not transmit. According to a variant opinion, however, the disciple may transmit it nevertheless. This opinion is based on an analogy between ḥadīth reporting (*riwāya*) and testimony (*shahāda*). Once a witness declares something, he can no longer control, allow or disallow others as to whether they transmit it or not. In response to this it is said that testimony is given in a court or a judicial tribunal (*majlis al-ḥukm*) and it differs from ḥadīth reporting in this respect. The ḥadīth teacher can, in other words, disallow his disciple from transmitting what he has declared to him.[22]

7. Bequest (*al-Waṣiyya*). This is rather a rare method of ḥadīth transmission. What it obviously means is that a ḥadīth teacher leaves instructions upon departing on a journey or at the time of death addressed to someone asking him to transmit the contents of a particular collection or book from him. This is the weakest method of *taḥammul* and many have advised against its admissibility. There is a difference, however, between this and a simple bequest of a book to someone which is not accompanied by permission to transmit its contents. For this would only transfer ownership of the book to the legatee, which is a different matter to ḥadīth transmission. It is as if to say that when the author bequests his book to someone, he does not necessarily assign his copyright to that person.[23]

8. Finding (*al-Wijāda*). This is where a person finds ḥadīth in the handwriting of his teacher or under his instruction which he has not heard from his teacher. The one who has found the materials may then transmit them to others provided that he recognises the handwriting of his teacher, or when he is assured of the reliability of his finding. He may then speak about it and say, for example, that "I found this in so and so's handwriting" or that "so and so said in his book ..." or something similar to that effect. The *Musnad* of Imām Ibn Ḥanbal contains many ḥadīth reports which have been recorded by ʿAbd Allāh b. Ḥanbal in such words that "I found in my father's handwriting ..." and then states the ḥadīth in question. Thus it was only proper for him to say so and it would not have been correct if he transmitted ḥadīth directly from his father, but to say that he found it in his father's

collection. Direct reporting in that situation would amount to a form of *tadlīs*.[24]

As a method of *taḥammul*, *wijāda* is rather rare in the works of the early writers and transmitters of ḥadīth and some *ʿulamā'* of ḥadīth and jurists of the Mālikī school have considered it impermissible to transmit ḥadīth on its basis. However, it is probably the most common form of *taḥammul* now as it has been ever since the documentation on a large scale of ḥadīth in the third century hijra. Most people nowadays find a ḥadīth in one of the reliable collections and quote it while mentioning the source where they found the ḥadīth. This is possible partly due to the reliability of the major compilations of ḥadīth which are widely known as the best receptacles of ḥadīth from where to quote and transmit the ḥadīth by students and scholars alike.[25]

In conclusion it may be said that ḥadīth transmitters are required to transmit ḥadīth in words that are indicative of the manner in which they received it. Thus, when the transmitter had heard the ḥadīth directly from his immediate source, he is expected to use words such as 'I heard, we heard' (*samiʿtu*, *samiʿnā*) and not, as it were, that so and so said (*qāla*), or 'mentioned to me' (*dhakara lī*) and the like, as these are vague and would cast doubt on the facts of direct hearing. It is also rare for ḥadīth teachers to use such particles as '*ʿan*' (from him) in the case of direct hearing as it would cause confusion.

Similarly a transmitter who received the ḥadīth from his source through *qirā'a* (reading or rehearsal) should use words that convey his manner of reception such as 'I read this to so and so' or 'it was read to so and so while I was listening', or expressions which convey that purpose. Similarly when the transmitter has received the ḥadīth through *munāwala* or *ijāza* or correspondence, the words he uses in transmitting the ḥadīth should make a reference to them. It is even more important to mention the source where one finds the ḥadīth in the case of *wijāda* (finding) and avoid using terms that would cast doubt between this and other varieties of *taḥammul*.[26]

[03] Documentation of Ḥadīth – Early Developments

IT is generally known that the Prophet, peace be on him, discouraged documentation of his own sayings and *Sunna* at the early stages of his mission in order to preserve the purity of the Qur'ān and prevent the possibility of confusion between the Qur'ān and his *Sunna*. The Prophet is thus reported to have said to his Companions: "Do not write what I say. Anyone who has written from me anything other than the Qur'ān, let him blot it out. You may speak about me and there is no objection to that, but one who attributes a lie to me deliberately should prepare himself for a place in Hell."[1]

لاتكتبوا عني ومن كتب عني غير القرآن فليمحه. وحدثوا عني ولاحرج، ومن كذب علي متعمدا فليتبوأ مقعده من النار.

Many of the leading Companions including ʿUmar b. al-Khaṭṭāb, ʿAbd Allāh b. Masʿūd, Zayd b. Thābit, Abū Mūsā al-Ashʿarī, and Abū Saʿīd al-Khudrī were against the writing of ḥadīth whereas ʿAlī b. Abī Ṭālib, his son, al-Ḥasan, Anas b. Mālik, ʿAbd Allāh b. ʿAmr b. al-ʿĀṣ considered it to be permissible. Some among this latter group also wrote what they heard of the Prophet's sayings for their own collections. There are also reports that during the latter part of his mission, that is, at a time when much of the Qur'ānic text had already been documented, the Prophet responded positively to the request of some of his Companions to write his sayings. By the time when most of the Qur'ān was received, memorised and documented, the Prophet permitted documentation of his *Sunna* and addressed the Companions to "preserve knowledge through writing."[2] He also employed the prisoners of war after the Battle of Badr to teach basic writing and literacy to the Muslim children and even accepted this as ransom for their eventual release. This also confirms that there were more writers in Makka than there were in Madīna. Some have in fact noted that there was a severe shortage of writers in Madīna. This may also explain the fact that the Masjid al-Nabī in Madīna combined a mosque and a literacy school for early Muslims. Some commentators have drawn the conclusion that prohibition of the writing of ḥadīth was actually meant to prevent the writing of the Qur'ān and the *Sunna* indistinguishably on the same page or collection but that writing was otherwise permitted if the two were clearly separated.[3] There is also the opinion that the initial prohibition of writing the *Sunna* was subsequently set aside and abrogated by the Prophet himself. Some support for this can be found in the practice of the Companions who actually wrote ḥadīth with the explicit permission of the Prophet.[4] This opinion has, however, been disputed by those who noted that the prohibitive position concerning the writing of ḥadīth was practised and observed by the Companions for quite a long time and it may therefore be inaccurate to say that it was abrogated. The more likely interpretation that can combine these various positions might therefore be that the original prohibition was the general (*ʿāmm*) ruling of ḥadīth and the permission that the Prophet subsequently granted to some of his Companions like Abū Shāh and ʿAbd Allāh b. ʿAmr. b. al-ʿĀṣ was specific and given for particular reasons. Abū Shāh al-Yamānī was weak of memory but was eager to retain the ḥadīth so he told the Prophet about it and the Prophet replied "seek the help of your right hand". ʿAbd Allāh was a literary figure who was well read in Arabic, had some knowledge of Assyrian, and was considered a reliable writer to document the sayings of the Prophet.[5] The proponents of the view that there was an abrogation of the original ruling have added that after the initial period, the *umma* as a whole and the *ʿulamā'* and jurists have unanimously accepted basic permissibility of writing the ḥadīth. This is undoubtedly the position that has prevailed ever since and represents general consensus, or *ijmāʿ*, of the *umma*. It is established beyond doubt that there was a change of direction and whether one subsumes it under the umbrella of abrogation, particularisation, or of *ijmāʿ*, it probably does not make much difference. These positions are also *ijtihād* – oriented positions, which help to explain certain factual developments within the rubric of a juristic formula. The fact thus remains that documentation of ḥadīth became a major preoccupation of the *ʿulamā'* which they pursued as a form of service to Islam and a means of gaining the pleasure of God Most High. The view thus prevailed that memories are liable to forgetfulness and the possibility therefore of error and inaccuracy in ḥadīth was bound to increase without documentation. As time passed, the chains of *isnād* became longer and details of names, places and dates therein became burdensome for anyone's memory.[6]

Commentators have often given the impression that there was very little documentation of the *Sunna* during the time of the Prophet and that of the Companions. There are also reports which suggest the opposite of this and maintain that documentation of ḥadīth during the lifetime of the Prophet was not as trifling or negligible as it is often assumed. Some of the reports on both sides may be less than conclusive. Yet the fact seems to be established beyond doubt that the writing of ḥadīth started during the lifetime of the Prophet, although not many of the early collections of ḥadīth have actually reached us. To reach a more accurate understanding of this, we need to review the relevant evidence.

Al-Tirmidhī has reported that the renowned Companion, Saʿd b. ʿUbāda, who was a leading figure of the *Anṣār* in Madīna had in his possession a *Ṣaḥīfa* collection wherein he documented the sayings and *Sunna* of the Prophet, and that his son used to narrate ḥadīth from that *Ṣaḥīfa*.[7] Al-Bukhārī has also reported that this same *Ṣaḥīfa* was later integrated into the collection of ḥadīth that another leading Companion, ʿAbd Allāh b. Abī Awfā, compiled in his own handwriting and the people used to read his manuscript and often verified its content with him.[8]

Another Companion, Samura b. Jundub (d. 60 H), is also noted to have documented ḥadīth in his own handwriting, which was later inherited by his son Sulaymān, who in turn reported ḥadīth from it. It is probably the same collection which came to the attention of Muḥammad b. Sīrīn (d. 110 H) who said concerning it that "the epistle which Samura transferred to his son contained a great deal of knowledge."[9]

Another Companion, Jābir b. ʿAbd Allāh (d. 78 H), is also noted to have compiled a collection of ḥadīth specifically on the subject of the rituals of the *ḥajj* in which he also quoted the Prophet's Farewell Sermon on the occasion of the last pilgrimage (*ḥajjat al-wadāʿ*). One of the leading *tābiʿī*, Qatāda b. Diʿāma al-Sadūsī (d. 118 H), spoke highly of the *Ṣaḥīfa* of Jābir even to the extent to say that "I remember the *Ṣaḥīfa* of Jābir better than the sūra al-Baqarah."[10] It is possible that ḥadīth narrated by Sulaymān b. Qays al-Yashkurī, who was a disciple of Jābir, were taken from the *Ṣaḥīfa* of Jābir. Jābir's collection became well-known and it is very likely that some of his disciples copied and wrote some of it for their own collections, even though none of it has actually reached us.[11]

One of the best known collection of ḥadīth that was written during the Prophet's lifetime was *Al-Ṣaḥīfa al-Ṣādiqa* (the true collection) by ʿAbd Allāh b. ʿAmr b. al-ʿĀṣ (d. 65 H).[12] It contained one thousand *aḥādīth*, and although the actual manuscript has not reached us, its contents have been quoted almost entirely in the *Musnad* of Imām Aḥmad b. Ḥanbal.[13] This has often been described as one of "the most reliable historical documents to prove the writing of ḥadīth during the Prophet's lifetime."[14] It is reported that ʿAbd Allāh b. ʿAmr b. al-ʿĀṣ used to write everything the Prophet would say and he was consequently told by some people that he should not do so, which was why ʿAbd Allāh b. ʿAmr asked the Prophet for permission to write his sayings:

> May I write all that I hear? The Prophet said "Yes". When you are calm and when angry? To this the Prophet said "Yes, for even in that state I do not say anything but the truth".[15]

فقد جاء عبد الله يستفتي رسول الله صلى الله عليه وسلم في شـــأن الكتابة قائلا: أكتب كل ما أســـمع؟ قال: نعم، قال: في الرضـى والغضب؟ قال: نعم، فإني لا أقول في ذلك إلا حقا.

The encouraging tone of this ḥadīth naturally bore fruit and ʿAbd Allāh b. ʿAmr became even more assiduous in what he was doing. This was also noted by his fellow Companion, Abū Hurayra, who is quoted to have said that "None of the Companions of the Prophet, peace be on him, has taken more ḥadīth from him than myself, except for ʿAbd Allāh b. ʿAmr who used to write, but I did not."

It is similarly reported that ʿAlī b. Abī Ṭālib wrote down the sayings of the Prophet. Abū Juḥayfa has thus stated that "I asked ʿAlī: Do you have anything written with you, and he said 'no', except for the Book of God ... or what is in this *Ṣaḥīfa*. I asked: What is in this *Ṣaḥīfa* then? He said: (It is about) blood money, release of war prisoners, and (the ḥadīth to the effect) that 'a Muslim is not executed for killing a disbeliever'."[16]

Another well-known document and probably the earliest on record was the constitution of Madīna (*dustūr al-Madīna*, also known as *ṣaḥīfat al-Madīna*) which was written in the first year of the Hijra. This document is concerned mainly with relations among the three major groups of Madīna, namely the Migrants, the Helpers and the Jews, which forged unity between them all and declared them as "one *umma* (community) to the exclusion of others." The document actually begins with the phrase "this is a document (*kitāb*)" and that document which is spelled out in (47) articles has survived in its original form, and is sufficiently well known to be ranked as ḥadīth *mutawātir*.

Moreover, the prominent Companion, ʿAbd Allāh b. ʿAbbās (d. 69 H) wrote the sayings of the Prophet and his *Sunna* on plates (*alwāḥ*) which he used to carry to his teaching circles. One of his students, Saʿīd b. Jubayr (d. 95 H) also wrote from his teacher, and in the course of time the collection of Ibn ʿAbbās became well-known and many of the ḥadīth reports that Ibn ʿAbbās transmitted were based on his written records.[17] Another prominent figure among the Companions, Anas b. Mālik, is also reported to have documented ḥadīth in a *Ṣaḥīfa* which he used to carry with him and showed it to the people he met.[18]

The *Ṣaḥīfa* collection of Hammām b. Munabbih (d. 101), a disciple of Abū Hurayra (d. 58 H) consists of ḥadīth that Abū Hurayra narrated and has actually attributed it to his teacher. This collection, also known as *al-ṣaḥīfa al-ṣaḥiḥa*, has survived and has been documented by Muhammad Hamidullah from the two near-identical manuscripts that he obtained in Damascus and Berlin respectively. It has also been documented in the *Musnad* of Imām Aḥmad b. Ḥanbal. Ṣubḥī al-Ṣāliḥ has concluded, however, that Hammām wrote the collection after the Prophet's demise as he was born in the year 40 Hijra and his teacher Abū Hurayra died in the year 58. Thus it is likely that Hammām's collection was written around the mid-first century Hijra. This collection contains 138 *aḥādīth* and is indicative of the high level of care and accuracy that Hammām gave to the content of the ḥadīth which he recorded.[19] Ṣubḥī al-Ṣāliḥ thus concluded from the evidence he has discussed that ḥadīth writing began at a very early stage, that is, during the Prophet's lifetime, and not, as many orientalists have held, at the beginning of the second century Hijra.

Another contemporary author, ʿUmar Hāshim, has quoted Abū'l-Ḥasan al-Nadwī and Aḥsan al-Kaylānī in support of his own conclusion that if these early collections of ḥadīth are put together they would comprise the greater part of the *aḥādīth* that were subsequently compiled in the larger collections during the third century Hijra. The fact that only the subsequent collections became well-known is due largely to their superior methods of compilation. These later collections showed a distinct improvement, in terms of classification and consolidation of themes, over the earlier collections, which consisted of unclassified *aḥādīth* that were simply put together. This situation is seen as a contributing factor to the orientalists' assertion that ḥadīth began to be written and compiled only in the second century. Even the history books began to mention only leading works and compilations of the subsequent period and almost totally ignored the earlier collections.

Another factor that contributed to this misgiving is the somewhat exaggerated references by the authors of subsequent works to ḥadīth collections, citing figures in the order of hundreds of thousands of ḥadīths, which somehow overshadowed and minisculed the significance of the earlier collections. It is remarkable to hear that Imām Aḥmad Ibn Ḥanbal collected seven hundred thousand *aḥādīth*, and similar figures are mentioned in conjunction with the works of the two leading scholars of ḥadīth, al-Bukhārī and Muslim. It may be that these figures consisted mainly of the number of reports and reporters rather than of actual *aḥādīth*. For the ḥadīth *innamā'l-aʿmāl bi-nniyyāt* alone has been transmitted through seven hundred channels. If we were to eliminate repetition and reduce all of this to the actual number of ḥadīth, we would have a much smaller number of *aḥādīth* left, that may or may not exceed ten thousand in number.[20]

The Caliph ʿUmar b. al-Khaṭṭāb considered the documentation of *Sunna* and consulted with the Companions, many of whom supported the idea, but as ʿUrwa b. al-Zubayr reported "ʿUmar delayed the matter and thought over it for a month as he remained doubtful about it himself",[21] but after a month of deliberation, he addressed the Companions and told them that he was apprehensive that this might distract people's attention from the Book of God. The Caliph ʿUmar eventually decided not to write the *Sunna*. This position basically remained unchanged during the period of the Pious Caliphs until the advent of the turmoil and *fitna* which followed the assassination of the third Caliph ʿUthmān and the civil war that broke out between the Caliph ʿAlī and the governor of al-Shām, Muʿāwiya. Military conflict led in turn to the emergence of political and theological differences among various groups, and some individuals resorted to ḥadīth forgery in order to promote their particular viewpoints.

With the subsequent expansion of the territorial domain of Islam and the travelling to remote places, or demise, of many of the Companions, concern gained ground once again for the documentation of ḥadīth. Among the successors, the Umayyad Caliph, ʿUmar b. ʿAbd al-ʿAzīz (d. 101 H) was the first to take up the issue and assigned to the governor of Madīna, Abū Bakr Muḥammad b. Ḥazm (d. 117 H) the task to collect and document the *Sunna* of the Prophet, and to "accept nothing other than the ḥadīth of the Prophet, peace be on him, and write therein the ḥadīth of ʿAmrah bt. ʿAbd al-Raḥmān al-Anṣāriyya (d. 98 H)." Reports also suggest that another learned man of ḥadīth, al-Qāsim Muḥammad b. Abī Bakr (d. 107 H) was also asked by the Caliph to assist Ibn Ḥazm, but the Caliph passed away at this juncture and did not live long enough to see the fruits of his important initiative.[22] Among those that the deceased Caliph had asked to document the *Sunna* was Muḥammad b. Muslim b. Shihāb al-Zuhrī (d. 124 H) of Madīna, the teacher of Imām Mālik, who responded to the call and attempted what proved to be the first major collection of ḥadīth, marking the early beginning of the extensive ḥadīth collections that were later accomplished during the second and third centuries. Al-Zuhrī's work was continued by scholars like Ibn Jurayj (d. 150) and Ibn Isḥāq (d. 151) in Makka, Imām Mālik (d. 179) in Madīna, Abū ʿAmr al-Awzāʿī (d. 157) in al-Shām, Sufyān al-Thawrī (d. 160) in

Kūfa, Ḥammād b. Salama (d. 167) in Baṣra and the movement spread far and wide to the Yemen and Khurāsān.

Al-Zuhrī's method of writing was subject-oriented and consisted of a separate book each on *Sunna* pertaining to an individual subject, such as the ritual prayer (*ṣalāh*), fasting and *zakāh*, etc., in which he also collected relevant data from the sayings of the Companions and the *tābiʿūn*, without giving exclusive treatment to the ḥadīth of the Prophet. He documented all that he had heard from the Companions. This manner of writing was generally followed by other writers on *Sunna* during the second century. The *Muwaṭṭa'* of Imām Mālik also conformed to this style of writing.[23]

Whereas the early years of the second century saw works on the *Sunna* that were in conformity with al-Zuhrī's method, the latter part of that century witnessed writings in ḥadīth that were different in style and format. Ḥadīth collections that were authored during the late second century by Imām Mālik, Ibn Jurayj and Sufyān al-Thawrī, for example, brought the various themes of ḥadīth within a single volume instead of the separate volumes that were devoted to individual themes. But these works still continued al-Zuhrī's method of joining the sayings and *fatwā* of the Companions and Followers with the ḥadīth of the Prophet on particular subjects. This can be seen, for example, in the *Muwaṭṭa'* of Imām Mālik, and the *Musnad* of Imām Shāfiʿī, the only two works that have reached us of that period. There are also references in earlier writings to a work entitled *al-Āthār* by Muḥammad b. Ḥasan al-Shaybānī and similar other contributions which have not survived but it seems likely that much of their contents have been covered by subsequent works that were written some years later.

The *Muwaṭṭa'* of Imām Mālik is often described as the leading work among the famous ḥadīth collections, even preceding, in some ways, that of al-Bukhārī. The Imām wrote his *Muwaṭṭa'* in response to a request by the ʿAbbāsid Caliph al-Manṣūr who solicited a work of authority on the *aḥkām* of *Sharīʿa* that were founded in authentic *Sunna*. The Imām revised and consolidated his work many times and it is said to have taken him forty years to complete. The classification of its contents are organised in an order that is typical of the works of *fiqh*, which is why it is sometimes identified as a work both of *fiqh* and ḥadīth.

The third-century hijra marked, yet again, a new phase of development in the documentation of ḥadīth. One of the distinctive features of the writings of this period was to isolate the *Sunna* of the Prophet from the sayings of the Companions and *fatwās* of the learned figures among the Followers. The earliest works of this period were the *Musnad* of Abū Dāwūd al-Ṭayālīsī (d. 204 H) and then the much larger work of that genre, the *Musnad* of Imām Aḥmad b. Ḥanbal (d. 241 H). Ḥadīth writers during the third century on the whole observed the principles of *uṣūl al-ḥadīth* that had already gained recognition and the methodological guidelines that were developed were consequently put into effect. By the beginning of the fourth century, writers drew a clear distinction between a sound or *ṣaḥīḥ* ḥadīth and a defective or *muʿallal* ḥadīth. Then came the period of the *muta'akhkhirūn* or latecomers of the ḥadīth writers, which marked the beginning of reproductive writings, glosses and commentaries on existing works that were authored by the pioneers, or *mutaqaddimūn*, of the ḥadīth literature.[24]

[04] Ḥadīth Literature – The Major Collections

THE different stages of development in the compilation of ḥadīth and their classification may be summarised under ten headings as follows. It may be said at the outset, however, that these categories are not exclusive in that they tend to overlap and are, in any case, meant to be used as aids to a better understanding of the vast literature of ḥadīth. The ḥadīth literature has thus been classified as follows.

1. The *Ṣaḥīfa* (lit. booklet) collections which marked, as already discussed, the earliest stage in the documentation of ḥadīth. At this stage, *aḥādīth* were simply put together in writing, often for purposes of personal use, without any order or classification. This period actually started during the lifetime of the Prophet and continued until the early second century and it is generally known as the *Ṣaḥīfa* period.

2. The *Muṣannaf* collections manifested the second stage in the development of ḥadīth literature. Unlike the *ṣaḥīfa* collections which were not classified, the *muṣannaf* (lit. classified) consisted of thematic classification of ḥadīth. Starting at about the middle of the second century, during this stage, ḥadīth belonging to particular themes were classified under separate titles and chapters. Famous in the *muṣannaf* category are the *Muwaṭṭa'* of Imām Mālik (d. 179), the *Muṣannaf* of Maʿmar b. Rāshid (d. 154) and the *Muṣannaf* of ʿAbd al-Razzāq b. Humām al-Ṣanʿānī (d. 211).[1]

3. The *Musnad* (lit. supported) compilations marked the next stage in the documentation of ḥadīth, and it signified a stage wherein greater attention was paid to the chain of transmission or *isnād* which linked the ḥadīth to the Prophet through the reports of reliable narrators that usually started with a Companion. All ḥadīth that were narrated by one Companion, regardless of the subject matter, were put under his or her name. The main purpose of the *musnad* writing was obviously to compile the largest possible number of ḥadīth for the sake of preservation and record. All *aḥādīth* that were transmitted by particular individuals on any subject were put together without much attention to classification on the basis of subject matter. This stage is considered as the richest of all. It began during the latter half of the second century and famous in this category was the *Musnad* of Imām Aḥmad b. Ḥanbal (164-241) which contains 40,000 *aḥādīth* including 10,000 repetitions reported by about 700 Companions. It was derived from a much larger mass of 750,000 *aḥādīth*, and it took the Imām some twenty years to complete. Even then, the work was unconsolidated and in separate parts, until the Imām's son, ʿAbd Allāh, consolidated the work to which he also added some of his own findings. Other works in this category are the *Musnad* of Ibn al-Najjār (d. 262), the *Musnad* of Abū Dāwūd Sulaymān b. Dāwūd al-Ṭayālīsī (d. 204 H) and many others.

The *musnad* compilers differed in their arrangement of names of Companions. Some of them begin with the four Pious Caliphs followed by the remaining six of the ten who had the tiding of Paradise from the Prophet (i.e. *al-ʿashara al-mubashshara*). These are followed by the Companions who embraced Islam first, then by those who migrated with the Prophet, those who participated in the Battle of Badr, and then in the treaty of Ḥudaybīya, those who embraced Islam on the occasion of the conquest of Makka, then women among the Companions until it reaches the generation of the Followers, or *tābiʿūn*. Some of the books are arranged alphabetically and some according to regions and tribes. The *musnads* are not easy to use since their contents are not classified subject-wise.[2]

4. The *Ṣaḥīḥ* (sound/authentic) collections represented the fourth and basically the last stage in the development of ḥadīth literature. This is manifested in the third-century compilations through the

works mainly of al-Bukhārī and Muslim, referred to as *ṣaḥīḥayn*, or the two authentic collections. The term *ṣaḥīḥayn* is, however, not used in the exclusive sense as there are *ṣaḥīḥ aḥādīth* in all the other major collections of ḥadīth. Nor did al-Bukhārī include in his work all the qualified narrators of ḥadīth, for he only planned to compile a short book (*mukhtaṣar*) on ḥadīth which was not all-inclusive of either the narrators or the ḥadīth. Since al-Bukhārī did not intend his collection to be all-inclusive, it would follow that no one may call a ḥadīth unreliable or weak simply because it has not appeared in al-Bukhārī. This is also true of *Ṣaḥīḥ Muslim*.[3]

Muḥammad b. Ismāʿīl al-Bukhārī (194-256 H) travelled widely and devoted sixteen years to the compilation of *Ṣaḥīḥ al-Bukhārī* which has remained to this day the most authoritative of all collections. Al-Bukhārī interviewed over 1,000 ḥadīth transmitters, or *shaykhs*, in the Ḥijāz, Egypt, Nishapur, Merw and Iraq and allegedly collected a vast number of about 600,000 *aḥādīth* from which he then selected 9,082 *aḥādīth*. He has repeated *aḥādīth* which had more than one chain of *isnād* as the strength and reliability of the *isnād* is deemed to increase with the plurality of its chains of transmission. When such repetitions are taken into account, the original figure of 600,000 is also likely to be drastically reduced. For a single ḥadīth is sometimes transmitted through ten different chains of transmission all of which would in the end establish just one ḥadīth. Al-Bukhārī went on record to say that he offered two units of prayer each time he selected a ḥadīth to include in his *Ṣaḥīḥ al-Bukhārī*. It seems that al-Bukhārī wrote a good portion of his book during his residence in Makka and Madīna and the rest in Baṣra, Kūfa, and Bukhārā. Another report has it that he completed the first draft of his work in the Holy Mosque in Makka and the rest in Bukhārā. When al-Bukhārī completed his work, he showed it to some of the leading *ʿulamāʾ* of his time, the Imām Aḥmad b. Ḥanbal, Yaḥyā b. Maʿīn and ʿAlī b. al-Madīnī, among others, who were among the important sources, or *shaykhs*, of al-Bukhārī, and they were pleased with it and verified it except for four *aḥādīth*, but it is said that al-Bukhārī kept those and verified them to be reliable.[4] ʿAlī b. al-Madīnī was the most learned man of his time especially on defects (*ʿilal*) of ḥadīth and he expressed full confidence in al-Bukhārī.

Al-Bukhārī was meticulous in the verification of ḥadīth and yet tactful and gentle in regard to those whom he impugned as unreliable. Some of his expressions such as *sakatū ʿanhu* (many remained silent concerning him) or *fīhi naẓar* (one has to look into him) or *tarakūhu* (abandoned) and similar other epithetic descriptions of al-Bukhārī are noted in this regard as being generally clear of backbiting or defaming others. He was affluent and had inherited wealth which he generously spent on students and other charitable causes.[5]

Discounting all repetitions, *Al-Bukhārī* contains 2,602 *aḥādīth*. It is divided into 106 books and a total of 3,450 chapters. Each chapter bears a heading which is descriptive of its contents. It seems that al-Bukhārī usually took a portion of the ḥadīth for the heading of the chapter. Some of these headings are reflective of al-Bukhārī's personal insight and knowledge of ḥadīth that is not found in other collections. Yet it has also meant rather too many headings and chapters which are, however, too numerous and tend to make the work somewhat difficult to use.

Works that preceded that of al-Bukhārī tended to mix the sayings of Companions and Followers with the ḥadīth proper as they did not draw a clear distinction between them. Al-Bukhārī committed himself to include only the Sound ḥadīth in his collection and classified them subject-wise. Al-Bukhārī included ḥadīth with an unbroken *isnād* narrated by upright and retentive individuals (*al-ʿudūl al-ḍābiṭīn*) which were also free of defect (*ʿilla*) and oddities (*shudhūdh*), and the narrators had met with one another.[6] He continued the work of Shihāb al-Zuhrī (d. 124) and in many ways took al-Zuhrī as a point of reference in his methodology and selection. Al-Bukhārī paid greater attention to narrators from al-Zuhrī's generation who were disciples of al-Zuhrī, travelled with him, or remained in his company, as compared to those who did not benefit from al-Zuhrī's teaching and influence. Al-Bukhārī's (and Muslim's) chain of *isnād* has been characterised as to rely in the first place on the narration of ḥadīth from the Prophet by a verified Companion whose identity as a Companion is free of doubt. This is narrated in turn by two upright Followers, or by one Follower who is verified by at least two narrators for having transmitted ḥadīth from the Companions. The third link in al-Bukhārī's chain of *isnād* consists of an upright and retentive Successor (*tābiʿ tābiʿī*) from whom other narrators (in the fourth generation) have also reported. The fifth link in al-Bukhārī's *isnād* is likely to be al-Bukhārī's own *shaykh*/teacher who is an upright and retentive narrator. He did not record ḥadīth from narrators whose trustworthiness he doubted. It was important for al-Bukhārī to ensure that at least two people had narrated ḥadīth from the preceding links, be it a Companion, Follower, Successor and so on. This is a general characterisation as exceptions are found, for example, in the case of a Companion, Mirdās al-Aslamī, whose ḥadīth al-Bukhārī has recorded but only one person (Qays b. Hāzim) has reported ḥadīth from him.[7]

Al-Bukhārī himself entitled his work as *Jāmiʿ Ṣaḥīḥ al-Musnad al-Mukhtaṣar min Ḥādīth Rasūl Allah wa-Sunanihi wa-Ayyāmih*. This is indicative of al-Bukhārī's methodology and approach. The word '*al-Jāmiʿ*' (lit. comprehensive) signifies that the coverage of al-Bukhārī extends to all the eight areas that *al-Jāmiʿ* are generally known to cover. These are the *ʿaqā'id* (dogmatics), *aḥkām* (legal rules), *al-riqāq* (moral teachings), *ādāb al-ṭaʿām wa'l-sharāb* (etiquette of eating and drinking), *al-tafsīr wa'l-tārīkh wa'l-siyar* (Qur'ān commentary, history and biography of the Prophet), *al-safar wa'l-qiyām wa'l-quʿūd* (travel and movement), *al-fitan* (tumults), and *al-manāqib* (the virtues of the Prophet and his Companions). *Sunan al-Tirmidhī* is also a *Jāmiʿ* collection as it comprises ḥadīth on all of these various themes. "*Al-Ṣaḥīḥ*" in al-Bukhārī's title signified that he has not included in his collection a weak (*ḍaʿīf*) ḥadīth that he might have known as such. Whereas the term *musnad* implied that the *aḥādīth* he compiled were all connected with a sound chain of *isnād* up to the level of the Companion reporting from the Prophet. Al-Bukhārī was thus the first to compile a comprehensive (*jāmiʿ*) collection of this kind on ḥadīth. The only work that preceded him was the *Muwaṭṭa'* of Imām Mālik, which was, however, not a *jāmiʿ* as it was basically confined to the *aḥkām* or legal ḥadīth only. Al-Bukhārī isolated the sayings of Companions and *tābiʿūn* from the Prophetic ḥadīth, and this is also a distinctive feature of his work when compared, for example, to the *Muwaṭṭa'* of Imām Mālik.[8]

Al-Bukhārī has explained how he was inspired to undertake the writing of his *Ṣaḥīḥ al-Bukhārī* when he noted that he was in the company of his teacher, Isḥāq b. Rāhawayh, together with some of his other disciples when he mentioned in passing "if you were to compile a compendium (*kitāban mukhtaṣaran*) of the authentic *Sunna* (*li-Ṣaḥīḥ al-Sunna*) of the Messenger of God, peace be on him." Al-Bukhārī says that the idea occurred to him then and his inspiration became stronger when he dreamt one night that he stood in front of the Prophet and al-Bukhārī had a fan in his hand. This he understood to mean that he was blessed with the task of removing doubts and impurity from the *Sunna* of the Prophet.[9]

Ṣaḥīḥ Muslim

Muslim b. al-Hajjāj al-Nīsābūrī (206-261 H) compiled his *Ṣaḥīḥ Muslim*, which contains 10,000 *aḥādīth* (3,030 without repetitions), derived from a much larger mass of about 300,000 *aḥādīth*.[10] Muslim was in many ways a follower of al-Bukhārī, which he has acknowledged himself and has to a large extent also utilised al-Bukhārī's methods. When al-Bukhārī came to Nishapur, then one of the finest cities of Khurāsān, Muslim kept him company and he held al-Bukhārī in affection and esteem. Muslim also learned from al-Bukhārī's teacher, Isḥāq b. Rāhawayh, who was one of the leading scholars of Khurāsān. This may partly explain why *Ṣaḥīḥ Muslim* generally ranks second next to *Ṣaḥīḥ al-Bukhārī*, except for the *ʿulamā'* of North Africa and the Maghreb who tend to rank Muslim first. This reverse order of ranking refers basically to the superior classification of Muslim which is based on subject matter and compiles all *aḥādīth* on the same subject, together with their various chains of *isnād* under one heading or chapter. *Ṣaḥīḥ Muslim* is consequently better consolidated and easier to use compared to *Ṣaḥīḥ al-Bukhārī*.

Those who knew Muslim spoke highly of his retentive memory, his piety, and dedication to scholarship. He went to *ḥajj* at the age of twenty and he learned from some of the leading figures in Makka. He also went to Baghdad on several occasions. Many of the leading figures of his time, including Abū Ḥātim al-Rāzī, Abū ʿIsā al-Tirmidhī, Abū Bakr b. Khuzayma, among others, have narrated ḥadīth from Muslim, and held him in affection and esteem.[11]

One of the reasons that prompted Muslim to write his work, *Ṣaḥīḥ Muslim*, was that works of ḥadīth that were available then were somewhat difficult to use, and he addressed himself to the task of writing a reliable work that is easy to utilise. Although al-Bukhārī's work was classified subject wise, it left room for improvement, which Muslim had obviously targeted for his own work. He completed his work in fifteen years and showed it to Abū Zurʿa al-Rāzī and implemented his suggestions concerning ḥadīth that were defective (*maʿlūl*) and included, as a result, only ḥadīth that were clear of *ʿilla*. Muslim went on record to say that his work consisted of Sound/*Ṣaḥīḥ* ḥadīth but noted "I did not say that what I have verified in this book is devoid of weak reports." The other purpose that motivated Imām Muslim was the same as motivated al-Bukhārī, which was to purify the *Sunna* of the Prophet from the accretions of story-tellers, the *Zanādiqa* (heretics) and those who were moved by ignorance and prejudice. He also tried to confine his selection of ḥadīth to a manageable size as he considered it to be easier to ensure the accuracy of a smaller bulk compared to a much larger one.[12]

Muslim's classification resembles that of al-Bukhārī in regard to its main headings but Muslim's division of chapters is better consolidated and self-contained. It has fewer repetitions and does not summarise ḥadīth in the way al-Bukhārī has done. He is known for his careful use of the terms *ḥaddathanā* and *akhbaranā*, in that he reserves the former for direct hearing by the disciple from the *shaykh* whereas the latter is used when the disciple has read back to the *shaykh* for his approval and verification. This is generally adopted but there are many among ḥadīth scholars who have used these two terms interchangeably.[13]

Al-Bukhārī tends to be more stringent in qualifying ḥadīth as *Ṣaḥīḥ*/authentic. Al-Bukhārī's conditions of admitting a ḥadīth as a *Ṣaḥīḥ* ḥadīth signified not only that the immediate links in the chain of *isnād* were contemporaries of one another, but also that they had actually met and direct hearing took place between the teacher and disciple. For Muslim it was sufficient if the two were contemporaries even if they had not actually met one another. Muslim was content, in other words, with the possibility of personal encounter whereas al-Bukhārī required proof of an actual encounter between the transmitter and recipient of ḥadīth.[14]

A comparative evaluation of the transmitters of al-Bukhārī and Muslim also reveals that more of al-Bukhārī's transmitters qualify for the requirements of just character (*ʿadāla*) and retentiveness (*al-ḍabṭ*) than that of Muslim's, and there are consequently fewer transmitters in al-Bukhārī that are considered weak (*ḍaʿīf*) than there are in Muslim.

Thus it is noted that of the total of 430 or so of al-Bukhārī's transmitters, only about 80 have been questioned or labelled as weak, whereas of the total of 620 narrators of Muslim, the critics have raised questions over 160. About 89 of al-Bukhārī's *aḥādīth* have been identified to have some defect, whereas in Muslim's collection, such ḥadīth have been numbered at 100.[15]

Al-Bukhārī and Muslim have not claimed to contain an exhaustive collection of the ḥadīth and some *aḥādīth* which are not recorded in their collections have been compiled in the four collections namely of *Sunan Abū Dāwūd*, *Sunan al-Nasāʾī*, *Sunan al-Tirmidhī*, and *Sunan Ibn Māja*.

5. The *Sunan* Collections: Works that fall under this classification specialise in the legal ḥadīth, or *aḥādīth al-aḥkām*. The various chapters of *Sunan* are thus devoted to practical rules (*aḥkām ʿamaliyya*) that pertain, for example, to cleanliness, ritual prayer, the legal alms, the pilgrimage, marriage and divorce and so forth. *Sunan Abū Dāwūd* of Sulaymān b. Ashʿath al-Sijistānī (d. 275), which consists of 4,800 legal *aḥādīth*, stands out for its comprehensive treatment of legal *aḥādīth*. Abū Dāwūd did not confine his *Sunan* to the collection of Sound/*Ṣaḥīḥ* ḥadīth alone but included with it Fair/*Ḥasan* in both its varieties, that is *Ḥasan* in its own right (i.e. *li-dhātih*), and *Ḥasan* due to an extraneous factor (i.e. *li-ghayrih*). He wrote that whenever he included weak ḥadīth he identified it as such and explained it by identifying the point of weakness in its *isnād*. This would imply that when he does not specify weakness in a ḥadīth that he has recorded, it is deemed to be acceptable and sound. In the chapter on cleanliness (*al-Ṭahārah*), for example, Abū Dāwūd records a ḥadīth from Naṣr b. ʿAlī, from Abī ʿAlī al-Ḥanafī, from Hammām, from Ibn Jurayj, from al-Zuhrī, from Anas that "whenever the Prophet, peace be on him, intended to pass a motion, he would remove his ring (on which God's name was inscribed)". Abū Dāwūd then says that this ḥadīth is *munkar* (confused), as it is probably mixed up with another ḥadīth also narrated by Ibn Jurayj, from Ibn Saʿd, from al-Zuhrī from Anas that "the Prophet, peace be on him, made a ring from silver, then he threw

it off". The weak point in the former ḥadīth is Hammām; no one else except Hammām has reported this ḥadīth.[16] In connection with another ḥadīth, after giving two various versions of it, Muslim wrote "The one related by Anas is more accurate than the other."

Many have considered *Sunan Abū Dāwūd* to be so comprehensive on legal ḥadīth and on *ḥalāl* and *ḥarām* that "it is sufficient for the *mujtahid*"[17] to obtain the knowledge of *ḥalāl* and *ḥarām* from Abū Dāwūd. The author's effort to identify points of weakness in ḥadīth that he recorded is yet another distinctive feature of Abū Dāwūd's collection. Al-Suyūṭī wrote that when Abū Dāwūd remains silent concerning a weak ḥadīth, it is likely to belong to the *Ḥasan* category.[18] Being confined to legal *aḥādīth*, Abū Dāwūd's *Sunan* does not expatiate in historical narrative, stories, moral themes on pious and virtuous deeds (*al-zuhd wa faḍā'il al-aʿmāl*) and so forth. He is said to have extracted his collection of 5,274 *aḥādīth* (4,800 without repetitions) from a much larger mass of 500,000 *aḥādīth*. He went on record to say that he did not include in his *Sunan* ḥadīth from those that were identified as *matrūk al-ḥadīth* (abandoned for their careless reporting of ḥadīth), which is probably why it has been ranked next in order of reliability to the *ṣaḥīḥayn*. This may also be due to his erudition and scholarship as well as piety and dedication to worship. In this regard, many have compared Abū Dāwūd to Imām Aḥmad b. Ḥanbal. Abū Dāwūd resided during the last three years of his life (272-275) in Baṣra at the invitation of the Governor of Baṣra who was a brother of the ʿAbbāsid Caliph, al-Muwaffaq. Students came to his circle of teaching from all directions. Abū Dāwūd also travelled widely in the Ḥijāz, Egypt, Iraq, al-Shām, North Africa and Khurāsān. He died in Baṣra and was buried next to Sufyān al-Thawrī.[19]

One of the distinctive features of Abū Dāwūd's work is that he gives the various sources through which he received the ḥadīth and also the various versions of the ḥadīth he might have received. He frequently pointed out the weakness or strength of the various versions he recorded and also declared which version he considered to be more reliable.

Another work to be mentioned in the *Sunan* category is that of Muḥammad b. Yazīd al-Qazwīnī (d. 273 H), better known as Ibn Māja, bearing the title, *Sunan Ibn Māja,* which contains 4,341 *aḥādīth*, of which 3,002 *aḥādīth* have been recorded by the authors of the previous works, there remaining 1,329 *aḥādīth* which are recorded by Ibn Māja alone.

Ibn Māja travelled to the Ḥijāz, Iraq, Egypt and Syria and met with many of the leading scholars and transmitters of ḥadīth. He was the leading ḥadīth scholar of Qazwīn and was also equally well-known as a leading Qur'ān commentator (*mufassir*) of his time. His *Sunan* collection includes, in addition to Sound/*Ṣaḥīḥ* ḥadīth, also ḥadīth in the other two categories of Fair and Weak (*Ḥasan*, *Ḍaʿīf*) which is why his *Sunan* was not included among the six leading collections until the early sixth-century hijra when Abū'l-Faḍl Muḥammad b. Ṭāhir al-Maqdīsī (d. 507) included it as one of the reliable works on ḥadīth, and then other scholars also recognised it as one of the main collections. Up until that time, ḥadīth scholars tended to regard the *Muwaṭṭa'* of Imām Mālik (d. 179 H) as the sixth major work on ḥadīth in preference to the *Sunan* of Ibn Māja.

The reason that prompted the ḥadīth scholars into giving priority to *Sunan Ibn Māja* over the *Muwaṭṭa'* was mainly do to the fact that the former contained additional ḥadīth, and additional *isnād* on existing *aḥādīth*, to what was already documented in the first five collections, whereas the *Muwaṭṭa'* contained very little in addition to what was already known, although the *Muwaṭṭa'* still commanded higher ranking in terms of reliability and *ṣiḥḥa*. A leading 20th-century ḥadīth scholar, Muḥammad Fu'ād ʿAbd al-Bāqī, has concluded that *Sunan Ibn Māja* contains 1,339 additional *aḥādīth* most of which have been recorded by the other five collections, but Ibn Māja has recorded them through different chains of transmitters. Ibn Māja went on record to say that he showed his work to the leading ḥadīth scholar of his time, Abū Zurʿa al-Rāzī who was impressed with it and considered it in some ways superior to the existing works on ḥadīth but added that it may contain ḥadīth that were weak in *isnād*. Ibn Ḥajar al-ʿAsqalānī has also spoken about *Sunan Ibn Māja* along similar lines and confirmed the existence of weak ḥadīth therein.[20] Many commentators have noted, however, that the ḥadīth Ibn Māja has recorded on the virtues of his home town, Qazwīn, are fabricated. Among them was Ibn al-Jawzī who declared in his work on *Mawḍūʿāt* that nearly all the ḥadīth on the merit of individuals, tribes or towns were fabricated and many of them were found in *Sunan Ibn Māja*.

Sunan al-Nasā'ī by al-Ḥāfiẓ Abū ʿAbd al-Raḥmān Aḥmad b. Shuʿayb al-Nasā'ī (d. 303) is another work in the *Sunan* category which consists of 5,000 legal *aḥādīth* of which a great number had appeared in the previous collections. Nasā'ī compiled his *Sunan* in two stages. The initial work which he completed contained ḥadīth in all the three categories of sound, fair and weak but did not record ḥadīth from narrators that were generally abandoned (*matrūk*) by the ḥadīth critics. This work bore the title *Al-Sunan al-Kubrā* which the author presented to the ʿAbbāsid ruler of Ramla in Palestine. The latter then questioned al-Nasā'ī as to whether all of his collection consisted of Sound/*Ṣaḥīḥ* ḥadīth. To this the author responded that it consisted of *Ṣaḥīḥ* and *Ḥasan* ḥadīths and what came close to them and resembled them. He was then requested to compile a work that contained only *Ṣaḥīḥ* ḥadīth, and it was then that he revised his *Al-Sunan al-Kubrā* and extracted therefrom a smaller collection (*al-sunan al-ṣughrā*) which the author then entitled *Al-Mujtabā min al-Sunan* (the selected portion of *Sunan*) often summarised as *Al-Mujtabā*. This is the collection that is currently in use and it contains very little weak ḥadīth. It is considered as one of the most reliable works after the *Ṣaḥīḥayn* which is also one of the best in terms of classification of its subject matter. *Sunan al-Nasā'ī* is ranked equal to that of *Sunan Abū Dāwūd* as the author is known to have been scrupulous in isolating doubtful ḥadīth from his collection and also his classification is of a *fiqhī* style. *Sunan Abū Dāwūd* is still considered the first book in *Sunan* category as it tends to provide additional data on the textual subject matter (*matn*) of ḥadīth that is of interest to the *fuqahā'*.[21]

6. The *Jāmiʿ* collections: This genre of ḥadīth literature signifies a comprehensive approach to ḥadīth collection due mainly to the broad range of topics that it includes. As already noted, the *Jāmiʿ* collections are expected to include a chapter each on dogmatics (*aqā'id*), legal rules (*aḥkām*), moral teachings (*al-riqāq*), social etiquette (*al-ādāb*), exegesis of the Qur'ān and the *Sunna*, history and biography of the Prophet (*al-tafsīr wa'l-tārīkh wa al-siyar*), virtues of the Prophet and his Companions (*al-manāqib*) and crises (*al-fitan*). The collections

of al-Bukhārī, Muslim and that of al-Tirmidhī fall under the *Jāmiʿ* category as they comprise ḥadīth on all of these eight subjects. Al-Tirmidhī's collection is occasionally identified as a *Sunan* work, which is due to his juristic style of classification of chapters in line with the *fiqh* works. Al-Ḥākim al-Nīsābūrī (d. 405) referred to Tirmidhī's collection as "*al-Jāmiʿ al-Ṣaḥīḥ*" which later scholars have considered somewhat of an exaggeration due to the fact that it contains ḥadīth in all the three categories of *Ṣaḥīḥ* (sound), *Ḥasan* (fair) and *Ḍaʿīf* (weak). The work is generally known as *Jāmiʿ al-Tirmidhī*, which is accurate as already explained. He included not only Sound or *Ṣaḥīḥ* ḥadīth in his work but also ḥadīth which were accepted and practised by the jurists. This is a feature of his work in that he collected ḥadīth that were practised and accepted by the jurists and the community at large, except as it is noted, for two *aḥādīth* neither of which are followed in practice. The first of these provides that "the Prophet, peace be on him, combined the *ẓuhr* and *ʿaṣr* prayers and those of the *maghrib* and *ʿishā'* without fear or travelling" (normally combination (*jamʿ*) is valid in those two situations). The second ḥadīth has it concerning the wine drinker that "if he repeats for the fourth time, he shall be killed."[22] Another distinguishing feature of al-Tirmidhī's collection is that he gives the *isnād* of the ḥadīth and then also gives other alternative *isnāds* through which the same ḥadīth is narrated. Sometimes he does not give this latter *isnād* in full but merely identifies a well-known narrator therein. Although al-Tirmidhī contains weak and sometimes defective (*muʿallal*) ḥadīth, the fact that he records only *aḥādīth* that are narrated or practised by prominent jurists and Imāms has meant that it is reasonably clear of spurious and fabricated ḥadīth, as it would be unlikely that such *aḥādīth* would be accepted by knowledgeable individuals of prominence.[23]

Shāh Walīullāh al-Dihlawī placed *Jāmiʿ al-Tirmidhī*, *Sunan Abū Dāwūd* and *Sunan al-Nasā'ī* in the second rank next to the *Ṣaḥīḥayn* and the *Muwaṭṭa'* of Imām Mālik. Then he added that al-Tirmidhī has improved the methods of the earlier works and included additional information concerning views and opinions of the leading scholars among the Companions, the Followers and other scholars. He also specified the sound from the weak ḥadīth and explained the grounds of weakness in ḥadīth.[24]

Until Tirmidhī's time, ḥadīth scholars divided ḥadīth into the two categories of *Ṣaḥīḥ* and *Ḍaʿīf*. *Ḍaʿīf* was also of two types, one of which was the abandoned (*matrūk*) variety, and the other which was not abandoned; the latter was rarely called *Ḥasan* by the previous scholars of ḥadīth and it was al-Tirmidhī that used the term *Ḥasan* consistently and this was then added as an intermediate class to the binary classification of ḥadīth that had hitherto prevailed. Al-Tirmidhī also used *Ḥasan* in other combinations such as *Ḥasan Ṣaḥīḥ* and *Ḥasan Gharīb*, terms which were coined by al-Tirmidhī himself. These will be explained in our discussion of *Ṣaḥīḥ*, *Ḥasan* and *Ḍaʿīf* below.

It thus appears that each of the six leading collections of ḥadīth has characteristic features of their own. *Al-Bukhārī* stands out in regard to the in-depth knowledge and insight that it conveys concerning ḥadīth (*al-tafaqquh fi'l-ḥadīth*), whereas *Muslim* is better consolidated and applies a superior thematic arrangement to that of *al-Bukhārī*. *Al-Tirmidhī* offers much information on *uṣūl al-ḥadīth* and methodology of ḥadīth transmission, whereas *Abū Dāwūd* is comprehensive on legal ḥadīth or *aḥādīth al-aḥkām*. *Ibn Māja* is elegant and more refined in terms of classification of themes and chapters of ḥadīth, whereas *al-Nasāʾī* is said to have combined most of these qualities.[25]

7. *Al-Muʿjam* (pl. *maʿājim*) collections refers to books of ḥadīth in which the contents appear in alphabetical order under the names of the narrators and their teachers, or the cities and tribes to which the narrators might have belonged. An example of this is *Al-Muʿjam al-Kabīr* by Abū'l-Qāsim Sulaymān b. Aḥmad b. Ayyūb al-Ṭabarānī (d. 360 H) in which he compiled ḥadīth narrated by Companions under their names. The names are arranged in alphabetical order and it contains 25,000 *aḥādīth*. This author has also compiled two other *Muʿjam* works, known as *Al-Muʿjam al-Awsaṭ* and *Al-Muʿjam al-Ṣaghīr*. Jalāl al-Dīn al-Suyūṭī (d. 911) authored a *muʿjam* entitled *Ḥāṭib al-Layl wa-Jārif al-Sayl* concerning his own teachers and *shaykhs*, that numbered 150 persons, and also a smaller *Muʿjam* entitled *Zād al-Masīr fi'l-Fihrist al-Ṣaghīr* in which he listed fifty narrators of ḥadīth in alphabetical order.[26]

8. *Al-Mustadrak* (pl. *mustadrakāt*): *Mustadrak* which literally means 'discovered' or 'detected' refers to ḥadīth books and collections

in which the compiler has supplemented the work of a previous compiler or compilers. Having accepted the conditions laid down by previous compilers, the new compilers collect other *aḥādīth* which fulfil those conditions but have been left out of the previous works. The *Mustadrak ʿala'l-Ṣaḥīḥayn* of al-Ḥākim al-Nīsābūrī (d. 405) thus consists of ḥadīth additions to al-Bukhārī and Muslim which escaped those authors' attention but which conformed to their conditions. A critic has stated, however, that the conformity of some of these additions to the conditions of al-Bukhārī and Muslim is not free of doubt. Thus on occasions, al-Ḥākim identified a ḥadīth as *Ṣaḥīḥ* on questionable grounds, or that he brought out ḥadīth which al-Bukhārī and Muslim themselves have not validated due to some weakness therein.[27]

9. *Al-Mustakhraj* (pl. *mustakhrajāt*). The *mustakhraj* (lit. extracted) are collections of ḥadīth in which a later compiler collects fresh *isnāds* for the same *aḥādīth* that were compiled in the previous works. The fresh attempt usually draws attention to transmitters that did not feature in the initial *isnād*. The two versions may be identical after the addition of the new link or links or may consist of two different chains of *isnād* altogether. The *Mustakhraj* of Abū Bakr b. Ibrāhīm al-Ismāʿīlī (d. 371) on *Ṣaḥīḥ al-Bukhārī* and that of Yaʿqūb b. Isḥāq b. Ibrāhīm al-Isfarā'īnī (d. 316) on *Ṣaḥīḥ Muslim*, and also the *Mustakhraj ʿala'l-Ṣaḥīḥayn* by Abū ʿAbd Allāh Muḥammad b. Yaʿqūb b. Yūsuf b. al-Shaybānī al-Nīsābūrī, known as Ibn al-Akhram (d. 344) are examples.

10. *Al-Juz'* (pl. *ajzā'*). *Al-juz'* (lit. section) refers to a book or collection in which ḥadīth is narrated by a single narrator among the Companions and others. Ḥadīth that are narrated by Abū Bakr and put in one collection is thus called *Juz' Abī Bakr*. It also refers to monographic collections of ḥadīth on a single theme or subject. Thus *aḥādīth* on night rising collected by al-Marwazī are known as *Juz' fi Qiyām al-Layl li'l-Marwazī*. A *juz'* consists, in other words, of what may be seen as a single chapter or section of a *jāmiʿ* collection.[28]

At about the middle of the fourth century hijra, the two *ṣaḥīḥs* of al-Bukhārī and Muslim and the two *Sunans* of Abū Dāwūd and al-Nasā'ī were recognised as the best collections of ḥadīth. After some time, the *Jāmiʿ* of al-Tirmidhī was added and the five books together were given the distinguished title of *Al-uṣūl al-khamsa* (the five source books).

It is not accurately known as to when the *Jāmiʿ* of al-Tirmidhī received the recognition and general approval of ḥadīth scholars. Ibn Ḥazm al-Ẓāhirī in the mid-fifth century criticised it for having recorded ḥadīth from al-Maslūb and al-Kalbī who were unreliable. It is likely that al-Tirmidhī's work was recognised well before that of Ibn Māja's collection, which was the last to be added to the five collections. Abū al-Faḍl Muḥammad b. Ṭāhir (d. 505/1111) appears to have been the first to support Ibn Māja's addition to the five collections and this was later endorsed by other ḥadīth scholars. By the seventh century hijra, the six books had been generally recognised by the world of Islam as the reliable collections of ḥadīth. Equally well recognised was the fact that among the six works, the first two, namely *al-Bukhārī* and *Muslim*, occupied the first rank.[29]

The main criteria that guided the ḥadīth scholars in their selection of the six works may be summarised as follows:

a. The compilers of these works employed certain principles of criticism and selection in their collections.
b. The six collections consisted mainly of Sound and Fair ḥadīth and if they added weak *aḥādīth*, they identified them as such, or that they were negligible in number.
c. The compilers had examined the value, merit and demerit of the ḥadīth they collected, discussed the reliability of their narrators, and explained the rare ḥadīth, if any, in their collections.
d. Subsequent experts of ḥadīth examined these works and considered them to be reliable.

The *musnad*, *muṣannaf* and other collections that were compiled before or after the *ṣaḥīḥs* of al-Bukhārī and Muslim contained both reliable and weak ḥadīths, which had not, however, been thoroughly examined by the ḥadīth scholars nor were they widely used by the jurists, and they were generally overshadowed by the six main collections.[30]

[05] Biographies of Ḥadīth Transmitters

ʿIlm Tārīkh al-Ruwāt

THIS branch of ḥadīth studies is sometimes referred to as *ʿilm al-rijāl al-ḥadīth*, and also *ṭabaqāt al-ruwāt* (classes of narrators), and *asmāʾ al-rijāl* (names of authorities). It is concerned mainly with biographical data, chronology, and life histories of ḥadīth transmitters, their academic achievements, their teachers, their students, school of following, political leaning and views of other people concerning them. All information that has a bearing on reliability or otherwise of their narration of ḥadīth, indeed any information that helps to explain and identify the personality and character of the ḥadīth transmitter is of concern to this branch of *ʿulūm al-ḥadīth*. Biographical data on ḥadīth transmitters is also concerned with precise identification of the generation (*ṭabaqa*) and time frame in which ḥadīth transmitters lived.

Ḥadīth transmitters have occasionally acted against the normal order of ḥadīth transmission. Sometimes a Companion narrates ḥadīth from a Follower (*tābiʿī*), or a father from son, in which case it is important that one is able to identify instances of this kind in the *isnād*. The normal order that is expected of *isnād* is that a person in the lower generation or *ṭabaqa* narrates ḥadīth from the preceding generation. It is also expected that the transmission occurs on a vertical line in an order where each generation is represented by one narrator. But this normal order frequently changes in parts of the *isnād* where, for example, two or three Companions, or two or three Followers, or Successors narrate from one another before the *isnād* shifts to a lower level. Sometimes relatives and family members narrate from one another horizontally in one generation. These and similar other factors have prompted the ḥadīth scholars to identify the classes/generations (*ṭabaqāt*) of ḥadīth narrators.

The Companions are basically one *ṭabaqa*, yet they have been classified in more than a dozen classes based on their seniority and closeness to the Prophet, their precedence in embracing Islam, time of migration to Madīna and participation in the various battles, beginning, for example, with the battles of Badr, Uḥud and so forth. Two persons may sometimes belong to the same *ṭabaqa* from a certain perspective, but fall under different *ṭabaqa* from a different perspective. The Companion, Anas b. Mālik al-Anṣārī, for example, is one of the junior Companions (*min aṣāghir al-ṣaḥāba*), but he joins the leading Companions for being one of *ʿashara mubashshara*.

Other factors that are brought to light by the biographers are exact identification of names especially when a person may be known by various names. The identification also of who is a Companion or *tābiʿī*, or *tābiʿ tābiʿī* and so on, are not self evident concerning the narrators of ḥadīth and it is the concern of this branch of ḥadīth to provide them as accurately as possible. Then the *tābiʿūn* are also sub-divided on the basis, for example, of the fact of their encounter with one of the *ʿashara mubashshara*, that is, the ten Companions to whom the Prophet gave the tiding of entry to Paradise. This is followed by the leading *tābiʿūn* that include the seven leading jurists of Madīna (*al-fuqahāʾ al-sabʿa*) and so on.[1]

It is possible, as experience shows, that a person is most pious and trustworthy yet weak in respect of retention and memory. Ḥadīth transmitted by such persons may not be admitted on the merit only of their piety. It is also possible, as ḥadīth scholars have noted, that a person is sound and reliable at one time and his condition changes due to personal situations, adoption of controversial views, illness and the like which may cast doubt on his reliability, and his transmission, therefore, of ḥadīth.[2] The *ʿulamāʾ* of ḥadīth are normally careful not to accept narration of ḥadīth from unknown people and persons of obscure identity and character. It is therefore not enough if a ḥadīth narrator is not known for transgression and doubtful statements but also that his propriety and trustworthiness is supported by positive evidence together with all relevant factors relating to their knowledge, piety, truthfulness, soundness of memory and association with others. This is in conformity with the widely-quoted statement of an early ḥadīth scholar, ʿAbd Allāh b. al-Mubārak (d. 181/797) who said that "*isnād* is a part of the religion, for without the verification of *isnād*, people may say what they wish to say." *Isnād* is concerned with accurate recording of the facts of ḥadīth and chronology (*al-tārīkh*) and plays a particularly important role in it. Investigation of the relevant dates has often revealed that spurious and careless statements have been made by individuals concerning the *isnād*. An early scholar of ḥadīth and a leading figure of al-Shām (Syria), Ismāʿīl b. ʿAyyāsh (d. 182/898) is quoted to have asked a man concerning a ḥadīth he had narrated from a Follower (*tābiʿī*), Khālid b. Maʿdān "When did you write the ḥadīth from Khālid b. Maʿdān?" and the answer given was "the year 113 hijra." This invoked the comment from Ibn ʿAyyāsh "Do you suppose that you heard the ḥadīth from him seven years after his death? – for Ibn Maʿdān died in 106 H."[3] Ḥafṣ b. Ghiyāth, a judge and ḥadīth scholar of Kūfa (d. 194/810) has been quoted to the effect "when you suspect a transmitter of ḥadīth, then judge him by the years," that is, his age, and the age of his immediate source, and time of encounter with his *shaykh* over the ḥadīth in question. Sufyān al-Thawrī (d. 161/778) who is known as *amīr al-mu'minīn fi'l-ḥadīth* (prince of the believers in ḥadīth) also went on record to say that "where the transmitters resorted to lying, we resorted to chronology (to judge them by it)."[4]

This sphere of ḥadīth studies is thus concerned primarily with biographical information which often begins with the date and place of birth and death, although it is the date of death which is the focus of attention rather than the date of birth. The information that is so documented is vast and it begins with the generation of the Companions, the Followers, and so on, while giving prominence to the leading scholars of ḥadīth and their contributions. The earliest works on the *Tārīkh al-Ruwāt* is that of Ibn Saʿd al-Zuhrī's (d. 230/845) *Kitāb al-Ṭabaqāt al-Kabīr* in fifteen volumes, and that of Imām Muḥammad b. Ismāʿīl al-Bukhārī (d. 256/871) *Al-Tarīkh al-Kabīr*, and Abū Ḥātim Muḥammad Ibn Ḥibbān al-Bustī's (d. 354/965) *Mashāhīr ʿUlamā' al-Amṣār*, and many others. Ibn Ḥajar al-ʿAsqalānī's (d. 852 H) *al-Iṣāba fi Tamyīz al-Ṣāḥāba* is very well-known, and a more recent work of acclaim on the subject is *Al-Risāla al-Mustaṭrifa* by Muḥammad b. Jaʿfar al-Kattānī (d. 1345/1927).[5] Al-ʿAsqalānī's *Al-Iṣāba* was subsequently summarised by his disciple al-Suyūṭī (d. 911) under the title *ʿAyn al-Iṣāba*. *Usd al-Ghāba* of ʿIzz al-Dīn Ibn al-Athīr (d. 630) is another well-known work on *ʿIlm Rijāl al-Ḥadīth*.[6]

The *Ṭabaqāt* of Ibn Saʿd contains biographies of most of the important narrators of ḥadīth. It is a rich mine of valuable information, not only on ḥadīth but also on the early history of Islam. It contains biographies of more than 4,000 traditionists. Ibn Saʿd was born in Baṣra in 169 H; he travelled in Kūfa, Makka and Madīna before he settled in Baghdad. Here he came in close contact with Muḥammad b. ʿUmar al-Wāqidī, one of the early Arab historians and prolific writers of his time. Ibn Saʿd worked as al-Wāqidī's literary secretary for many years, which gave him his title, Kātib al-Wāqidī, by which he is generally known. Ibn Saʿd was a man of great accomplishment in learning who attracted many distinguished students to his teachings. One of the most prominent among them was al-Balādhurī, the author of *Futūḥ al-Buldān*, who has relied extensively on Ibn Saʿd. Ibn Saʿd's own reliance on al-Wāqidī's works has, however, been criticised as the latter has been said to have been less than accurate in reference to ḥadīth.

Ibn Saʿd is known to have written two other works entitled *Al-Ṭabaqāt al-Ṣaghīr* and *Kitāb Akhbār al-Nabī* respectively. They are in effect not separate works as almost all the information they contain has been included in the first two volumes of his *Kitāb al-Ṭabaqāt al-Kabīr*.

Ibn al-Ṣalāḥ commented on Ibn Saʿd's *Ṭabaqāt*, saying that it is "an extensive work of great benefits, and its author is also reliable (*thiqa*), except that he has frequently recorded information from weak narrators (*al-ḍuʿafāʾ*), one among whom is (his teacher) Muḥammad b. ʿUmar al-Wāqidī."[7]

It seems that one of Ibn Saʿd's disciples, probably al-Ḥusayn b. Fahm (d. 289/901) wrote portions of the *Ṭabaqāt* as the text in some sections contains phrases such as "*ḥaddathanā Ibn Saʿd*" (Ibn Saʿd spoke to us). Ibn Fahm completed the book according to the plan of its author, added short notations to it concerning names that were already included by the author, and read the work to his own students. The first two volumes of this work are devoted to the geneology of the Prophet Muḥammad, and his biography where the author also gives information gives information on many of the previous prophets. The Prophet Muḥammad's early life in Makka, the beginning of his mission, migration to Madīna, his various battles, illness and death, etc., are expounded in considerable detail. The rest of this voluminous work is devoted to biographical data on the Companions, which he divided into five *ṭabaqāt*, beginning with the Migrants who participated in the Battle of Badr, Companions who had migrated to Abyssinia, those who converted to Islam before the conquest of Makka, Companions who settled and lived in Kūfa, or in Baṣra, Baghdad and other places, and then the Followers and the Successors. Biographical notations on the Companions are long and generally contain their geneologies on both their father and mother's side, the names of their wives and children, time of conversion to Islam, the part taken by them in the important events during the Prophet's lifetime, the dates of their death and so forth. There is a certain degree of overlap and inclusion of the same names in different classes in his divisions, some of which is, however, considered to be inevitable. The very last volume of this work is devoted to women among the Companions and the Followers.[8] Ibn Saʿd pays a great deal of attention to geneologies with an unusual emphasis on tribal origins and descent in a way that is reminiscent of the pre-Islamic era. In this regard Ibn Saʿd's work stands in contrast to that of his teacher al-Wāqidī. Ibn Saʿd's biographies are generally premised on the time factor and dates such as those of migration to Abyssinia, the Hijra proper, the Battle of Badr, the conquest of Makka and so forth. Yet he also refers frequently to place names in the biographical data he has compiled.[9] Siddiqi has quoted Prof. Sachau's remark on Ibn Saʿd who has "shown impartiality and honesty, thoroughness and minuteness, objectivity and originality."[10]

Writers have taken different approaches to biographical literature on the classification of ḥadīth transmitters. Some writers classified them in accordance with categories, or *ṭabaqāt*, that lived in the same era or generation. Famous in this category is the *Ṭabaqāt* of Ibn Saʿd. Whereas Ibn Saʿd's work provides detailed information on biographies, the *Ṭabaqāt al-Ḥuffāẓ* of al-Ḥāfiẓ Shams al-Dīn al-Dhahabī (d. 748) contain extremely short notices on the classes and individuals of ḥadīth transmitters. There are also some who confine their works only to the names, appellations, titles and geneologies.

Still others have classified their biographies in alphabetical order in accordance with the names of narrators and this appears to be easier to use. One of the well-known works in this category is Ibn Ḥajar al-ʿAsqalānī's *Tahdhīb al-Tahdhīb* in ten volumes. Imām al-Bukhārī's *Al-Tarīkh al-Kabīr* is another work of this type.

There are also those who based their biographies on the chronological factor of the dates of deaths of the transmitters, and yet others who used the names of cities and localities to which the narrators belonged. Makka, Madīna, Kūfa, Baṣra, Wāsiṭ, Damascus, Baghdad, Alleppo, Qayrawan, Bukhārā, Merw, etc., were also home to ḥadīth transmitters and literary figures. This data provides basic tools for ḥadīth criticism and the application of rules pertaining to impugnment and validation (*al-jarḥ wa'l-taʿdīl*).[11]

The magnitude of these biographical dictionaries is seen from the large number of persons whose biographies they contain. Al-Bukhārī's *Al-Tarīkh al-Kabīr*, which is the next landmark work after that of Ibn Saʿd dealt with over 40,000 traditionists. No complete manuscript of this work is, however, known to exist. Only sections of it have been preserved. Al-Khaṭīb al-Baghdādī (d. 463 H) gave in his *Tārīkh Baghdād*, short biographies of 7,831 persons, whereas Ibn Ḥajar al-ʿAsqalānī in his *Tahdhīb al-Tahdhīb* and *Mizān al-Iʿtidāl* recorded biographies of 12,415 and 14,443 traditionists respectively.

The initial phase of the *ṭabaqāt* literature, which was general and recorded biographies of all narrators of ḥadīth soon led to the writing of more specialised works that focused on certain classes thereof. These works specialised in the biographies of the Companions, or of persons in other periods, and in respect of cities and localities, or according to their ranking on the various criteria of reliability or weakness and so forth.

The results of this research was collected and put together by ʿIzz al-Dīn Ibn al-Athīr (d. 630/1230) in *Usd al-Ghāba* which compiled biographies of 7,554 persons in the category of Companions, some of whom were only discovered by him. *Usd al-Ghāba* is considered a work of authority and it was followed in the ninth-century hijra by a more comprehensive work on the subject, namely, *Al-Iṣāba fī Tamyīz al-Ṣaḥāba* by Shihāb al-Dīn ʿAlī Ibn Ḥajar al-ʿAsqalānī (d. 852/1448). Ibn Ḥajar has put together the results of the labours of his predecessors on the biographies of Companions, criticising them in certain cases and adding to them some of his own findings. His work thus combines a part where correct biographies are recorded of persons who have been wrongly identified as Companions in some other biographical dictionaries.

In the *Iṣāba* and his other works on ḥadīth narrators, Ibn Ḥajar has altogether identified twelve classes of narrators from the time of the Companions down to the time when the six major collections were written. All of his biographies are of persons whose ḥadīth have been quoted in one or the other of the six collections. These may be summarised as follows. It will be noted at the outset, however, that all of the twelve categories actually fall under the basic three, namely, the Companions, the Followers (*tābiʿūn*) and the Successors (*tābiʿ tābiʿūn*). The twelve categories are:

1. Companions, who are sub-divided into various categories.
2. Leading figures among the Followers (*kibār al-tābiʿīn*), such as Saʿīd b. al-Musayyib, ʿAlqama and Ḥasan al-Baṣrī.
3. The upper middle category of Followers, such as Muḥammad b. Sīrīn, Ḥafṣa bint Sīrīn, and ʿAmra bint ʿAbd al-Raḥmān.
4. Lower middle category of the Followers, who narrated mostly from the Followers (not Companions), such as al-Zuhrī and Qatāda.
5. The junior category of Followers, who may not have heard directly from the Companions, such as Aʿmash.
6. Those who accompanied the fifth category but who have not met with the Companions, such as Ibn Jurayj.
7. The leading Successors (*kubbār atbāʿ al-tābiʿīn*), such as Mālik b. Anas and Sufyān al-Thawrī.
8. The upper middle category of Successors, such as Ibn ʿUyayna and Ibn ʿUlayya.
9. The junior category of Successors, such as al-Shāfiʿī, and Abū Dāwūd al-Ṭayālisī.
10. Leading literary figures who narrated from junior Successors who had not met the Followers, such as Aḥmad b. Ḥanbal.
11. Upper middle among the tenth category, such as al-Bukhārī.
12. Junior figures among the tenth who quoted the Successors, such as al-Tirmidhī.

A perusal of this list is enough to show that the categories tend to overlap and grey areas have persistently been noted and invited attention from researchers who tried to minimise them. The overlap that is noted is not necessarily a function of ambiguity but a combination of factors that renders the same person eligible to be listed in more than one category. Note, for example, the first *ṭabaqa*, namely of the Companions, who are classified in about a dozen sub-categories on the basis either of their seniority in embracing Islam, migration to Madīna, participation in the various Battles, the ten to whom the Prophet gave the tiding of admission to Paradise (*al-ʿashara al-mubashshara*) and so on, and now consider the first Caliph Abū Bakr or his Successor ʿUmar, who belonged to many of these categories. Overlaps of a similar order can also be seen among the Followers and Successors.[12]

It is suggested that the last of the Companions was Abū Ṭufayl ʿĀmir b. Wāthila al-Laythī who died in the year 100 of the hijra, and the last of the Followers is one who has seen the last living Companion. Abū Ṭufayl ʿĀmir b. Wāthila died in Makka and the last person among the Followers who met him was Khalaf b. Khalīfa who died in 181 hijra and this also marked the ending of the period of the Followers. The Successors' period is considered to have ended at the year 220 H; included among them were the Imāms Mālik and al-Shāfiʿī. Imām Aḥmad b. Ḥanbal (d. 241) belongs to the succeeding generation, that is, next to the Successors, whereas Imām Abū Ḥanīfa (d. 150 H) belongs to the category of the Followers as he met some of the junior Companions like Anas b. Mālik, Jābir b. ʿAbd Allāh and others.

About seven persons among the Companions are known to have narrated a major portion of ḥadīth from the Prophet, a fact which earned them the epithet *mukththirū al-ḥadīth* (prolific narrators of ḥadīth) as opposed to those who transmitted little notwithstanding their recognised status as leading figures among them. Anyone who narrated more than one thousand ḥadīth from the Prophet belongs to the category of prolific narrators and these are Abū Hurayra who narrated (5,374) *aḥādīth*, ʿAbd Allāh b. ʿUmar (2,630) *aḥādīth*, Anas b. Mālik (2,286) *aḥādīth*, ʿĀ'isha Ṣiddiqa (2,210) *aḥādīth*, ʿAbd Allāh b. ʿAbbās (1,660), Jābir b. ʿAbd Allāh (1,540) and Abū Saʿīd al-Khudrī (1,170) *aḥādīth*.[13] The most learned among the Companions were ʿUmar b. al-Khaṭṭāb, ʿAlī, Ubayy b. Kaʿb, Zayd b. Thābit, Abū al-

Dardā' (some say Abū Mūsā al-Ashʿarī instead of Abū al-Dardā), and ʿAbd Allāh b. Masʿūd, and the two selected names from among these were ʿAlī and Ibn Masʿūd.[14]

Abū Bakr, the first Caliph, and lifetime friend and Companion of the Prophet has narrated about one hundred and forty-two *aḥādīth*, which is said to be due to his early death at a time when ḥadīth narration had not yet become the focus of attention.

[06] Ḥadīth Terminology

Muṣṭalaḥ al-Ḥadīth

"*MUṢṬALAḤ al-ḥadīth*" denotes two different meanings, one of which is general and the other more specific. As a general term, "*Muṣṭalaḥ al-ḥadīth*" is often used as an equivalent term to *ʿulūm al-ḥadīth*, both of which refer to the entire body of ḥadīth methodology and science. The whole discipline began with the purpose mainly of stemming the tide of forgery in ḥadīth with the aid of a carefully worked out methodology and rules by which to isolate the forgeries. More specifically "*Muṣṭalaḥ al-ḥadīth*" refers to technical terms, names and phrases that the discipline has developed over time, and it is in this latter sense that the term is used in the present context.

Ḥadīth literature is replete with technical terms of the kind that even a native Arabic speaker without expert knowledge of the subject cannot be expected to comprehend. Some of the technical terms pertaining to ḥadīth have already been discussed in the preceding sections of this book. As will be noted, matters pertaining to reliability of the chain of *isnād* and also the meaning and linguistic clarity of ḥadīth have moved from simple categories and classifications to shades of meaning and nuances of linguistic refinement over the various stages of development in ḥadīth literature. The terminology that is developed as a result has in the course of time gained general recognition so that the mere use of a term such as *musnad*, *muttaṣil*, *marfūʿ*, *mursal*, *maqṭūʿ*, *munqaṭiʿ*, *muʿallaq* and so on is enough to convey full identification of the type of ḥadīth and relative strength and weakness of its chain of *isnād*. From the dictionary perspective some of these words carry identical or near-identical meanings but technically they are very different.

Muṣṭalaḥ al-ḥadīth is one of the most, if not the most, significant areas of ḥadīth learning in that it consists mainly of the names of things. It is the embodiment in many ways of the sum-total of the rest of the ḥadīth sciences and communicative, as such, of the end-result of its related disciplines. *ʿIlm muṣṭalaḥ al-ḥadīth* also serves to depict the cumulative scholarship of the men of learning over the history of developments in ḥadīth studies. The refinement of thought and levels of distinction in ḥadīth terminology are also indicative of the nature of the issues that were encountered in these stages. Ḥadīth sciences have grown along different lines and directions which tend to be somewhat less than consolidated. *Muṣṭalaḥ al-ḥadīth* may be said to be the one branch of the ḥadīth studies that seeks to bring all of the other branches into focus and provide the reader with an efficient lead-in to the knowledge of the entire discipline.

The discussion that follows provides a brief description of the ḥadīth terminology relating to basic terms, ḥadīth literature, ḥadīth types and classification from the viewpoints of both transmission (*riwāya*) and meaning (*dalāla*). This also includes titles of the ḥadīth scholars, that is, the *alqāb al-muḥaddithīn*, whereas the genres of ḥadīth literature, or *asmāʿ kutub al-ḥadīth,* have been discussed under the documentation of ḥadīth in a previous chapter.

Basic Terms: *Sunna*, *Khabar*, *Athar*, *Ḥadīth* and *Ḥadīth Qudsī*

Sunna literally means a trodden path, or *ṭarīqa*, a precedent and exemplary conduct. Although *Sunna* can mean a bad example or precedent as well as a good one, it is often the latter which the *Sunna* conveys. *Bidʿa* (innovation), which is the opposite of *Sunna* is used often in the sense of a pernicious innovation which departs from the accepted precedent, or *Sunna*. Although many have considered *Sunna* and ḥadīth to be synonymous, others have reserved *Sunna* for practical examples and ḥadīth for verbal expressions of the *Sunna*. *Sunna* also differs from ḥadīth in that *Sunna* refers to the ruling or *ḥukm* that is conveyed in a ḥadīth, whereas ḥadīth is the verbal carrier of *Sunna*, the words and phrases, in other words, in which the *Sunna* has been communicated and expressed.

Ḥadīth literally means 'speech' and also 'new', which is the opposite of '*qadīm*'. Since speech is created as it is uttered by the speaker, it is known as ḥadīth. Thus the sayings of the Prophet were known as ḥadīth in contradistinction with the Qur'ān, which was *qadīm*. Ḥadīth as such is the verbal embodiment and vehicle of *Sunna*. After the demise of the Prophet, people engaged in speech about him so much that the word ḥadīth was eventually reserved for speech concerning the Prophet, including his own speech. This may also explain that in the early stages, the sayings of Companions and even Followers were included in 'ḥadīth', which is still the case to some extent. Although ḥadīth is the verbal carrier of *Sunna*, not every ḥadīth contains *Sunna*, that is, a *ḥukm* and exemplary conduct. This distinction between *Sunna* and ḥadīth is still valid, but it was more significant in the early stages of the development of ḥadīth studies. The distinction has lost some of its meaning after al-Shāfiʿī who insisted that every *Sunna* must be verified and established by an authentic ḥadīth, which to all intents and purposes was equivalent to saying that there is no *Sunna* if it cannot be proven through a validly transmitted ḥadīth that is supported by a reliable *isnād*.

The view has generally gained ground among the scholars of ḥadīth, especially the latecomers (*muta'akhkhirūn*) among them that ḥadīth and *Sunna* are two words for the same meaning and that both include the saying, act and tacit approval of the Prophet. Yet background historical developments tend to draw subtle distinctions between them which may now be said to be of historical interest and would carry little, if any, religious or juridical weight. Yet a brief review of background developments in terminology is useful for purposes of understanding. *Sunna* was seen to have a stronger base in actual reality and practice, and it was basically in this sense that the word occurred in the saying, as it is reported, of the Prophet:

> You are to follow my *Sunna* and the *Sunna* of the rightly-guided caliphs after me.[1]

> عليكم بسنتي وسنة الخلفاء الراشدين من بعدي.

Some have even asserted that *Sunna* basically means actual conduct and that *Sunna* does not include verbal statements. They say that this was what *Sunna* had meant during the time of the Prophet and the Companions. This is, however, not accepted and it is generally held that *Sunna* is a general term that includes both the saying and action of the Prophet. To say this is also in harmony with the Qur'ān: When the Qur'ān assigns to the Prophet the role to explain to the people what God has revealed (al-Naḥl, 16:44), it is understood that the Prophet explained the messages of the Qur'ān in words and action both. Besides, a person's statements, words, and conduct often become a part of one another and a realistic distinction would be difficult to maintain between them.

Sunna has meant different things to the ḥadīth scholars, the jurists, and the *uṣūl* scholars respectively. To the *ʿulamā'* of *uṣūl*, *Sunna* primarily signifies a proof and source of the *Sharīʿa* next to the Qur'ān and it comprises the sayings, acts and tacit approval of the Prophet which contain evidence to establish a ruling or *ḥukm* of *Sharīʿa*. Some *uṣūl* scholars have included in *Sunna* acts and precedent of the Companions whether they followed the Qur'ān or the directives of the Prophet or followed their own *ijtihād*, such as their action to collate and compile the Qur'ān, for example. Imām Mālik has shown this tendency as he considered the *Sunna* of the Prophet and the practice of the Companions an extension of one another. Imām Shāfiʿī has, however, criticised his teacher, Imām Mālik, for mixing the *Sunna* of the Prophet with the conduct of the Companions.[2]

For the jurists and *fuqahā'*, *Sunna* primarily signifies a value point below the level of obligation, including everything which the Prophet has authorised by way of recommendation that does not convey an emphatic demand. *Sunna* as such is equivalent to *mandūb* that merits a reward when it is followed but omitting it is not punishable. *Sunna* in this sense is also used in the expression that so and so is a follower of the *Sunna*, or *Ahl al-Sunna wa'l-Jamāʿa*, and also as ritual prayer, such as performing two units of supererogatory prayer, or *Sunna*.

For the ḥadīth scholars and *muḥaddithūn*, *Sunna* is not confined to that which conveys a *ḥukm* or ruling of *Sharīʿa*, nor to a proof and source thereof, but comprises all the sayings and acts of the Prophet and his tacit approval, his biography and description of personal attributes, events such as reports of his battles, and news and stories of interest concerning him. The jurists tend to preclude description of the personal attributes of the Prophet from their perception of *Sunna*. The *ʿulamāʾ* of ḥadīth thus tend to include in *Sunna* almost everything that is attributed to the Prophet and this is *Sunna* in its widest sense as compared to the *ʿulamāʾ* of *uṣūl* who discuss *Sunna* in the context mainly of the proofs of *Sharīʿa*.

The *fuqahāʾ*, refer to *Sunna* in the context mainly of the rulings, or *aḥkām*, of *Sharīʿa* in the determination of what is obligatory (*wājib*), recommendable (*mandūb*), permissible (*mubaḥ*), reprehensible (*makrūh*) and forbidden (*ḥarām*). The ḥadīth scholars and jurists have recognised the distinction between *Sunna* and ḥadīth in the typical statement, for example, that "this ḥadīth is contrary to *qiyās*, *Sunna* and consensus" (*hadhāʾl-ḥadīth mukhālif liʾl-qiyās wal-Sunna waʾl-ijmāʿ*).[3] *Sunna* as such refers to the normative and exemplary conduct of the Prophet which is a recognised source of the *Sharīʿa*.

Sunna is divided into three types, namely verbal *Sunna* (*Sunna qawliyya*) which is now synonymous with ḥadīth and, by far, the largest part of *Sunna* consists of this type. This is followed by actual *Sunna* (*Sunna fiʿliyya*) which consists of reports concerning the acts of the Prophet. What the Prophet has tacitly approved falls under the tacitly approved *Sunna* (*Sunna taqririyya*). This too is a broad category as it included customary practices of the Arabs which came to the Prophet's attention but which he did not overrule. Tacit *Sunna* also included acts and conduct of the Companions that the Prophet allowed or did not overrule when they caught his attention.

Khabar literally means a report or verbal communication and announcement of a factual event, and it thus bears a meaning that is closer to ḥadīth than *Sunna*. For there can be no ḥadīth without a *khabar*, as ḥadīth basically consists of a report of the saying and exemplary conduct of the Prophet. Yet there is a difference between *khabar* and ḥadīth in that every ḥadīth consists of what originates from the Prophet and comes from him, whereas *khabar* is what comes from others concerning him. Every ḥadīth may also be said to be a *khabar* but not every *khabar* is a ḥadīth. "*Khabar*" in the expression "*ikhbārī*" is employed in reference to a historian in contradistinction to a *muḥaddith*, that is, a scholar of ḥadīth. The Shīʿī *ʿulamāʾ* tend to use *khabar* more widely than their Sunnī counterparts often in preference to ḥadīth. This is because the Shīʿīs include within the general meaning of ḥadīth and *khabar* the sayings, not only of the Prophet, but also of their recognised Imāms as they are deemed to have inherent knowledge of the *Sunna* of the Prophet. Ḥadīth to the Shīʿīs thus signifies a wider meaning, and *khabar* as a term is used by them to include ḥadīth proper as well as the sayings of the Imāms. Yet there is a tendency among Shīʿī writers to use the word *Sunna* in reference to the *Sunna* of the Prophet only.

Athar literally means imprint, relic or vestage that is inherited from the past. It is often used synonymously with ḥadīth, both of which imply valid precedent, but *athar* is wider than ḥadīth in that it includes all that is attributed to the Prophet, his Companions, Followers and other leading figures. However, some scholars of ḥadīth, especially the non-Arabs from Khurāsān and Persia, have reserved *athar* for the sayings and precedent of the Companions only. An equivalent term to *athar*, which is commonly employed, is *khabar mawqūf*, that is, what a Companion has indicated to be a part of the *Sunna* but whose chain of *isnād* does not reach the Prophet himself.[4]

Ḥadīth Qudsī: This is a variety of ḥadīth in which the Prophet speaks to his community and relates what he says directly to God Most High. *Ḥadīth Qudsī* (also known as *Ḥadīth Ilāhī* and *Ḥadīth Rabbānī*) is thus distinguished from *al-Ḥadīth al-Nabawī*, or ḥadīth of the Prophet, in that the speaker in the former is God Most High whereas in the latter it is the Prophet himself. When the Prophet says, for example that "God Most High said" and in what follows there are also parts which read such as "O my servants (*yā ʿibādī*)" – the question arises as to whether this should be regarded as part of the Qur'ān or of the ḥadīth of the Prophet. Some have said such ḥadīth partially resembles the Qur'ān and it also partakes in ḥadīth. It is called *Ḥadīth Qudsī* because the speech is attributed to God Most High wherein the Prophet simply acts as a carrier of the divine message. Although the word "*quds*" in the Qur'ān has been used in reference to the Archangel Gabriel (cf. al-Naḥl, 16:102) *qudsī* in the present context is used in its literal sense which conveys the sense of purity and holiness in reference to God Most High. But even so there is a difference between *Ḥadīth Qudsī* and the Qur'ān, which is that the Qur'ān is the speech of God that is conveyed to the Prophet by the Archangel Gabriel in the form of manifest *waḥy* (*waḥy ẓāhir*) in the words of God, whereas the words of

Ḥadīth Qudsī are those of the Prophet himself and they are not revealed in the form of *waḥy ẓāhir*, but revealed to him through inspiration of idea and concept.

The words of the Prophet do not command the same spiritual ranking as the text of the Qur'ān. This also explains why only the Qur'ān, but not the *Ḥadīth Qudsī*, may be recited in the five daily prayers, or any other *ṣalāh* that a Muslim performs. It is a requirement also that the Qur'ān should be read in a state of ablution, but this is not required for *Ḥadīth Qudsī*. A total of just over 100 *Qudsī* ḥadīth have been transmitted and there are some ḥadīth collections that consist exclusively of this type of ḥadīth. The early *ʿulamā'* (*salaf*) usually opened the *Ḥadīth Qudsī* with a phrase such as "*qāla Rasūl Allah fimā yarwī ʿan rabbih*" (the Messenger of God said while reporting from God). But the scholars of the later period (*khalaf*) substituted this by the typical statement *qāla Allahu taʿālā fimā rawāhu ʿanhu Rasūl Allah* (God Most High said in what the Messenger of God narrated from Him). The source in both cases is God Most High. *Ḥadīth Qudsī* may be illustrated as follows:

1. God Most High said: O My servants! I have forbidden injustice unto Myself and also prohibited it to you. So do not be unjust amongst yourselves.

قال الله تعالى: يا عبادي! إنّي حرمت الظلم على نفسي وجعلته محرماً بينكم، فلا تظالموا ...

2. Sometimes a ḥadīth *Qudsī* is merged into a ḥadīth *nabawī*, as in the following example:

All deeds of the progeny of Adam are multiplied, the good deeds are multiplied ten-fold upwards to seven hundred times. God Most High said except for fasting, for this is for Me alone and I reward it Myself. It is for My sake that My servant abandons his sexual desire and food. One who fasts experiences two joys, one when he opens his fast and the other when he meets Me.

كل عمل ابن آدم يضاعف، الحسنة عشر أمثالها إلى سبعمائة ضعف، قال الله تعالى: "إلا الصوم فإنه لي وأنا أجزي به، من يدع شهوته وطعامه لأجلي..."

From the viewpoint of its authenticity, ḥadīth *Qudsī* is measured by the same criteria as any other ḥadīth, and it may thus be classified as Sound, Fair or Weak, just as it may be classified as elevated (*Marfūʿ*), suspended, or broken (*Mawqūf, Maqṭūʿ*) and also as *Mutawātir* or *Āḥād*. This is also indicative of a difference between ḥadīth *Qudsī* and the Qur'ān in that the text of the Qur'ān is authentic beyond question, all of which is *Mutawātir*, whereas this is not the case with most of the ḥadīth *Qudsī*.[5]

Al-Riwāya wa'l-Dirāya (Transmission and Meaning)

Riwāya (lit. reporting or narration), refers to transmission of ḥadīth and the soundness and continuity or otherwise of its *isnād*, and also the manner in which the ḥadīth was received, retained and delivered, or subjected to validation and impugnment, etc., without looking into the meaning and implications of the text of ḥadīth. *Dirāya* on the other hand is concerned with the truth, meaning and message of the ḥadīth, and the law or ruling that is conveyed by the text. To establish the accuracy of the text of ḥadīth is naturally the end-result of the enquiry over the transmission and meaning. *Riwāya* and *dirāya* are therefore not separate from one another as they both seek to establish the authenticity of ḥadīth and accuracy of its message.

Sanad, Isnād, Musnad

Literally '*sanad*' means a pillar or support, and in reference to ḥadīth it refers to all the individuals and persons who transmitted ḥadīth from the Prophet and then from one another until it reaches us. *Musnid*, which is the active participle of the same root word (*sanada*) refers to the individual narrator that is included in the *sanad*, whereas *isnād*, which is the verbal noun of the same root refers to the chain of transmission of ḥadīth and it is, in this sense, synonymous with *sanad*. *Musnid* is thus the carrier of ḥadīth and it is synonymous with *rāwī* (narrator). '*Isnād*' is sometimes used to signify the activity that is involved in attributing the ḥadīth to its narrators in every generation.

'*Musnad*' which is the passive participle of *sanada* refers to ḥadīth that is supported by a chain of transmission or *isnād*. According to the preferable view, the chain of transmission in *Musnad* is also connected from beginning to end all the way back to the Prophet. It is a ḥadīth, in other words, that is both *Muttaṣil* (connected) and *Marfūʿ* (elevated). *Musnad* as such precludes ḥadīth with a broken *isnād* or one that does not reach the Prophet himself. *Musnad* in other words, precludes *Mawqūf* (suspended), *Mursal* and disconnected (*ghayr muttaṣil*) ḥadīth. To say that the *isnād* of *Musnad* ḥadīth is connected all the way means that every narrator therein heard or received it through a valid method of reception from his teacher or *shaykh*. *Musnad* is not synonymous with *Marfūʿ* in that every *Musnad* is a *Marfūʿ* but every *Marfūʿ* does not necessarily qualify as *Musnad*. Al-Ḥākim al-Nīsābūrī also adds that the *isnād* of *Musnad* must also be clear of *tadlīs* or hidden ambiguity that causes doubt about its reliability.

Although some ḥadīth scholars have equated *Marfūʿ* with *Musnad*, it is a weak opinion. This is because *Marfūʿ* can also include disconnected ḥadīth which cannot therefore qualify as *Musnad*.[6]

Al-Matn

Literally *matn* means support. It is the verbal noun of *matana* which means strengthening or fortifying something, and in this context it refers to a ḥadīth that is supported by a text. *Matn* refers to the text or body of ḥadīth and it is used in contradistinction with *isnād*, which is a different aspect of providing support for *ḥadīth*, namely, through a chain of transmission.

Ranking and Titles of Ḥadīth Scholars (*alqāb al-muḥaddithīn*)

The *ʿulamā'* have identified a number of ranks in the accomplishment and erudition of ḥadīth in an ascending order, beginning with the *musnid*, as follows:

a. *Musnid* (the active participle of *isnād*) refers to a person who engages himself in the transmission of ḥadīth and this is acceptable even if he has little knowledge either of the *isnād* or the meaning that is conveyed by the ḥadīth. Sometimes the term *mubtadi'* (novice) is used as an equivalent. A step more advanced to *Musnid* is the *ṭālib al-*

ḥadīth (lit. seeker of ḥadīth), an expression which is used in reference to a student of ḥadīth who engages himself in acquiring knowledge of the *riwāya*, *dirāya* and other aspects of *uṣūl al-ḥadīth*.

b. *Muḥaddith* (learned in ḥadīth): This title is given to one who knows the strengths and weaknesses both of the *isnād* and the text of the ḥadīth and hidden defects (*al-ʿilal*) therein. A *muḥaddith* is also expected to be familiar with the six renowned collections of ḥadīth and has, it is said, committed to memory at least one thousand *aḥādīth* from the six collections.[7]

c. *Ḥāfiẓ*: Literally retentive of memory or a memoriser, one who has committed to memory all the *Ṣaḥīḥ*/Sound *aḥādīth* and cites it from memory when the occasion arises. The term refers to one who possesses wider knowledge of ḥadīth than that of a *muḥaddith*. A *Ḥāfiẓ* is a person who is well-informed about the conditions of the transmitters and *isnād* and can evaluate reliability or weakness of the narrators of ḥadīth in every generation just as he can ascertain strength and weakness in the *ijtihād* of other scholars. He is knowledgeable of the terminology of ḥadīth and can ascertain nuances of expression in ḥadīth literature with regard especially to narrators of ḥadīth. A *Ḥāfiẓ* conveys a reference to memory, which is naturally important, and even if recourse is made to writing and written record, the role of committing to memory is still emphasised. Some *ʿulamāʾ* have specified that a *ḥāfiẓ* is expected to have committed to memory 100,000 *aḥādīth* and some have said even more, whereas others have mentioned a minimum of 20,000 *aḥādīth*. But it is suggested, rightly perhaps, that these specifications have to some extent been dictated by the prevailing conditions of earlier generations. With the advancement of literacy and other aids to memory, and use of computer, the requirements may be open to adjustment, for it would otherwise be difficult to find people who would qualify for these requirements.[8] It would be equally untenable to say that no one would qualify. Such a conclusion would be patently false as it is certain that people of great standing in the knowledge of ḥadīth existed in the past as they also continue to exist. It would thus be advisable for us to attach greater credibility to the knowledge and insight, to *dirāya*, rather than to *riwāya*, in our own times. For the titles that were specified in the past may not even be accurate to apply after the compilation and documentation of ḥadīth on a massive scale. What is important now is to carry the meaning and message of those evaluative designations and not be too specific perhaps on their quantitative specifications, which might in any case, have been mentioned for the sake of emphasis rather than literal application. Would it not be taxing for any one person to memorise hundreds of thousands of *aḥādīth* with their *isnāds*? What we are saying here also applies to the next two ranks, namely of *Ḥujja* and *Ḥākim*.

d. *Ḥujja*: literally proof, and it refers to a degree of erudition in ḥadīth that ranks above that of the *ḥāfiẓ*. *Ḥujja* thus refers to a person whose knowledge of ḥadīth is comprehensive and insightful in addition, that is, to possessing the necessary qualifications of a *ḥāfiẓ*. Some have specified committing to memory for a *Ḥujja* of 300,000 *aḥādīth* together with their *isnāds*.

e. *Ḥākim*. *Ḥākim* signifies the highest degree of erudition in ḥadīth which is all-round and comprehensive and comprises a high level of competence in ḥadīth in all of its various branches such as *al-jarḥ wa'l-taʿdīl*, *ʿilal al-ḥadīth*, *gharīb al-ḥadīth*, the abrogator and abrogated and so forth. A *ḥākim* is also described as one who has committed to memory all the reported ḥadīth on record together with their *isnāds* in all the *Ṣaḥīḥ* as well as the *Ḥasan* and *Ḍaʿīf* categories and can distinguish and isolate the fabricated or *mawḍūʿ* from other *aḥādīth*.

These were some of the basic terms in *Muṣṭalaḥ al-Ḥadīth*, which are by no means exhaustive. The various classifications of ḥadīth in the three varieties of *Ṣaḥīḥ*, *Ḥasan* and *Ḍaʿīf* as well as their sub-varieties into a much larger range and, of course, *Mutawātir*, *Mashhūr* and *Āḥād* also fall within the purview of *Muṣṭalaḥ al-Ḥadīth*. These are not discussed here as they will be addressed in their appropriate contexts in the various sections of this book. What follows next is an extension basically of ḥadīth terminology, or *Muṣṭalaḥ al-Ḥadīth*. I continue first with the classification of ḥadīth into Sound, Fair and Weak (*Ṣaḥīḥ*, *Ḥasan*, and *Ḍaʿīf* respectively), whereas the section that follows addresses a variety of other classifications ranging from elevated (*Marfūʿ*), to suspended (*Mawqūf*), solitary (*Fard*), strong (*ʿAzīz*) to *Mutawātir* and *Āḥād*.

[07] Ḥadīth Forgery

Waḍʿ al-Ḥadīth

EXTENSIVE forgery in ḥadīth was commonly known and acknowledged to have occurred in the early decades of the advent of Islam. It is believed to have begun following the turmoil over the murder of the third caliph, ʿUthmān, which dealt a heavy blow to the unity of the *umma*. This momentous event is held responsible for the emergence of serious political differences and partisan groups such as Shīʿa, Kharijites and Muʿtazila, as well as the onset of forgery in ḥadīth. Ḥadīth forgery was to a large extent an epiphenomenon of these developments and the conflicts they precipitated eventually led to the collapse of the early caliphate barely forty years after its inception.

A forged ḥadīth or *al-mawḍūʿ*, may be defined as a report, invented by a liar, who has attributed it to the Prophet and it may include either the text or both the text and *isnād* of the report.[1] Even if this is done with a pious purpose in order to promote what is deemed to be a good cause, it would still count as a forgery and no credibility would be given to the motive and purpose of a deliberate forgery. Ḥadīth forgery has not been confined to isolated cases but took rather a wide dimension barely before the end of the first generation of Muslims in Madīna. A part of this phenomenon has been associated with the expansion of the territorial domains of the Islamic state and the ever-increasing number of new immigrants of Persians, Romans, Egyptians, Syrians and others who were easy prey to misguided influences against ḥadīth.[2]

The historical origins of forgery in ḥadīth are somewhat uncertain. While some observers have given the caliphate of ʿUthmān as a starting point, others have dated it a little later, at around the year 40 hijra, when political differences between the fourth caliph, ʿAlī, and the governor of al-Shām, Muʿāwiya, led to military confrontation and the division of Muslims into various factions. According to a third view, forgery in ḥadīth started even earlier, that is, during the caliphate of Abū Bakr when he waged the war of apostasy (*ridda*) against the refusers of *zakāh*. But the year 40 is considered the more likely starting point for the development of serious and persistent differences in the community. Muslims were thus divided and hostility between them acquired a religious dimension when they began to use the Qur'ān and *Sunna* in support of their claims. When the misguided elements among them failed to find any authority in the sources for their views, they either imposed a distorted interpretation on the source materials, or embarked on outright fabrication. *Aḥādīth* that were transmitted by the advocate of *bidʿa* (pernicious innovation) and those who were embroiled in controversy thus came under suspicion and were, for the most part, isolated or abandoned as a result of these developments.

Ḥadīth forgery may be divided into two types: (1) deliberate forgery, which is usually referred to as *ḥadīth mawḍūʿ*; (2) unintentional fabrication, which is usually referred to as *ḥadīth bāṭil* and is due mainly to error and recklessness in reporting. For example, in certain cases it is noted that the chain of narrators ended with a Companion or a Successor only but the transmitter instead extended it directly to the Prophet. The result is the same and fabrication whether deliberate or otherwise must in all cases be abandoned.[3] The present discussion is, however, mainly concerned with deliberate fabrication in ḥadīth.

Forgery in ḥadīth is believed to have begun in the context of personality cults (*faḍā'il al-ashkhāṣ*) which aimed to credit or discredit leading political figures with exaggerated claims. An example of this is the following statement attributed to the Prophet: "Whoever wishes to behold Adam for his knowledge, Noah for his piety, Abraham for his gentleness, Moses for his commanding presence and Jesus for his devotion to worship – let him behold ʿAlī."[4]

Political differences between ʿAlī and Abū Bakr, ʿAlī and Muʿāwiya, ʿAlī and ʿĀ'isha, between ʿAbd Allāh b. Zubayr and ʿAbd al-Malik b. Marwān, and generally between the Umayyads and ʿAbbāsids were among the causes of ḥadīth forgery. Numerous fabricated *aḥādīth* have thus been recorded in condemnation of Muʿāwiya including, for example, the one in which the Prophet is quoted to have ordered the Muslims "When you see Muʿāwiya on my pulpit, kill him." The fanatical supporters of Muʿāwiya and the Umayyad dynasty are, on the other hand, known to have fabricated ḥadīth such as "The trusted ones are three: I, Gabriel and Muʿāwiya."[5] Political motives also seem to be behind the so-called ḥadīth, for example, that "When the caliphate reaches banī al-ʿAbbās, it will not leave them until they surrender it to Jesus the Son of Mary."[6]

The Kharijites are on the whole considered to have avoided fabricating ḥadīth, which is due mainly to their belief that the perpetrator of a grave sin is no longer a Muslim. Since they saw the fabrication of ḥadīth in this light, they avoided indulgence in forgery as a matter of principle and a requirement of their doctrine.[7]

The heretic faction known as al-Zanādiqa, (pl. of Zindīq), owing to their hatred of Islam, fabricated ḥadīth which discredited Islam in the view of its followers. Included among such are: "eggplants are a cure for every illness"; and "beholding a good-looking face is a form of *ʿibāda*". It is reported that just before his execution at the time of Caliph al-Mahdī, one of the notorious fabricators of ḥadīth, ʿAbd al-Karīm b. Abū al-ʿAwjā', confessed that he had fabricated 4,000 *aḥādīth* in which *ḥalāl* was rendered *ḥarām* and *ḥarām* was rendered *ḥalāl*. It has been further reported that the Zanādiqa have fabricated a total of 14,000 *aḥādīth*,[8] a report which may or may not be credible. For a statement of this nature tends to arouse suspicion as to its veracity: even in fabricated matters, it is not a facile task to invent such a vast number of ḥadīth on the subject of *ḥalāl* and *ḥarām*.

Racial, tribal and linguistic fanaticism is yet another context in which ḥadīth has been fabricated. *Aḥādīth* were thus fabricated on the superiority of Arabs over non-Arabs, which were then reciprocated by forgeries on the superiority of Persians and Romans, Abyssinians and Turks over the Arabs. Note for example the following: "Whenever God was angry, He sent down the revelation in Arabic but when contented, He chose Persian for this purpose." The Arab fanatic too matched this anathema by claiming that "Whenever God was angry, He sent down the revelation in Persian, but when contented He chose to speak in Arabic."[9] These and similar other forgeries relating to the virtues or superiority of certain tribes, cities and periods of time over others have been isolated by the *ʿulamāʾ* of ḥadīth and placed under the category of *al-mawḍūʿāt*.[10]

Known among the classes of forgers are also professional story-tellers and preachers (*al-quṣṣāṣ wa al-wāʿiẓūn*) whose urge for popularity through arousing an emotional response in the audience led them to indulge in forgery. They made up stories and attributed them to the Prophet. Included in these are the so-called ḥadīth:

- "The first thing that God created was the light (*nūr*) of the Prophet Muḥammad."
- "God revived the Prophet's parents and they embraced Islam before him."
- "Intercession is obligatory for one who is named by the name Muḥammad."

It is reported that once a story-teller cited a ḥadīth to an audience in the al-Ruṣāfa mosque of Baghdad on the authority of Aḥmad b. Ḥanbal and Yaḥyā b. Maʿīn that ʿAbd al-Razzāq b. Maʿmar reported from Qatāda from Anas that the Prophet, peace be on him, said: "Whoever says 'there is no god but Allah', Allah will reward him, for each word uttered, with a bird in Paradise, with its beak of gold and feathers of pearls." At the end of his long sermon, the speaker was confronted by Aḥmad b. Ḥanbal and Yaḥyā b. Maʿīn who were present on the occasion and told the speaker that they had never related any ḥadīth of this kind. They were ridiculed and told that there were many reporters by those names and that he had come across "seventeen Aḥmad b. Ḥanbal and Yaḥyā b. Maʿīn". Another example is the so-called ḥadīth: "There is no tree in Paradise without the following being written on every one of its leaves: *lā ilāha illallāh, Abū Bakr al-Ṣiddīq*, *ʿUmar al-Fārūq wa ʿUthmān Dhū'l-Nūrayn*."[11]

Juristic and theological differences constitute another theme of forgery in ḥadīth. The *ʿulamāʾ* were thus divided into the *Ahl al-Sunna, Muʿtazila, Jabriyya, Murjiʾa*, etc., and they disagreed over many issues, such as the attributes of God, the definition of faith (*īmān*), whether faith is only a state of mind or that it relates to both belief and conduct, whether faith is liable to increase or decrease, whether the Qur'ān is created or uncreated and so forth. Some of these differences are known to have led to exaggerated statements, even forgery, in ḥadīth. This may be illustrated by the following statement attributed to the Prophet that "Whoever raises his hands during the performance of *ṣalāh*, his *ṣalāh* is null and void." In yet another statement, we read: "Whoever says that the Qur'ān is the created speech of God becomes an infidel ... and his wife stands divorced from him as of that moment."

Another category of fabricated ḥadīth is associated with the religious zeal of individuals whose devotion to Islam led them to careless ascription of ḥadīth to the Prophet. This is illustrated by the forgeries committed by one Nūḥ b. Abī Maryam on the virtues of the various sūras of the Qur'ān. He is said to have later regretted what he did and explained that he fabricated such ḥadīth because he saw people who were turning away from the Qur'ān and occupying themselves with the *fiqh* of Abū Ḥanīfa and the battle stories of Muḥammad b. Isḥāq and that he did so as part of carrying out *ḥisba*, that is promoting good and forbidding evil, and that he "lied for the Prophet and not against him". This is considered as one of the worst forms of forgery as it almost succeeds to be convincing and becomes difficult to isolate. Numerous other names occur in the relevant literature, including those of Ghulām Khalīl and Ibn Abī ʿAyyāsh of Baghdad, who were both known as pious individuals, but who invented ḥadīth on devotional matters.[12] Other examples of this kind include the so-called ḥadīth that "the superiority of Rajab over other months is like the superiority of the Qur'ān over other speech, and the superiority of Shaʿbān over other months is like that of mine over other Prophets, and the superiority of the month of Ramaḍān is like that of God over His servants." Furthermore, it is stated that "there is a certain day and a night in Rajab if one observes a fast on that day and offers prayer in that night, it is equivalent to fasting and prayer for one hundred years. This occurs during the last three days of Rajab. It was on this day that God sent Muḥammad as Prophet."[13]

Other themes of ḥadīth forgery include the urge on the part of courtiers who distorted ḥadīth so as to please and flatter their overlords. Similarly, the desire to establish the permissibility or virtue of certain varieties of food, beverages, clothes and customary practices has led to forgery in the ḥadīth. A number of fabricated *aḥādīth* have thus been recorded on the virtues of food items such as rice, lentils, aubergines, and places such as ʿAsqalān, months of the year, days and even certain times of the day, and also of personal names such as Aḥmad and Muḥammad, etc.

Numerous names are associated with forgery: Abān b. Jaʿfar al-Numayrī forged a large number of *aḥādīth* after Abū Ḥanīfa, and Ibrāhīm b. Zayd al-Aslamī did so in the name of Imām Mālik. Jābir b. Yazīd al-Jaʿfī, Aḥmad b. ʿAbd Allāh al-Juybārī, Muḥammad b. Shajjāʿ al-Thaljī and a string of other names have been identified and their forgeries isolated in separate works.

Al-Ḥāfiẓ Abū'l-Faraj ʿAbd al-Raḥmān Ibn al-Jawzī's (d. 597 H) book entitled *Al-Mawḍūʿāt* is a renowned work on forgeries, which became the focus of attention of several follow-up works. Jalāl al-Dīn al-Suyūṭī (d. 911) wrote a follow-up on this entitled *Al-Taʿaqqubāt ʿala'l-Mawḍūʿāt*, and also a summary of Ibn al-Jawzī's book bearing the title *Al-La'āli' al-Maṣnūʿa fi'l-Aḥādīth al-Mawḍūʿa*. Many have noted, however, that al-Jawzī all too readily classified even good *aḥādīth* as forgeries. Abū Ḥafṣ ʿUmar b. Badr al-Mūṣalī's (d. 622) *Al-Mughnī ʿan al-Ḥifẓ wa'l-Kitāb* isolated themes and chapters that had become liable to forgery, and Abū'l-Faḍl Muḥammad Ibn Ṭāḥir al-Maqdisī's (d. 507) *Tadhkirat al-Mawḍūʿāt* identified *aḥādīth* narrated by liars and discredited individuals and their abandoned works. Two other works to mention are Shaykh ʿAlī al-Qārī al-Ḥanafī's (d. 1014) *Al-Mawḍūʿāt*, and Yaḥyā b. ʿAlī al-Shawkānī's (d. 1250) *Al-Fawā'id al-Majmuʿa fi'l-Aḥādīth al-Mawḍūʿa*.[14] Numerous other works of a similar kind were written in which the *ʿulamā'* made a concerted effort to isolate the fabricated matter from the general corpus of ḥadīth. In view of these efforts, it is relatively easy now, according to Ṣubḥī al-Ṣāliḥ, to identify the fabricated ḥadīth. He also advises that one should be careful not to fall into the error of readily dismissing ḥadīth in the name of *mawḍūʿ* without valid evidence.[15]

Forgeries have infiltrated many disciplines of Islamic learning, including *fiqh*, *uṣūl al-fiqh* and *tafsīr*. Jurists and *ʿulamā'* who suffered from poverty of knowledge of ḥadīth have often quoted ḥadīth in their discussions which were subsequently identified to be fabrications and decidedly questionable. Some of the renowned works of *fiqh* such as the *Hidāya* of al-Marghīnānī are noted for making frequent references to ḥadīth without paying due attention to their *isnād*, a fact which led al-Ḥafiẓ Jamāl al-Dīn ʿAbd Allāh al-Zaylaʿī (d. 762) to write a book entitled *Naṣb al-Rāya fī Takhrīj Aḥādīth al-Hidāya*. Ibn Ḥajar al-ʿAsqalānī (d. 852) wrote a similar work on *Sharḥ al-Rāfiʿī* bearing the title *Talkhīṣ al-Ḥabīr fī Takhrīj Aḥādīth Sharḥ al-Rāfiʿī al-Kabīr*, in which he also supplemented al-Rāfiʿī's references to ḥadīth and ascertained its reliability and accuracy or otherwise of *isnād*. Al-Zaylaʿī also authored *Takhrīj al-Aḥādīth wa'l-Āthār al-Wāqiʿa fī Tafsīr al-Kashshāf li'l-Zamakhsharī* on Zamakhsharī's *Tafsīr al-Kashshāf*. On a similar note, Ḥāfiẓ Zayn al-Dīn al-ʿIrāqī wrote a compendium on Abū Ḥāmid al-Ghazālī's *Iḥyā' ʿUlūm al-Dīn* in which he identified numerous *aḥādīth* to be obscure, weak and unreliable.

Al-Zaylaʿī has considered the ḥadīth to the effect that the "Prophet vomited but did not refresh his ablution" to be very strange (*gharīb jiddan*), and Ibn Ḥajar also said that he did not find any correct ḥadīth anywhere to that effect. As for the ḥadīth that "prayer is invalidated by loss of blood the size of a dirham" – al-Bukhārī has said that it is null and void (*bāṭil*), and Ibn al-Jawzī has included it in his collection of forged *aḥādīth*.[16] Another ḥadīth which occurs in the works of *uṣūl al-fiqh* and even *uṣūl al-ḥadīth* has been identified to be a fabrication by the Zanādiqa heretics; the ḥadīth thus reads:

> When you find a ḥadīth from me, refer it to the Book of God; if it conforms with it, take it but reject it if it disagrees with it.

Similarly the ḥadīth which is quoted in some *fiqh* works to the effect that "My judgement on one is the same as on a multitude" – this has also been identified to be a fabrication.[17]

Abū Shahba has discussed these and drawn the conclusion that "researchers and those who base their reasoning on ḥadīth should not rely on ḥadīth that occur in *fiqh* works without verifying the authenticity and soundness thereof".[18] Abū Shahba went on to add that ḥadīth should be quoted from its verified sources, namely the six recognised collections and the *Muwaṭṭa'* of Imām Mālik and other reliable works.

Qur'ān commentaries (*tafāsīr*) in both the *tafsīr bi'l-mā'thūr* (commentary based on precedent) and *tafsīr bi'l-ra'y* varieties have not escaped forgeries especially in regard to what is known as Jewish anecdotes (*Isrā'īliyāt*). It is noted in this connection that prior to Islam when the Bedouin and illiterate strata of the Arabian people wanted to learn more about certain subjects such as the origins of creation and its mysteries, turmoil and *fitna*, and so forth they asked the Jews and Christians who had known of such subjects from the Torah and the Bible. Later when these people converted to Islam they conveyed the information they had in their commentaries and elaborations on Qur'ānic passages, especially on subjects outside the area of the *aḥkām*. Some of the recognised names among the *ahl al-kitāb* such as ʿAbd Allāh b. Salām, Kaʿb al-Aḥbār, and Wahb b. Munabbih were famed for their anecdotes and stories some of which then found their way into the context of the Qur'ānic commentaries. Since these were stories and anecdotes outside the *aḥkām*, their veracity was often overlooked. "The Qur'ān commentators treated these relatively lightly and filled their *tafsīr* works with such anecdotes ..." that were of questionable origin and content.[19]

The *ʿulamā'* of ḥadīth became so critical of such indiscriminate importation of *Isrā'īliyāt* into the body of *tafāsīr* that some of them, like Imām Aḥmad b. Ḥanbal and Ibn Taymiyya openly denied their authenticity. Imām Ibn Ḥanbal thus singled out "three subjects which are obscure of origin: *tafsīr*, tumults (*al-malāḥim*) and battle stories (*al-maghāzī*)". There is little of ḥadīth in these that can be found to be based on valid and properly connected *isnād*. They consist mainly of disconnected and isolated reports (*munqaṭiʿāt wa marāsīl*) that some Companions and Followers took from the converts among the *ahl al-kitāb*. Some of these discredited *Isrā'īliyāt* have been reported by Companions such as ʿAbd Allāh b. ʿAbbās and ʿAbd Allāh b. ʿAmr b. al-ʿĀṣ, often in sincerity and good faith which was, however, blemished by neglect as to the veracity and origin of their reports. The rule that applies to such information is as follows: If what the Companion has said is something that could not have originated in his own opinion, then it is considered as *Marfūʿ* (elevated) on condition, however, that the Companion in question is not known to have been influenced by *Isrā'īliyāt*. If he is known to have been so influenced, then his saying and report may never be attributed to the Prophet nor should it be classified as *Marfūʿ*.[20]

In Ibn Taymiyya's assessment "a significant portion of fabricated ḥadīth have found their way into the *tafsīr* works such as those of ʿAbd al-Raḥmān al-Thaʿālibī (d. 875 H), ʿAlī b. Aḥmad al-Wāḥidī (d. 468 H) and al-Zamakhsharī's *Tafsīr al-Kashshāf* in the context especially of the virtues of the various chapters of the Qur'ān. The *ʿulamā'* of ḥadīth are generally in agreement that these are altogether forgeries". Ibn Taymiyya went on to say that he had nothing to say personally against any of these, including al-Thaʿālibī who was a pious man but he was like a "wood collector in the night" who collected the sound and the weak as well as the fabricated into his *tafsīr*. Al-Wāḥidī was more knowledgeable of the Arabic language but was farther away from the chosen path of the predecessors (*al-salaf*). Al-Baghawī's *tafsīr* is shorter than that of al-Thaʿālibī but much to his credit "he guarded his work against fabricated ḥadīth and *bidʿa*-oriented views."[21]

Much of the literature on the occasions of revelation (*asbāb al-nuzūl*) of the Qur'ānic *āyāt* is similarly affected by forgeries. Even the well-respected *Tafsīr al-Ṭabārī* is affected by forgeries, and al-Suyūṭī (d. 911) has rendered a great service to evaluate and criticise it in his *Al-Durr al-Manthūr fi'l-Tafsīr bi'l-Ma'thūr*. Suyūṭī's other work, *Al-La'āli' al-Maṣnūʿa fi'l-Aḥādīth al-Mawḍūʿa* has identified and isolated the forgeries from many of these works. *Tafsīr al-Zamakhsharī* may not contain so much of the *Isrā'īliyāt*, yet it does contain forged ḥadīth on the virtues of the Qur'ān and its occasions of revelation. *Tafsīr al-Nasafī* is similar to that of al-Zamakhsharī in this regard except that it does not quote fabricated ḥadīth on virtues of the chapters of the Qur'ān. *Tafsīr al-Khāzin* contains a great many stories and reports of the bygone nations and tends to indulge in repeating the discredited stories of Hārūt and Mārūt, and those of the Arab idols, "*al-gharānīq*, and the story-teller's version of David and Solomon." Among the *tafāsīr* that are reasonably clear of forgeries are *Tafsīr Ibn Kathīr*, *Tafsīr al-Fakhr al-Rāzī*, *Tafsīr al-Alūsī*, the twentieth-century *Tafsīr al-Manār*, and probably also some of the more recent *tafāsīr*. *Tafsīr Ibn Kathīr* tends to stand out for its avoidance of the *mawḍūʿāt* and *Isrā'īliyāt*, and also for the attempt often to identify the source of the forgeries and their context.[22]

Works on moral teachings and mysticism (*taṣawwuf*) have also been affected by forgeries as they too quoted fabricated ḥadīth of unverified origin. Many works are cited in this connection, including, for example, the renowned *Iḥyā' ʿUlūm al-Dīn* of Abū Ḥāmid al-

Ghazālī. Al-Ghazālī has quoted *aḥādīth* on the superiority of intellect (*al-ʿaql*) which have come in for criticism and the critics maintain that nothing reliable on this subject exists in the ḥadīth. There is much evidence in the Qur'ān on the superiority of reason and Islam generally subscribes to that conclusion, but not through those so-called ḥadīth. Al-Ghazālī's work is also criticised for the forged *aḥādīth* it contains on the virtues of prayers during the various days and nights of the week. Al-Ḥāfiẓ b. Ḥusayn al-ʿIrāqī's (d. 806) *Al-Mughnī ʿan Ḥaml al-Asfār fi'l-Asfār fī Takhrīj mā fi'l-Iḥyā' min al-Akhbār* enquired into this and drew the conclusion that "nothing sound exists in ḥadīth on the days and nights of the week." Al-ʿIrāqī has enquired into the sound and weak ḥadīth of the *Iḥyā'* and warned that the reader of *Iḥyā'* should not accept the ḥadīth cited therein without consulting his (ʿIrāqī's) enquiry into them. Two other books that Abū Shahba has discussed in this connection are al-Jīlānī's *Ghunyat al-Ṭālibīn* which he described to be "even more hazardous – *ashaddu khaṭaran* – than *al-Iḥyā'*, whereas Abū Ṭālib al-Makkī's *Qūt al-Qulūb* contains the least of *mawḍūʿat* among the three."[23]

Without wishing to burden this discussion with further detail it may merely be added that hardly any area of Islamic learning, including the renowned histories by Ibn al-Athīr, al-Ṭabārī, al-Masʿūdī, and works on theology and *kalām* as well as works in Arabic language and literature have escaped the cancerous spread of forgeries. Abū Shahba has discussed these and warned in almost every part that the reader should exercise caution in accepting them in the name of ḥadīth. Ḥadīth should only be quoted from its reliable sources, including the six collections and the *Muwaṭṭa'* of Imām Mālik.[24]

Just as the *ʿulamā'* have classified the ḥadīth into various categories so as to identify its strengths and weaknesses from various viewpoints, they have also identified the signs of forgery in ḥadīth from the viewpoints respectively of transmission (*isnād*) and subject matter (*matn*), which may be summarised under two headings as follows:

a. Signs of forgery in transmission are identified mainly by reference to the reputation and biography of the transmitter. There is a wealth of literature on the names and biographies of the transmitters of ḥadīth and those who are known to have indulged in lying and forgery.

This information would normally be the first point of reference in identifying the signs of forgery in a particular ḥadīth. Another useful tool that the *ʿulamā'* have utilised in identifying forgery in the *isnād* is to ascertain the time factor and dates in the transmission of ḥadīth. This is done by verifying whether the reporter has actually met the person he has quoted as his immediate source or that personal contact between them had neither occurred nor was possible. When the transmitter mentions, for example, that he heard so and so in such and such a place reporting such a ḥadīth then the question of geographical location and verifying the facts as to whether they lived in the same period or generation become of vital significance in ascertaining signs of forgery in the chain of transmission. Forgery in *isnād* is also known sometimes by admission of the forger, such as the confession made by Maysara b. ʿAbd Rabbih al-Fārisī who admitted forging ḥadīth on virtues of the Qur'ān. Similarly, when the transmitter is known for lying and his ḥadīth stands alone in that no one else has reported it – this would be another way of detecting forgery in ḥadīth.[25] And lastly, signs of forgery in transmission are also detected by reference to personal interest and motive. An example of this is a so-called ḥadīth narrated by Muḥammad ibn al-Hajjāj al-Lakhmī which reads that "cookies (*al-harīsa*) strengthen the spine" and it turns out that he used to sell *al-harīsa*.

b. Signs of forgery in the text of a ḥadīth are identified by reference to at least seven factors as follows: Firstly, the language of ḥadīth: The Prophetic language is characteristically known for its eloquence and style. Speech of a particularly crude variety and style is taken as a sign of forgery. Al-Rabīʿ b. al-Khāthim is widely quoted to have said that "there is light in ḥadīth such as the broad daylight that we know it, or else it is dark like the dead of the night that we do not fail to denounce."[26]

Secondly, corruption in the purpose and meaning of a reported ḥadīth also provides evidence as to its fabrication. The report, for example, that "the ark of Noah circumambulated the Kaʿba seven times and then prayed two units (*rakʿah*) of *ṣalāh* at the end;" or the report that "God created the horse and raced it first and then created Himself from it" are evidently unreasonable and corrupt, and cannot be accepted in the name of ḥadīth. Ibn al-Jawzī is quoted as having said: "when you see a ḥadīth that is irrational, or in conflict with the text or basic principles then know that it is a forgery."[27]

Thirdly, statements that stand in clear opposition to the Qur'ān in such a way that no reasonable compromise and interpretation can be attempted are usually rejected. The so-called ḥadīth, for example, that "The offspring of *zinā* shall not enter Paradise down to seven generations" was rejected by the Prophet's widow, ʿĀ'isha, as it violated the clear text of the Qur'ān that "no soul shall carry the burden of another soul" (al-Anʿām, 6:164). Similarly the report "whoever begets a child and names him Muḥammad, he and his offspring shall go to Paradise" is clearly in conflict with numerous Qur'ānic promises of reward for good work and punishment for corruption and evil. Another example is the so-called ḥadīth that specifies the lifespan of the world at 7,000 years, which stands in contrast to the Qur'ānic declaration: "God only knows the time of the day of resurrection" (Luqmān, 31:34).

Similarly the so-called ḥadīth "when someone conveys to you my ḥadīth which is in conformity with the truth, follow it even if I have actually not said it." This is contrary to a clear *Mutawātir* ḥadīth that "one who attributes a lie to me deliberately must prepare himself for a place in Hell." Another example is the so-called ḥadīth "one who performs the obligatory prayers in the last Friday of Ramaḍān will be forgiven for all the prayers he has missed up to 70 years." This is in conflict with the general consensus that nothing replaces an act of *ʿibāda* that has not been duly performed.[28]

Fourthly, a report may be unhistorical and fail to pass the test of historical reality. The ḥadīth, for example, which is transmitted by Saʿd b. Muʿādh and Muʿāwiya that "the Prophet imposed the *jizya* (poll tax) on the Jews of Khaybar and relieved them of hardship (prospects of war)" is discredited on account of historical facts that *jizya* was not known at that time and that the Qur'ānic ruling on it was only revealed in the year of Tabūk, and that Saʿd b. Muʿādh had died before this last event. In yet another report Anas b. Mālik has stated that "I entered the public bath and saw the Prophet wearing a wrapper and said: O Anas, I have forbidden entry to the public bath without a wrapper." The facts of history show on the other hand that the Prophet never entered a public bath and that they did not exist in Madīna at the time.

Fifthly, when the ḥadīth smacks of scholastic fanaticism such as the report by Ḥibbān b. Juwayn that "I heard ʿAlī saying that I and the Prophet worshipped God six or seven years before anyone of this *umma*." It is known on the other hand that Ḥibbān was a fanatical Shīʿī and careless in the treatment of ḥadīth.

Sixthly, when a ḥadīth is supposed to have been known to vast numbers of people and yet only one person has reported it. The fact that no one else has confirmed it is taken as a sign of forgery. An example of this is the so-called ḥadīth that "Anyone who touches his sexual organ must take a fresh ablution." It is thus stated that if this were a true ḥadīth, the entire *umma* would have known it and practised it. Since this is not the case, it is likely to be a forgery.

And lastly, when the ḥadīth in question promises a disproportionate reward or an exceedingly severe punishment for a small act that does not warrant the stipulated consequence. Note for example the report "anyone who says 'there is no God but Allah', Allah will create for him a bird with 70,000 tongues each of which speaks 70,000 languages and all will be praying for him."[29]

These were some of the main, although not all, indicators of forgery in ḥadīth. Those who are particularly learned in ḥadīth may be able to detect signs of forgery in other ways that might be peculiar to their ability and understanding of the subject matter of their investigation. It is sometimes stated with regard to the category of ḥadīth known as *al-targhīb wa'l-tarhīb*, that is, ḥadīth which consists mainly of encouragement and warning – that forging this type of ḥadīth does not deserve condemnation and total disapproval. In response to this it may be said that the *ʿulamā'* of ḥadīth who made efforts to isolate the doubtful and corrupt elements from ḥadīth did not make any exception of this kind. The reason for this is not difficult to see: one who fabricates ḥadīth on one subject can also do that with another, and the effects of both are bound to be subversive by undermining the credibility of ḥadīth generally. All forgery must therefore be denounced regardless of subject matter.

Concerning the Khawārij, it has been said that they were usually candid and spoke the truth even at the expense of courtesy and finesse and they consequently stayed clear of resorting to forgery for the sake of promoting particular viewpoints. Ibn Taymiyya has even reached the conclusion that "they are known for their truthfulness and their ḥadīth is the most sound of all *aḥādīth*."[30]

The *ʿulamā'* have held it to be forbidden (*ḥarām*) for anyone to knowingly narrate fabricated ḥadīth in any context whatsoever, be it the rule of law, anecdote, or moral teaching. Whenever a forged ḥadīth is quoted or discussed, for teaching purposes or illustration, it should be clearly identified as a forgery.[31]

[08] Impugnment and Validation

al-Jarḥ wa'l-Taʿdīl

ALTHOUGH the Prophet, peace be on him, has in principle encouraged diffusion of the knowledge of his teachings and *Sunna*, he has in the meantime warned the believers in such terms: "If anyone tells a lie about me intentionally, let him be sure of his place in the Hell fire".[1] In another ḥadīth he is reported to have said: "If anyone speaks of a ḥadīth in my name while knowing that I have not said it, he is a liar".[2] These and similar other warnings influenced the Companions and subsequent generations of Muslims to exercise caution in the transmission of ḥadīth. The Companions were consequently careful not to narrate ḥadīth of which they were doubtful. Instances are on record to show that the Rightly-Guided Caliphs were careful, and often solicited evidence, to clarify doubt in the rendering and transmission of ḥadīth. Quoted in support of taking a cautious approach to the verification of ḥadīth was also the Qur'ānic *āya* addressing the believers "when a transgressor (*fāsiq*) comes to you with news, then investigate (its veracity) so that people are not afflicted with adversity due to ignorance and then you regret what you have done" (al-Ḥujurāt, 49:6). What is emphasised here is to investigate and verify reports in all cases especially when they are conveyed by persons of compromised integrity. Do not, in other words, dismiss such reports prior to investigation and out of ignorance. Since ḥadīth that is reported from the Prophet falls within the purview of this directive, taking an inquisitive approach toward ḥadīth was thus justified.

Another Qur'ānic passage that is quoted in this context is the one which validates the testimony of two persons for proof of unsubstantiated claims (al-Baqara, 2:282). Narration and transmission of ḥadīth are no less important than testimony and they are both accepted only from upright and trustworthy individuals. Owing to the great sensitivity of this matter, some *ʿulamāʾ* went so far as to say that intentional propagation of lies in the name of ḥadīth amounted to disbelief (*kufr*) and validated the death punishment for its perpetrator.[3] The spread of ḥadīth to the remote parts of the Islamic domain is also known to have given rise to apprehensions on the part of the *ʿulamāʾ* over error and distortion in ḥadīth, which is why they began to address the problem by recourse to rigorous criticism of the reliability of the narrator of ḥadīth and the textual accuracy of his reports. A separate branch of ḥadīth studies, known as *al-jarḥ waʾl-taʿdīl* (impugnment and validation – also known as *naqd al-ḥadīth*) was developed as a result and numerous writers contributed to the growth of interest and literature in this field.[4] This branch of the ḥadīth studies is concerned mainly with the reliability or otherwise of the transmitters of ḥadīth and compiles information which either proves them as upright and reliable, or else weak and unreliable. Ever since the time of the Companions scholars have continued to contribute to the development of *al-jarḥ waʾl-taʿdīl.*

A number of prominent Companions, including Abū Bakr, ʿUmar b. al-Khaṭṭāb, ʿAlī b. Abī Ṭālib, ʿAbd Allāh b. ʿAbbās (d. 96 H), Anas b. Mālik (d. 93), ʿUbāda b. al-Ṣāmit, and ʿĀʾisha as well as scholars among the *tābiʿūn*, such as Saʿīd b. Jubayr (d. 95), Saʿīd b. al-Musayyib (d. 99) al-Shaʿbī (d. 104 H) and Ibn Sīrīn (d. 110) are associated with the development of this branch of the ḥadīth and they are known to have spoken concerning the reliability of reports by individuals, whom they have either approved or disapproved. But works of scholarship on the subject were not written until the third century hijra. Yaḥyā b. Maʿīn (d. 233 H), Imām Aḥmad b. Ḥanbal (d. 241 H) and ʿAlī b. al-Madīnī (d. 234) were the early pioneers who wrote on the subject and then almost all the leading Imāms of ḥadīth including al-Bukhārī (d. 256), Muslim, Abū Dāwūd and al-Nasāʾī have to their credit written one or more books on the biographies of ḥadīth transmitters and their works and thus contributed to the development of *al-jarḥ waʾl-taʿdīl* during the third century.

A comprehensive work on *al-jarḥ waʾl-taʿdīl* is *Kitāb al-Ṭabaqāt al-Kabīr* of Ibn Saʿd al-Zuhrī al-Baṣrī (d. 230 H) in 15 volumes in which the author compiled biographies of over 4,000 narrators of ḥadīth. Due to the growth of literature, some writers specialised their works either to *al-jarḥ* (impugnment) or to *al-taʿdīl* (validation) and many others addressed both as two sides of the same coin. There were also works that only focused on the transmitters of the six famous collections, and some only on the narrators of al-Bukhārī, or of Muslim and so forth. Al-Bukhārī himself wrote three books on the subject of *al-jarḥ wa'l-taʿdīl*, one of which is entitled *Al-Ḍuʿāfā' wa'l-Matrūkīn* (the weak and abandoned) and compiled information on a much larger number of narrators. More recent works of authority on the subject included the four-volume *Mizān al-Iʿtidāl* by Shams al-Dīn Muḥammad b. Aḥmad al-Dhahabī (d. 748 H) which compiled data on (11,053) individuals, and Ḥāfiẓ Ibn Ḥajar al-ʿAsqalānī's (d. 852), *Lisān al-Mīzān* in six volumes containing data on (14,343) ḥadīth transmitters.[5] Works of scholarship that emerged after the third century generally followed and upheld the conclusions of the early pioneers of this discipline. The early scholars also tend to fare better on the scale of validation and reliability than their successors in the subsequent generations.

The *ʿulamā'* are not unanimous in their assessment of the character and qualifications of the transmitters of ḥadīth. While some like Yaḥyā b. Maʿīn (d. 233), and Yaḥyā b. Saʿīd al-Qaṭṭān (d. 198 H) were strict in their assessment of the reliability of narrators, others like Abū ʿĪsā al-Tirmidhī and al-Ḥākim al-Nīsābūrī (d. 405 H) were not so strict, while Aḥmad b. Ḥanbal (d. 241), al-Bukhārī (d. 256) and Muslim (d. 261) were considered to be moderate. Hence their respective assessments of the various narrators tend to vary. The Sunnī and Shīʿī scholars have, moreover, taken different approaches to the reliability of narrators of ḥadīth. There are also differences that emanate from *ijtihād*. The traditionists (*ahl al-ḥadīth*) have, rightly or wrongly, discredited some *ʿulamā'* among the Rationalists (*ahl al-ra'y*) because of their differential approaches to *ijtihād*.[6]

The assassination of the Caliph ʿUthmān and the ensuing civil war between the Caliph ʿAlī and Muʿāwiya in the year 41 hijra is widely known to have marked the beginning of forgery in ḥadīth primarily for political purposes of crediting or discrediting a certain individual, party or doctrine. This naturally led to greater restrictions and a more critical attitude toward the dissemination and transmission of ḥadīth.

With regard to ascertaining the textual accuracy of ḥadīth, the principal tool that the *ʿulamā'* applied was comparison and cross-examination. By gathering all the ḥadīth on a certain subject and other data relating to time, place and particular individuals and then carefully comparing the relevant parts with one another, the *ʿulamā'* were able to evaluate the accuracy of ḥadīth and reliability of their reporters. Some of the methods that were applied were as follows:

1. Comparison between the *aḥādīth* of the different students of one scholar.
2. Comparison between the statements of a single scholar at different times.
3. Comparison between oral recitation and written documents.
4. Comparison between the ḥadīth and the relevant text of the Qur'ān.

To give an illustration, Yaḥyā b. Maʿīn (158-233 AH) tried to authenticate the written work on ḥadīth of Ḥammād b. Salama of Baṣra (d. 167), and this took him to Baṣra where he checked the text with many of Ḥammād's students (18 students altogether) and then said in a conversation to one of them (Mūsā b. Ismāʿīl) that Ḥammād made mistakes and his students added some more to his, and that he wanted to distinguish who made which mistakes. Ibn Maʿīn tried to identify the source of the mistakes through comparison and cross reference: if all the students of Ḥammād had made the same error, Ḥammād was the likely source, but if they differed in making the same error, the error was likely to have originated with the student himself. Ibn Maʿīn's enquiry also enabled him, in addition to identifying the specific errors, to grade the various students of Ḥammād and determine their accuracy in reporting.[7]

Both Imāms, Muslim and his teacher al-Bukhārī, have authored separate works on ḥadīth criticism. In a ḥadīth that Muslim has investigated, Ibn ʿAbbās reported that on one occasion he prayed alone behind the Prophet and started to stand on his left side, but the Prophet turned him, to change sides from his left to his right side. This incident was then reported by the scholar Yazīd b. Abī Zinād, from Kurayb, from Ibn ʿAbbās stating that Ibn ʿAbbās stood on the right side of the Prophet and he was then made to stand on the left side. There was obviously an error. So Imām Muslim gathered all the statements of the students of Kurayb, and then he collected all the statements of Ibn ʿAbbās and established that Ibn ʿAbbās had changed sides from the left to the right, not vice versa. Then he compared this with other reports by the Companions who had prayed with the Prophet when alone, and found out that Yazīd b. Abī Zinād had made a mistake.[8]

Whenever the reliability of the ḥadīth transmitter is questioned and a probing is attempted into his character and knowledge, two possibilities are envisaged, one of which is that the available evidence supports his reliability and uprightness. This is referred to as *taʿdīl*, or proving someone to be upright and *ʿadl*. The other possibility is to establish by evidence that the transmitter is unreliable, or that his uprightness and *ʿadāla* is unproven. This is referred to as *al-jarḥ* which literally means wounding. The methods by which *al-jarḥ* is invoked and established are more rigorous than what is usually required in *taʿdīl*. The *ʿulamāʾ* of ḥadīth have often confirmed the transmitter of ḥadīth to be acceptable and upright without actually inquiring into the detailed grounds of their conclusions. To establish the reliability of a person may be due to numerous reasons which may be difficult to elaborate. For otherwise the validator (*muʿdil*) may be saying things such as "he did not do this, did not tell a lie, he did do such and such" and the list may become lengthy. Yet validation, or *taʿdīl*, is not accepted if it is too vague. Thus if a validator does not identify the narrator and simply writes that "a reliable person informed me," it is not enough, although according to a minority view, this may be acceptable from a prominent scholar.

As for the question whether validation or impugnment is acceptable from only one, or from a minimum of two persons, there is an opinion to the effect that like testimony in judicial disputes, the minimum requirement here too is affirmation by two persons. But the correct view is that *jarḥ* or *taʿdīl* can both be proven by the affirmation of one person.

As for the terminology that is used in *taʿdīl*, some *ʿulamāʾ*, including Ibn al-Ṣalāḥ and Ibn Abī Ḥātim al-Rāzī (d. 327 H), have used slightly different expressions to the six that are listed below. If someone approves of a narrator in words such as '*thiqa*' or '*mutqin*' (reliable, firm), his report is acceptable. Approval is also indicated by words such as '*thabtun*, *ḥujjatun*' (proof, strong evidence), and even more so if words such as '*ḥāfiẓ*' and '*ḍābiṭ*' (retentive, unwavering) are used. These expressions indicate the first degree of *taʿdīl*, whereas expressions such as '*ṣadūq*' and '*ṣāliḥ al-ḥadīth*' (fit to be a ḥadīth narrator) and '*lā-ba'sa bihi*' (no objection) tend to come next.[9]

Impugnment, or *al-jarḥ*, is also verified by the use of terms and expressions as will presently be discussed. In the case of *jarḥ*, it is necessary, as already noted, that a reference is made to the grounds or causes of *jarḥ*. People tend to vary in their assessment of what they may regard to be a valid ground of *jarḥ*, but even here, there has been a tendency toward avoidance of detail in specifying the grounds of *al-jarḥ*. The *ʿulamā'* have often made brief statements that "so and so is weak (*ḍaʿīf*) or *matrūk* (abandoned)" and the like without giving much detail. Brief comments of this type often fell short of explaining or specifying the grounds of *jarḥ*, but they succeeded nevertheless in casting doubt on the reliability of their subjects.[10] Ḥadīth critics are also noted for having paid attention to what may be called profane *mubāḥāt*, such as indulgence in jokes, eating on public thoroughfares, playing chess, listening to music, or playing a musical instrument. It is known that a narrator's indulgence in music and chess hardly failed to disqualify him from being a narrator of ḥadīth. It is of interest to note that al-Khaṭīb al-Baghdādī has a chapter in *Al-Kifāya* in which he elaborates on what is not suitable nor valid to be considered as a ground for *jarḥ*.[11]

Pursuit of pernicious innovation (*bidʿa*) and indulgence in capricious opinion (*hawā*) also counted as grounds of *al-jarḥ*. When a narrator of ḥadīth became known for these, or known for fraudulent dealings and dishonesty in financial transactions, his report did not fail to be downgraded or abandoned.[12] There has been a tendency on the other hand of taking a lenient view of any weakness that might have been noted concerning well-known figures whose uprightness had become common knowledge. The *ʿadāla*, for example, of the leading Imāms of jurisprudence, al-Awzāʿī (d. 157), ʿAlī b. al-Madīnī (d. 234), Yaḥyā b. Maʿīn (d. 233) and others was taken for granted and was hardly, if ever, questioned. Another tendency to be noted in the discussion of *al-jarḥ wa'l-taʿdīl* is that the higher links in the chain of transmission, who were closer to the source, were given greater credibility and recognition than the lower links. The scholars of ḥadīth thus tended to scrutinise reports by their contemporaries or narrators of later generations more stringently compared to, for example, narrators who belonged to the *tābiʿūn* or even the *tābiʿ tābiʿīn*.[13]

Yaḥyā b. Maʿīn has specified four qualities in a narrator of ḥadīth, namely truthfulness, willingness to authenticate ḥadīth, abandonment of pernicious innovations (*al-bidaʿ*), and avoidance of grave sins (*al-kabā'ir*). As for the truthfulness of a narrator or his avoidance of sin, it is generally acknowledged that no one is totally clear of sin and if one were to require total probity, no one is likely to qualify. It is also agreed that ḥadīth is not accepted from those who indulge in criminality and transgression. God Most High has ordained acceptance of reports by an upright person and rejection thereof by a transgressor.[14] There are clear statements in the ḥadīth of the Prophet on the identification of a number of sins into grave sins, but these *aḥādīth* are not exclusive. In one ḥadīth, the Prophet has warned the believers of seven devastating sins (*al-sabʿ al-mūbiqāt*). The Companions then asked as to what were they and the Prophet, peace be on him, said that they were "associating another deity with God, sorcery, slaying a life that God has made sacrosanct except in the cause of justice, usury, devouring the property of orphans, staying away from *jihād*, and slanderous accusation of chaste women with *zinā*."[15]

اجتنبوا السبع الموبقات، قيل: يارسول الله ماهي؟ قال: الشرك بالله والسحر وقتل النفس التي حرم الله إلا بالحق وأكل الربا وأكل مال اليتيم والتولي يوم الزحف وقذف المحصنات الغافلات المؤمنات.

In another ḥadīth on the same subject, it is provided that "the gravest of all sins before God on the Day of Resurrection is association with Him, slaying a believer without a just cause, escape from *jihād* in the way of God, and renunciation by one's parents."[16]

إن أكبر الكبائر عند الله يوم القيامة الإشراك بالله وقتل النفس المؤمنة بغير حق والفرار من سبيل الله يوم الزحف وعقوق الوالدين.

A similar ḥadīth on the subject of grave sins adds one more, namely false testimony (*shahādat al-zūr*).[17] To this list, the *ʿulamāʾ* of ḥadīth have added drinking, sodomy, fraud and other prescribed offences when they are proven by the testimony of two just witnesses.[18] Anyone who has deliberately lied concerning a ḥadīth or is involved in forgery is disqualified for ever and may never be admitted again even if he repents and corrects himself.[19] As for repentance from other major sins, it may qualify the repenter again when his sincerity and good conduct becomes known and established beyond doubt.[20]

When a reliable person narrates a ḥadīth from an equally reliable person and then the latter denies it in definite expressions such as "I did not narrate it, or he lied," or the like, then there would be a clash of two decisive statements, one of affirmation and the other of negation. Negation prevails in this case and the ḥadīth concerning affirmation is rejected. But if the teacher in question merely says "I do not recognise this, or I do not remember," this does not amount to impugnment and the ḥadīth is also not rejected because of it.[21]

When someone narrates a ḥadīth and subsequently forgets what he narrated, this does not amount to impugnment of himself and the ḥadīth he had narrated is also not affected by his forgetfulness. This is the position of the majority of the *ʿulamāʾ* of ḥadīth, with the exception of the Ḥanafīs who have rejected a ḥadīth on this very ground. This was the ḥadīth of Sulaymān b. Mūsā from al-Zuhrī – ʿUrwa – ʿĀʾisha from the Prophet: "When a woman concludes a marriage without the permission of her guardian, her *nikāḥ* is null and void ...".

الأيم إذا نكحت بغير إذن وليها فنكاحها باطل.

Ibn Jurayj has said concerning this ḥadīth that he asked al-Zuhrī about it but he did not recognise the ḥadīth. The correct view is, however, that of the majority as many learned authorities are known to have narrated a ḥadīth and then forgot their earlier report. People do tend to forget and this by itself does not amount to impugnment of either the person or of the ḥadīth he had narrated.[22]

As for a narrator who charges a fee for transmitting ḥadīth, some *ʿulamāʾ* of ḥadīth have considered this as a ground of impugnment. Ibn al-Ṣalāḥ confirmed this and wrote that Aḥmad b. Ḥanbal and Abū Ḥātim al-Rāzī have also held the same view. According to a minority view attributed to some scholars, including Abū Isḥāq al-Shirāzī, charging a fee in this case is like charging a fee for teaching the Qur'ān, which is not objectionable, especially for someone who may be in need of earning a fee. But even so, charging a fee for transmitting ḥadīth of the Prophet is considered demeaning of the integrity and *murū'a* of a person.[23]

The methods that were applied in ḥadīth criticism were clearly focused on the reliability of the narrator. To accept a ḥadīth according to the criteria of ḥadīth criticism, it is not sufficient for the text to be accurate and sound but that it should also be transmitted by an upright *ʿadl* person of undisputed credibility. The issue at stake is not, in other words, the narrator's accuracy and care in receiving, retaining and then transmitting the ḥadīth but also his upright character and *ʿadāla*. Individual narrators naturally varied in their abilities and attitudes. To ascertain these, the *ʿulamā'* developed a set of criteria that enabled the grading of ḥadīth transmitters initially on the binary scale of impugnment *al-jarḥ* and validation *al-taʿdīl*, each of which were then sub-divided into six sub-headings, or ranks, known respectively as the grades of validation *marātib al-taʿdīl*, and grades of impugnment *marātib al-jarḥ*. There were attempts at the use of uniform terminology for grading purposes, which tended to vary somewhat in the works of various authors and it has evidently taken time for a measure of uniformity to develop. Ibn Ḥajar al-ʿAsqalānī (773-852 H) has rendered the relevant terminology as follows:

1. The Companions who stand at the highest point on the scale of *taʿdīl*.
2. *Thiqāt Ḍābiṭūn*: Unwaveringly trustworthy, accepted beyond question.
3. *Thiqāt*: trustworthy and retentive, inspiring confidence.
4. *Ṣadūq*: truthful (the word *mutqin* is sometimes used by other writers as an equivalent).
5. *Ṣadūq yahīm*: truthful but prone to making mistakes.
6. *Maqbūl*: accepted; occasionally the phrase *in-sha' Allāh* (God willing) is added. What it means is that there is no proof why his report should not be accepted. The word *layyin* (of little weight) is also occasionally used.

Al-Nawawī and Ibn al-Ṣalāḥ have recorded a four-point scale in a descending order of probity, each of which consists of several terms. The first rank is identified by the following six terms: *thiqa* (trustworthy), *mutqin* (firm), *thabtun* (of proven record), *ḥujja* (proof), *ʿadlun ḥāfiẓun* (upright and retentive), and *ḍābiṭun* (retentive). The second rank is identified by *ṣadūq* (truthful), *maḥal al-ṣidq* (inclined to truth), *lā ba'sa bihi* (no objection). These three terms imply a second ranking next to the six terms above as they do not indicate the retentiveness (*al-ḍabṭ*) quality of the narrator. The third rank of probity is identified by the use of the term *shaykhun*, that is an acceptable transmitter but that one may need to look into his report and not to readily accept it. This is equivalent to *ṣadūq yahīm* in al-ʿAsqalānī's terminology, which we earlier identified as truthful but prone to indulging in untruth (*wahm*) and making mistakes. The fourth and last rank in this scale is identified by the phrase *ṣāliḥ al-ḥadīth* (fit to transmit ḥadīth but should be verified). This is said to be equivalent to the last point, that is *ṣadūq*, or *maqbūl in-shā' Allāh* in al-ʿAsqalānī's terminology.[24]

The probity (*ʿadāla*) of a person is established by his good reputation and acceptance of his ḥadīth by the *ʿulamā'* and scholars, or when the latter speak well of the narrator, praise him, and express confidence in his work. Leading figures such as Imāms Mālik, Shāfiʿī and Ibn Ḥanbal, Sufyān al-Thawrī, Yaḥyā b. Maʿīn, ʿAlī al-Madīnī and many others have established a reputation of *ʿadāla* to an extent that they stand beyond questioning and challenge. Many of them have in turn spoken well of the work of others or else have impugned and denounced them as being unreliable.[25]

The six grades of impugnment or *al-jarḥ* are:

1. *Majhūl al-ḥāl*: whose integrity is unknown, but there is nothing negative about him. As a general rule, obscurity (*jahāla*) is overruled when two upright individuals are known to have accepted the report of one who would otherwise be classified as *majhūl al-ḥāl*. The word *mastūr* (hidden) is occasionally employed as an equivalent.
2. *Ḍaʿīf*: weak, in the sense that no scholar has given him any credit and some have openly spoken against him.

3. *Majhūl*: unknown, obscure, no more than one person has narrated from him, and the person has little to his credit that can be said.
4. *Matrūk*: abandoned, mainly because someone reliable has discredited him. The abandoned person also fails to qualify the prerequisites of uprightness.
5. *Muttaham bi'l-kadhib*: accused of lying and forgery.
6. *Khadhdhāb* (liar), or *waḍḍāʿ* (forger).

Al-Nawawī uses a four-point scale of evaluation that implies degrees of weakness in the trustworthiness of a narrator. The first of these is *layyin al-ḥadīth* (of little weight) which does not necessarily imply that the ḥadīth is totally rejected yet it does imply impugnment of a type that represents a blemish in uprightness (*ʿadāla*) of the person concerned. The second expression is *laysa bi-qawiyyin* (not strong by any means) which is a degree below *layyin*, yet ḥadīth narrated by this type may still be considered and upheld subject to verification. This is followed by *ḍaʿīf al-ḥadīth* (weak in the narration of ḥadīth) which is a degree below that of *laysa bi-qawiyyin*, yet still not totally rejected. And lastly, the terms *matrūk al-ḥadīth* (abandoned), *wāhī* (careless, superficial) and *kadhdhāb* (liar). When these are used in the impugnment of a narrator, his ḥadīth is totally rejected and abandoned.[26]

These grades were mostly followed by earlier scholars, but some degree of laxity in their application had been noted in the works of the scholars of later ages. Many have used additional expressions for, and within, each grade. Scholars preceding al-ʿAsqalānī have often used different terms for grading but were generally assiduous in their assessment.[27]

Should there be conflicting information concerning a narrator of ḥadīth, some of which qualifies him to be reliable and the rest does not, the evidence on *al-jarḥ* takes priority over the evidence on *al-taʿdīl*. But if the negative evidence only relates to an earlier part of the narrator's life and he is subsequently known to have become upright and reliable, then his narration may be accepted. It is important to note that in situations of uncertainty such as this, greater attention will be paid to the grounds/reasons that are given for impugnment rather than validation. Although the evidence in support of *al-jarḥ* takes priority over that of *al-taʿdīl*, but if the number of validators exceed those of impugners, then validation may take priority over impugnment. The safer position, as Ibn al-Ṣalāḥ points out, is still the first one, which is supported by the majority, namely that *jarḥ* takes priority over *taʿdīl*.[28]

When a reliable person reports from another reliable person and later denies it himself or overrules what he had earlier reported, this is not exactly a form of *jarḥ* but the effect is similar in that two positions, one positive and the other negative have come about, and the latter therefore takes priority over the former. Forgetfulness is also not a form of *jarḥ* and therefore one who forgets what he has reported earlier and denies it because of forgetfulness – this does not invalidate the ḥadīth according to the majority, except for a group of the Ḥanafīs who do consider this as a form of impugnment. The correct view here is that of the majority as instances are noted when prominent scholars have forgotten ḥadīth, or comments on its narrator, which they had earlier rendered or confirmed.[29]

The *ʿulamā'* have differed as to the admissibility of impugnment and validation without any reference to the grounds thereof. Whereas some have considered specification of the grounds necessary in both validation and impugnment, others maintain this to be a requirement of validation but not of impugnment. According to yet another view, specifying the cause or ground of one's assessment is necessary in impugnment but not in validation. The correct view is that explanation of causes is not a requirement in validation but it is of impugnment. Impugnment is thus unacceptable without a clear reference to its cause simply because people tend to differ as to what they may or may not consider to be a ground for impugnment. This view is upheld by Ibn Maʿīn, Ibn al-Ṣalāḥ, and al-Nawawī among others, whereas al-Khaṭīb al-Baghdādī has identified it as the *madhhab* of all the leading scholars of ḥadīth. It is thus unacceptable to judge a narrator to be weak, or unreliable, without explaining the ground of his weakness.[30]

Ibn Ḥajar al-ʿAsqalānī has held that impugnment without explanation is unacceptable concerning a person who is considered upright by even a single learned scholar of ḥadīth. For once a person is validated he retains that qualification unless it is set aside by clear evidence. It is generally known that the leading Imāms of ḥadīth do not validate nor impugn a person unless they are assured of the grounds of their assessment. This is also confirmed by al-Dhahabī who went on record to say that "never have two learned scholars of ḥadīth validated a weak narrator nor have they impugned a reliable one." Abū Shahba who quoted both al-Dhahabī and Ibn Ḥajar has observed that Ibn Ḥajar's position represents a mature stage of developments in ḥadīth sciences on this.[31]

Moreover, validation is unacceptable even from a reliable authority without naming of the person concerned. Thus if a reliable figure narrates ḥadīth from "a trustworthy person (*al-thiqa*)" whom he does not mention by name, his validation is not acceptable, as it is possible that the same person is not considered trustworthy by someone else who might know of a ground of impugnment concerning the same anonymous "*thiqa*".[32] Narration of ḥadīth from a person by an upright narrator without mentioning that person's name does not amount to validation (*taʿdīl*) either. An exception to this is made, however, concerning well-known authorities who are known to have narrated ḥadīth only from reliable persons.[33]

There is a difference of opinion as to whether impugnment and validation is acceptable from only one person or two. Those who maintain that two persons constitute the necessary minimum to establish an assessment on one side or the other do so by analogy to the testimony of witnesses. The correct view is, however, that impugnment and validation by one person is acceptable in the narration of ḥadīth, a view which has prevailed among the *ʿulamā'* of ḥadīth.[34]

When a reliable person narrates ḥadīth from someone whom he has mentioned by name, this by itself does not amount to validation of the person so named, although some have held that it does amount to validation. The correct position is, however, the first one, for it is impermissible in principle to narrate ḥadīth from a person who may not pass the test of probity (*ʿadāla*) and narration by itself does not establish his *ʿadāla*.[35]

Among the grounds of impugnment that some scholars have listed are (1) attribution of lies and false reports to the Prophet and narrating something from him which no reliable person has verified; (2) suspicion of lying especially concerning someone who has a reputation of telling lies even if he is not specifically known to have lied concerning a ḥadīth; (3) reputation for making frequent errors; (4) when one is known for neglect and oversight (*ghafla*); (5) sinful conduct whether consisting of words or action that falls short of unbelief (*kufr*); (6) when one is known for incredulity and imaginary indulgence (*wahm*) contrary to truth; (7) disagreement with reliable authorities and narrators; (8) obscurity in regard to personal identification or in regard to uprightness; (9) advocacy of pernicious innovation (*bidʿa*) consisting of views and beliefs that are contrary to well-known precedent owing to confusion and doubt but not to hostility and arrogance; and (10) bad memory of the kind that gives rise to doubt whether the person is accurate or the opposite thereof.[36]

Ḥadīth scholars are in agreement as to the permissibility of what may amount to backbiting (*ghība*) in the context of impugnment. Although *ghība* is normally forbidden, it is permitted on grounds of necessity in this context, for it would otherwise be difficult to distinguish the truthful from the liar and the upright from the transgressor. The same exemption from *ghība* is granted, on the basis of general consensus (*ijmāʿ*) with regard to witnesses before the courts of justice. The purpose in both cases is to protect the community against harm and to avail them of the best means that would uncover the truth and avert indulgence in falsehood and evil.[37]

Validation and impugnment are only acceptable from persons who are knowledgeable of this subject to a degree that inspires confidence in their ability and insight. The person who validates or impugns narrators of ḥadīth must be dedicated to truth and act in the capacity of a judge of high integrity. The majority of ḥadīth scholars have held that impugnment by a learned and upright person is acceptable even without any further explanation as to its grounds, but that such explanation is necessary in the event where impugnment is attempted by a commoner (*ʿāmmī*). It is thus reported that when the Imām al-Shāfiʿī learned that someone had impugned another, he enquired into the grounds of his accusation. The man said that he saw the accused urinating in a standing position. The Imām then asked as to what did that have to do with impugnment, to which the man replied that the urine would splash onto his clothes and praying in such clothes became questionable. The Imām then asked the man whether he had actually seen the accused praying in those clothes, to which the man said 'no'. The Imām then said that a learned man would not impugn another on weak grounds such as this.[38]

Some Examples of Impugnment (*al-Jarḥ*)

As a result of the efforts at developing the criteria of impugnment, the leading scholars of ḥadīth were able to apply them to particular transmitters and their reports as the following illustrations indicate.

1. A ḥadīth narrator, Aḥmad b. al-Ḥasan b. al-Qāsim b. Samura al-Kūfī died in Egypt in 262 H; al-Dāraquṭnī and others said concerning him that he was "*matrūk*" and Ibn Ḥibbān said he was a liar "*kadhdhāb*". A so-called ḥadīth that is reported by him from Wakīʿ, from Sufyān, from Ibn Jurayj, from ʿAmr b. Dīnār from Ibn ʿAbbās, labelled as a *marfūʿ* (elevated) ḥadīth, has it that "on the Day of Resurrection a caller will call from beneath the Throne (*ʿarsh*) and will mention the names of Abū Bakr, ʿUmar, ʿUthmān and ʿAlī." This report was consequently isolated and abandoned.

2. Another ḥadīth transmitter of the third century, Aḥmad b. Badīl al-Kūfī al-Qāḍī (d. 286), was evaluated and discredited by al-Nasā'ī (d. 302) by the phrase "*la ba'sa bihi*" (of little weight), whereas Aḥmad b. ʿAbd Allāh Ibn ʿAdī (d. 365/976) said of him that he transmitted ḥadīth from Ḥafṣ b. Ghiyāth and others that were known to be weak and unacceptable.

3. Aḥmad b. ʿAbd al-Jabbār al-ʿAṭārudī (d. 272 H) who has reported ḥadīth from persons such as Abū Bakr, Ibn ʿAbbās and others, has generally been considered to be weak. Al-Dāraquṭnī (d. 385 H) said of him as "*la ba'sa bihi*" and Ibn Abī Ḥātim al-Rāzī (d. 327/938) said of him that he is "not strong – *laysa bi'l-qawī*", whereas Ibn ʿAdī (d. 315) said that the reason he is considered as weak is that he did not meet the people from whom he narrated ḥadīth although the ḥadīth he reported are not necessarily condemned "*munkaran*" as such.[39]

4. Ḥabīb b. Abī Ḥabīb (d. 280 H) whose father's name is Zarīq or some said to be Marzūq Abū Muḥammad al-Miṣrī. Aḥmad b. Ḥanbal (d. 241) said of him that he was "unreliable – *laysa bi-thiqa*", whereas Abū Dāwūd went so far as to say that he was "the greatest of liars – *akdhab al-nās*". Abū Ḥātim al-Rāzī said that he ostentatiously narrated ḥadīth from his nephew al-Zuhrī which he actually fabricated. Ibn ʿAdī (d. 315) said that virtually all of his *aḥādīth* were forgeries. Ibn Ḥibbān said concerning him that he attributed ḥadīth to reliable people and chains of transmitters, such as Mālik – Nāfiʿ – Ibn ʿUmar which were forgeries. One such forgery by him was the so-called ḥadīth: "The beauty of this world would be lost as of the year 225 H."

5. Another name among the ḥadīth transmitters of the early third century was that of Hajjāj b. Nuṣayrat al-Fasāṭiṭī of Baṣra (d. 214 H). This person was evaluated by Yaʿqūb b. Shayba who said that he asked Yaḥyā b. Maʿīn about him and he said that he was "*sadūq* – truthful" but that some had expressed doubt as to his reliability especially concerning ḥadīth he narrated from Shuʿba. ʿAlī Ibn al-Madīnī said of him that "his ḥadīth is dismissed – *dhahaba ḥadīthuhu*" whereas Abū Ḥātim al-Rāzī, Abū Dāwūd, and al-Nasāʾī have considered him weak and said that his ḥadīth was abandoned. Al-Bukhārī said that many remained silent concerning Hajjāj, "*sakatū ʿanhu*," whereas Ibn Ḥibbān mentioned him among the *thiqāt*.[40]

The *ʿulamāʾ* of ḥadīth have on the whole classified as weak ḥadīth the work of someone who is regarded as being of doubtful reliability. They have not, in other words, given the benefit of doubt to weak transmitters unless they found evidence that supported the work of the individual concerned through some other and more reliable channels.

[09] Hidden Defects I

ʿIlal al-Ḥadīth

THE *ʿulamāʾ* of ḥadīth have designated *ʿilal al-ḥadīth* as a separate branch of ḥadīth studies. The discussion here is primarily concerned with the study of defects of a less than obvious type in ḥadīth, defects that often escape the naked eye in that they may be present in a ḥadīth even if the ḥadīth appears to be otherwise intact.[1] A defect (*ʿilla*) may relate either to *isnād*, such as elevating a suspended ḥadīth (*rafʿ al-mawqūf*) or connecting a disconnected ḥadīth (*ittiṣāl al-mursal*), or to the subject matter (*matn*) such as a subtle change of a word, superfluous addition or insertion of words that do not belong to the text, known as *idrāj*, and insertion sometimes of one ḥadīth into another (*idkhāl ḥadīth fī ḥadīth*), or indeed the *ʿilla* may relate to both the text and the *isnād*. The defects are often related to the *isnād* and detecting them often begins with the verification of the manifest conditions of a *ṣaḥīḥ* ḥadīth. A defect is often suspected when there is something odd about the *isnād*, which may be due to its variance with other reports or criticism it might have invoked from others. The method that the *ʿulamāʾ* have applied in order to detect the *ʿilla* in ḥadīth is to look into all the relevant information concerning a particular ḥadīth and ascertain discrepancies therein and then to verify the reliability or otherwise of the transmitter who comes under suspicion. The defects are often such that only the expert would be likely to detect them.[2] Al-Ḥākim al-Nīsābūrī (321-405 AH) has stated that the focus of attention in this branch of the ḥadīth studies is not on ḥadīth which clearly falls under the rejected (*mardūd*) category, nor is impugnment (*al-jarḥ*) of concern to *ʿilal* (*al-ḥadīth*), for a rejected ḥadīth is usually set aside and abandoned. Rather, in *ʿilal al-ḥadīth* one often looks into the works of reliable narrators who might have themselves failed to notice the defect in the ḥadīth they have narrated. *ʿIlal al-ḥadīth* basically looks into the retentiveness, comprehension, and knowledge (*al-ḥifẓ, al-fahm, al-maʿrifa*) of the qualified narrators of ḥadīth.[3] Because of its sensitivity and refinement, the *ʿulamā'* of ḥadīth have often considered *ʿilal al-ḥadīth* as the most meticulous and worthwhile of all the ḥadīth sciences, and one who masters it is often compared to a keen craftsman who can distinguish the pure from the adulterated by dent of valuable experience.[4] To illustrate this, it is noted that when the *isnād* of a ḥadīth combines transmitters from different places, such as when a Madīnese transmits a ḥadīth from one who resided in Kufā, this often gave rise to suspicion.

The *ʿulamā'* have spoken at length about *ʿilal al-ḥadīth* and some have written specialised works on the subject. The focus is often on the skill, reliability, and knowledge of the narrators, their personal details, works, contacts and teachers. The earliest known work on *ʿilal al-ḥadīth* is that of Yaḥyā b. Maʿīn (158-233 H) bearing the title *Al-Tārikh Wa'l-ʿIlal*; followed by Imām Aḥmad b. Ḥanbal's (164-241 H), *ʿIlal al-ḥadīth*; *Al-ʿIlal* by Muḥammad Ibn ʿĪsā al-Tirmidhī (209-279 H), and many others.[5]

Numerous examples of defective ḥadīth have been recorded. To give one or two brief examples, it is provided in a ḥadīth, narrated by Yūnus, from al-Zuhrī, from Sālim, from Ibn ʿUmar from the Prophet who said: "One who captures one unit of the Friday or other prayers, has captured the whole".

Abū Ḥātim al-Rāzī has stated that this ḥadīth is defective both in respect of transmission and subject matter. The correct names in the chain of transmitters (from al-Zuhrī upwards) are al-Zuhrī, from Abū Salama, from Abū Hurayra, from the Prophet, and also the word "Friday" in the text is superfluous. The correct rendering of the text therefore is "Whoever captures one *rakʿa* of (a congregational) prayer has captured (all of) it".

The defect (*ʿilla*) of this ḥadīth has thus been located in both the subject matter and the *isnād*.[6]

Another example of a defective ḥadīth is as follows: Abū ʿAbd Allāh Muḥammad reported from Aḥmad b. Muḥammad b. ʿĪsā – Abū

Ḥudhayfa – Zuhayr b. Muḥammad b. ʿUthmān b. Sulaymān – from his father who heard the Prophet, peace be on him, reciting the Sūra al-Ṭūr in the *Maghrib* prayer (this is contrary to normal practice of silent recitation). Al-Nīsābūrī has identified three defects in this ḥadīth: firstly that ʿUthmān's last name is "Ibn Abī Sulaymān", and not "ʿUthmān Ibn Sulaymān", second that ʿUthmān reported it "from Nāfiʿ b. Jubayr, from his father", and third that Sulaymān's father did not hear anything from the Prophet as he never saw the Prophet.[7] Hidden defects of this kind are not infrequently found in the works of even senior scholars who often discuss a ḥadīth without noticing the defects therein. It is always recommendable for the transmitter and critic to expose and explain any hidden defect that they know in a ḥadīth. Al-Ḥākim al-Nīsābūrī identified ten different varieties of *ʿilal*, which will presently be reviewed, but has in the meantime mentioned that he only mentioned some varieties, or grounds, of *ʿilal* and that in reality the ways in which *ʿilla* can find its way to a ḥadīth cannot be exclusively enumerated nor defined. But the *ʿulamā'* have not neglected the subject and most of these have, in fact, been identified and exposed from early times by scholars such as ʿAbd al-Raḥmān b. Abī Ḥātim al-Rāzī (d. 327 H), *ʿIlal al-Ḥadīth*, and ʿAlī b. ʿUmar al-Dāraquṭnī (d. 385), *Al-ʿIlal al-Wārida fi'l-Aḥādīth al-Nabawiyya*, and many others. The *ʿulamā'* of ḥadīth have also considered certain works such as the three collections of al-Ṭabarānī, namely, *Al-Kabīr*, *Al-Awsaṭ*, and *Al-Ṣaghīr*, Dāraquṭnī's work *Al-Afrād*, compilations of ḥadīth by al-Khaṭīb al-Baghdādī, and Abū Nuʿaym al-Iṣfahānī's *Ḥīlyat al-Awliyā' wa Ṭabaqāt al-Aṣfiyā'* to contain many a weak ḥadīth and should therefore not be relied upon.[8]

To illustrate a defect that relates only to the text or *matn*, one may refer to a ḥadīth, recorded by al-Bukhārī, in which the Prophet said in response to some news that had broken out in Madīna that considerable wealth had arrived from the collection of poll-tax (*jizya*) in Bahrain. The following day when the Prophet ended his morning prayer in congregation, the attendants had apparently expected an announcement over the distribution of those assets. The Prophet then said:

> By God! I do not fear poverty for you. I only fear that when this material world has been opened to you, as was opened to those who came before you, it may distract you from the right path, just as it distracted them (*fa-tulhikum kamā alhathum*).

In another version of the same ḥadīth the last three words have been recorded as *fatuhlikukum kamā ahlakathum* (it will destroy you as it destroyed them).[9]

It has been suggested that a Companion who might have been closer to the Prophet on that occasion had heard this phrase differently to the one standing a little farther away, as the two phrases sounded very similar and their meanings could also equally fit into the context.[10]

For an example of an *ʿilla* that is detected in the *isnād*, one may refer to a ḥadīth narrated by Yaʿlā b. ʿUbayd al-Ṭanāfusī, from Sufyān al-Thawrī, from ʿAmr b. Dīnār, from Ibn ʿUmar, from the Prophet that "The buyer and seller have the option to (retract their agreement) until they part company".

Other scholars have reported the same ḥadīth from the associates of Sufyān al-Thawrī, including Abū Nuʿaym al-Faḍl b. Dakīn, Muḥammad b. Yūsuf al-Fāryābī and Mukhlid b. Yazīd. It has been discovered that Yaʿlā had mistakenly recorded ʿAmr b. Dīnār, instead of ʿAbd Allāh b. Dīnār. There is no defect in the text of the ḥadīth.[11]

Another example of *ʿilla* in the *isnād* is the ḥadīth narrated by Mūsā b. ʿUqba, from Suhayl b. Abī Ṣāliḥ, from his father, from Abū Hurayra that the Prophet, peace be on him, said: "One who sits in a meeting where he speaks excessively, he should say before he leaves the meeting 'praise be to God, there is no god but Allah, I seek your pardon and I repent'; if he recites this, God would grant him pardon for all of his misgivings in that meeting." Al-Ḥākim al-Nīsābūrī wrote concerning this ḥadīth: One day Imām Muslim visited his mentor, Imām al-Bukhārī, and asked him concerning this ḥadīth, to which the learned al-Bukhārī replied "it is an elegant ḥadīth and it is the only one that I know of concerning this subject, except for the fact that it is defective (*maʿlūl*): Mūsā b. Ismāʿīl narrated it from Wuhayb, from Ṣuhayl, from ʿAwn b. ʿAbd Allāh... which means that the ḥadīth in question is a statement of ʿAwn b. ʿAbd Allāh and not of the Messenger of God. This is a preferable reading as it also appears that Mūsā b. ʿUqba has not actually heard it from Ṣuhayl."[12]

Moreover, al-Ḥākim al-Nīsābūrī also gives the following instances of defective (*maʿlūl*) ḥadīths:

a. where a *mursal* (disconnected) ḥadīth is partially joined by a *musnad* (complete *isnād*) ḥadīth thus ending a *mursal* with a *musnad*. An example of this is the ḥadīth narrated by Abū Qulāba that the Prophet said: "The most compassionate of my *umma* is Abū Bakr, and the most stringent in God's religion is ʿUmar; the most truly modest is ʿUthmān; the most literate is Ubayy b. Kaʿb; and the most knowledgeable on *ḥalāl* and *ḥarām* is Muʿādh b. Jabal. Verily every *umma* has a trustee and the trustee of this *umma* is Abū ʿUbayda (b. al-Jarrāḥ)."

The larger part of this ḥadīth is a *mursal* as it is said that Abū Qulāba may have heard it from Anas b. Mālik but this is uncertain. Only the last portion that adds something to the text concerning Abū ʿUbayda is *musnad* (as known from other reports) and it is a separate ḥadīth which is joined to a larger ḥadīth, thus ending a *mursal* with a *musnad*. The separate ḥadīth here is: "Verily every *umma* has a trustee, and the trustee of this *umma* is Abū ʿUbayda."

b. *Isnād* becomes defective, according to al-Nīsābūrī, wherein the Madīnese narrate from Kufians. The doubt here obviously relates to distance and location and doubt will persist unless it becomes known that the one link travelled to the locality of the other to meet the latter. An example of this is the ḥadīth wherein the Prophet has reportedly said: "I ask God for forgiveness and repent a hundred times a day." Al-Nīsābūrī wrote concerning the *isnād* of this ḥadīth: "It is the type of *isnād* that I would not look into, if I report a ḥadīth, that is. For one who knows the conditions of authenticity of ḥadīth would also know that when the Madīnese narrate from Kufians, they tend to slip (*zalaqū*)."[13]

c. *Isnād* becomes defective if it omits a link which may be very well known, and the fact of its omission is known through another chain of *isnād* concerning the same ḥadīth. An example of this is the ḥadīth narrated by Yūnus b. Zayd, from Ibn Shihāb (al-Zuhrī), from ʿAlī b. al-Ḥusayn, from men of the *Anṣār* (*rijāl min al-Anṣār*) that one night they were with the Messenger of God "when we saw a comet that enlightened the sky...".

أنهم كانوا مع رســـول الله صلى الله عليه وسلم ذات ليلة فرمى بالنجم فاستنار.

Al-Nīsābūrī wrote that notwithstanding his eminent retention and status as a reliable narrator, Yūnus b. Zayd unduly condensed the *isnād* of this ḥadīth. The first link in the chain of *isnād* was Ibn ʿAbbās who said that he had heard this ḥadīth "from men of the Anṣār". The ḥadīth has been confirmed to be *ṣaḥīḥ* due to the correct information obtained concerning the missing link as it has also been reported from al-Zuhrī by Ibn ʿUyayna, Shuʿayb, Ṣāliḥ, Awzāʿī and others.[12]

d. *Isnād* is defective if the narrator omits a link that may be unknown and replaces it with another name so as to make it look more reliable. An example of this is the ḥadīth reported by al-Zuhrī, from Sufyān al-Thawrī, from Ḥajjāj b. Farāfisa, "from Yaḥyā b. Kathīr, from Abū Salama," from Abū Hurayra that the Prophet said "A believer is dignified and generous whereas a transgressor is secretive and ignoble."

المؤمن غرٌّ كريم والفاجر خبئٌ لئيم.

Al-Nīsābūrī commented that there is a distortion in this *isnād* and it occurs between Ḥajjāj and Abū Salama. The correct version is verified to be "from Hajjāj b. Farāfisa, from a man (*ʿan rajul*), from Abū Salama ...". The defective *isnād* has thus substituted "a man" with "Yaḥya b. Kathīr".[15]

e. Sometimes the narrator quotes his immediate source, or *shaykh*, who is his contemporary and the two have met, but the narrator has not actually heard the particular ḥadīth from him. An example of this is the ḥadīth narrated by Yaḥyā b. Kathīr, from Anas b. Mālik that "when the Messenger of God broke his fast in someone's house, he would say: observers of fast opened their fast with you and ate your pure food and the angels prayed for you (or peace descended on you)."

إن النبي صلى الله عليه وسلم إذا أفطر عند أهل بيت قال: أفطر عندكم الصائمون وأكل طعامكم الأبرار وصلت عليكم الملائكة (أو نزلت عليكم السكينة).

In this *isnād*, it is known from other relevant evidence that although Yaḥyā b. Kathīr met with Anas he did not hear this particular ḥadīth from him.[16]

f. A ḥadīth may be considered defective due to its report via two separate chains of transmission, one of which is elevated (*marfūʿ*) and the other suspended (*mawqūf*). Thus it becomes difficult to establish whether it is a ḥadīth proper or the saying of a Companion. An example of this is the ḥadīth narrated by Abū Farwa Yazīd b. Muḥammad, from his father, from his grandfather, from Aʿmash, from Abū Sufyān, from Jābir that the Prophet peace be on him said "One who laughs during prayer must repeat the prayer but need not take a new ablution."

This is the elevated version of the ḥadīth wherein Jābir narrated from the Prophet. But the same ḥadīth is reported through a second *isnād* in which Abū'l-Ḥusayn ʿAlī al-Subayʿī of Kūfa narrated it from Ibrāhīm b. ʿAbd Allāh al-ʿAbsī, from Wakīʿ, from Aʿmash, from Abū Sufyān who said that "Jābir was asked concerning a person who laughs aloud in *ṣalāh*, and he said that only the *ṣalāh* may be repeated but not the ablution".[17]

It is quite obvious that defects of this type can easily pass unnoticed by readers who are not knowledgeable on the narrators of ḥadīth, their contemporaries and the expectation therefore of the place of particular narrators in the relevant *isnād*. Defect (*ʿilla*) is identified when something unexpected or unusual is noted concerning the *isnād* or the actual text of the ḥadīth.

Instances are also found of plausible additions of a phrase to an originally shorter ḥadīth, which phrase either explained the ḥadīth or gave additional detail, but was found, upon closer examination, to have been added by the narrator himself. There is a ḥadīth, for example, wherein Anas b. Mālik has stated that he had prayed in congregation behind the Prophet, as well as Abū Bakr, ʿUmar and ʿUthmān and they all used to start the prayer with the recitation of "*al-ḥamdu li-llāh rabbi al-ʿālamīn* and did not recite *bismillāh al-raḥmān al-raḥīm*". It was later found out that the latter portion of the ḥadīth (i.e., and they did not recite ...) was not mentioned in the original version of the ḥadīth that was transmitted by Anas b. Mālik, but was added by other transmitters somewhere down the line. Al-Bukhārī and Muslim have consequently recorded the shorter version of this ḥadīth.[18]

[10] Hidden Defects II

Tadlīs al-Ḥadīth

TADLĪS literally means concealment, especially in reference to a fault that a merchant does not reveal in order to sell his goods. It is the verbal noun of *dalasa* which originally means the mixing of light and dark colours. *Tadlīs* is usually attempted by one who knows what he chooses not to reveal and remains silent. The *ʿulamā'* of ḥadīth have used *tadlīs* somewhat technically in reference to a transmitter who has narrated a ḥadīth from an authority whom he met but from whom he did not learn that particular ḥadīth, but learned it from someone else going through the same authority. It also refers to a narrator who was a contemporary of his immediate source but has not met him, yet he makes out as if he did. At other times, the narrator, who might or might not have met with his immediate source uses a term which can imply both direct and indirect learning. In such situations, the narrator tends to avoid using such terms as "so and so informed, or spoke to me" and uses terms such as "so and so said, or it is reported from so and so". Note for example, the ḥadīth which reads: "Abū ʿAwāna narrated (*rawā Abū ʿAwāna*) from Aʿmash, from Ibrāhīm al-Taymī, from his father, from Abū Dharr that the Prophet, peace be on him, said ..." Abū ʿAwāna then went on record to say that he asked Aʿmash whether he heard the ḥadīth in question from Ibrāhīm. To this Aʿmash answered that he actually heard it from Ḥakīm ibn Jubayr who quoted Ibrāhīm. Aʿmash had thus concealed his direct source, but the fact that he actually declared so when he was asked about it exposes the concealed element and effectively changes the *Mudallas* into a *Mursal*.[1] This form of concealment is known as *tadlīs al-isnād*, or hiding some weakness in the *isnād*, as opposed to concealment in the identification of the teachers, or *tadlīs al-shuyūkh*, wherein the transmitter has used a scholar's name which was not commonly known, instead of using the name for which he was well known. The transmitter may have used the first name of his authority, or an appellation, or a description of some kind, which somehow fails to clearly identify his source. An example of this is the report by one Abū Bakr b. Mujāhid al-Muqri' who narrated from "ʿAbd Allāh b. Abī ʿAbd Allāh", by which he meant Abū Dāwūd, the author of *Sunan Abū Dāwūd*, but Abū Dāwūd was hardly well known by this appellation (*kunya*) of his. Another variety of *tadlīs al-shuyūkh* occurs when the transmitter exaggerates in the praise of his teacher and refers to him by such terms as *al-ḥāfiẓ al-ḍābiṭ, al-ʿallāma al-thābit*, etc., which may be less than accurate. A similar *tadlīs* can be seen with reference to places, such as mentioning the name of a village without mentioning the nearest city or country, or using a name that could apply to different places. An example of this is the use by al-Khaṭīb al-Baghdādī of "so and so from Mā-Warā' al-Nahr reported" by which he simply meant the other side of the river Tigris. Such ambiguities have occurred occasionally in the reports of people who had not travelled widely in search of the ḥadīth, as opposed to those who had, but made out as if they had. This situation was obviously encountered frequently, so much so that Ibn Ḥajar has given it the name '*tadlīs al-bilād*' (concealment of cities).[2]

The *ʿulamā'* have strongly condemned *tadlīs* of the first type and have spoken disapprovingly of the second, although they have disagreed in their acceptance/rejection of ḥadīth in which *tadlīs* might have occurred. The *ʿulamā'* have often equated *tadlīs al-isnād* with lying and have disqualified the person committing it from the transmission of ḥadīth, even when committted only once. At times words and expressions that the transmitter has used are such that can equally imply direct or indirect hearing, and this creates ambiguity, but it is often read in the light of the general reputation and record of the transmitter so as to determine the reliability of his report. Reports that contain *tadlīs* are generally suspect, yet in the more milder cases of *tadlīs*, scholars do not disqualify the transmitter altogether and tend to accept only those of his reports in which the words used are indicative of direct hearing from the source. To give an example, one of al-Zuhrī's reliable pupils, Sufyān b. ʿUyayna (107-198) transmitted a ḥadīth from him saying *qāla al-Zuhrī* (al-Zuhrī reported, or al-Zuhrī said), and he was asked the question, by one ʿAlī b. Khashram, whether he heard that particular ḥadīth from al-Zuhrī; he remained silent but Khashram repeated the question to which the reply came "No, I did not hear it from al-Zuhrī, nor from the one who heard it from al-Zuhrī, I heard it from ʿAbd al-Razzāq, from Maʿmar, from al-Zuhrī". As it is generally known, the two Sufyāns, namely Sufyān b. ʿUyayna and Sufyān al-Thawrī, both well-known and reliable figures, are associated with this kind of dubious usage of words, but the *ʿulamā'* of ḥadīth have still accepted their reports. This is because the two Sufyāns are otherwise known to be reliable and have usually transmitted ḥadīth from trustworthy narrators; their version of *tadlīs*, especially that of Sufyān al-Thawrī, is often said to consist of little more than a use of appellation for the first or full name, and the ambiguity is generally ignored.[3] This kind of *tadlīs* is also known in the narrations of such other personalities among the *tābiʿūn* as Qatāda, Ḥasan al-Baṣrī and Aʿmash, and even the prominent Companion, Ibn ʿAbbās, for the latter had heard only a handful of *aḥādīth* directly from the Prophet and heard the rest from fellow Companions, and yet he often quoted the Prophet directly. But once again these are not discredited altogether as the ambiguity is considered to be slight on the whole when seen in the light of their generally acknowledged integrity and accomplishment. The collections of both al-Bukhārī and Muslim comprise *aḥādīth* transmitted by these well-known figures notwithstanding their involvement in some mild forms of *tadlīs*. Some have compared *tadlīs* by Companions to *Mursal* ḥadīth, which should actually be classified as *Mursal*. Be that as it may, Ṣubḥī al-Ṣāliḥ is right in saying perhaps that few narrators of ḥadīth were able to avoid *tadlīs* altogether in all respects. The traces of *tadlīs* that are found in al-Bukhārī and Muslim are often said to consist of mild forms of ambiguity in the use of words and concern the precise import of expressions such as '*haddathanā*' and '*akhbaranā*' as to whether they might conceal the difference between direct and indirect hearing. It is probable, however, that al-Bukhārī and Muslim may have ignored such levels of uncertainty on account of the sound reputation and reliability of the persons that might have been implicated in *tadlīs*.

Some critics have drawn a distinction between *Mudallas* and the type of *Mursal* known as *Mursal Khafī* (hidden *Mursal*) in that the *Mudallas* involves transmission of ḥadīth from someone who is known to the transmitter and the two have met or that they were contemporaries but who have not communicated concerning the ḥadīth at issue, yet it is made out as if they had. *Mursal Khafī* on the other hand involves a missing link and the likelihood therefore that the two were contemporaries but have not met nor spoken to one another. *Mursal Khafī* differs from *Mursal* in that *Mursal* consists of a broken link at the level of the Companion and there is no concealment in it whereas *Mursal Khafī* consists of a noted broken link at a lower level and it is concealed. Al-Khaṭīb al-Baghdādī held that it is the element of concealment which distinguishes the *Mudallas* from *Mursal Khafī*. When a person transmits ḥadīth from another and makes out that he heard the ḥadīth directly from him and then it turns out that this was not the case, or that he intentionally conceals the name of his immediate source, this is *tadlīs*. This is different from *Mursal*, which is not likely to involve concealment but it does involve omission. A *Mursal*, in other words, does not involve *tadlīs* but *tadlīs* may on the other hand involve *irsāl*, that is, jumping the link, or omission. This may explain why the *ʿulamāʾ* disapprove of *tadlīs* much more strongly than they do of *irsāl*. When *tadlīs* is committed by someone who is not known to be reliable (i.e. *thiqa*), it must be abandoned.[4]

Various reasons have been detected for *tadlīs*, some of which are more objectionable than others. *Tadlīs* may sometimes be due to a certain amount of confusion on the part of a transmitter who has heard many things from his immediate source and cannot distinguish with clarity exactly what he had heard, so he uses a word that is less than categorical on the fact of direct hearing and thus falls into *tadlīs*. The transmitter may also happen to be a more senior person than his immediate source and may thus be reluctant to quote him clearly and refers to him instead by a name other than what he is commonly known by, or some such description for which he is not well known. Sometimes the transmitter, who has quoted another person on numerous other occasions, may refer to him vaguely so as to show that he has transmitted ḥadīth from more than one teacher or *shaykh*. *Tadlīs* may also involve an attempt to hide one particularly weak link in an otherwise reliable *isnād*. And lastly a certain ambiguity in *tadlīs* may be due to a desire on the part of the transmitter to make out that he had travelled widely or met with more scholars than he actually did in his search for the ḥadīth of the Prophet.[5]

The *ʿulamā'* of ḥadīth have written at length on transmitters of ḥadīth who have committed *tadlīs* and their detailed investigations have led them to grade these individuals into four categories of concealers (*mudallisūn*) ranging from those who committed *tadlīs* rarely but were otherwise trustworthy, to those who only left out the names and details of well-known figures, and then those who left out the names of weak and unknown links, and finally those who did this and were weak narrators themselves. As a general rule, transmission from these last two groups of people is rejected altogether, but narration of the first two grades in the four-point scale may be accepted unless there is specific evidence to suggest otherwise. There is general agreement as to the disqualification absolutely of the perpetrator of *tadlīs al-isnād* in which a weak link is deliberately omitted. Some *ʿulamā'* have also held that the ensuing disqualification is permanent, whereas others have held that ḥadīth which is clear of *tadlīs* may be accepted from one who has committed *tadlīs* previously provided there is no ambiguity of any kind in his report and the person is otherwise upright. This is the view of the majority of the leading *madhāhib*, including the Shāfiʿīs.[6]

A branch of the ḥadīth literature which relates closely to some aspects of *tadlīs* is knowledge of the names of ḥadīth transmitters who are known by different names (*maʿrifatu mā dhukira bi-asmā' aw ṣifāt mukhtalifa*). For example, Sālim Abū ʿAbd Allāh al-Madīnī, who narrated ḥadīth from Abū Hurayra, Abū Saʿīd al-Khudrī and ʿĀ'isha is known by no less than eight other variations of the same basic name, including Sālim Mawlā Mālik b. Aws, Sālim Abū ʿAbd Allāh al-Dawsī, Sālim Mawlā Daws, Abū ʿAbd Allāh Mawlā Shaddād and others. Ibn al-Jawzī has noted that this name has been rendered in fifty variations or more and this has given rise to numerous instances of *tadlīs*.[7]

[11] Conflict in Ḥadīth

Mukhtalif al-Ḥadīth

THIS branch of the ḥadīth studies, which is also known as *mushkil al-ḥadīth*[1] (the difficult in ḥadīth) is concerned with the study of conflict in *aḥādīth* and proposes methods by which to reconcile them. In the event of an apparent conflict which can be resolved by recourse to interpretation (*ta'wīl*), the latter is often attempted through the application of the rules of *takhṣīṣ,* that is, particularisation of the general, or whenever appropriate, by qualifying the absolute (*taqyīd al-muṭlaq*). A conflict may also be resolved by attempting reconciliation (*al-jamʿ wa'l-tawfīq*), or by providing factual information so as to distinguish the context and application of each ḥadīth with the purpose of retaining both and applying each in their respective capacity. This area of ḥadīth studies is also concerned with clarification of the meaning of difficult and unfamiliar terms and expressions in ḥadīth even when there are no other conflicting ḥadīth. This is why the expression '*mushkil al-ḥadīth*' is sometimes preferred to '*mukhtalif al-ḥadīth*' as the former can include conflict in ḥadīth as well as ḥadīth which is not in conflict with any other ḥadīth but difficult nevertheless to comprehend. The difficulty in *mushkil al-ḥadīth* may also be due to an apparent conflict between a ḥadīth and a Qur'ānic text, or with human experience and natural sciences. We still retain the more commonly applied term (i.e. *mukhtalif al-ḥadīth*) here with a reminder perhaps that the term 'conflict' is used in rather a loose sense and in reference sometimes to cases that do not strictly amount to a conflict situation. Resolving conflict and clarifying difficulties in ḥadīth is admittedly not a facile task and the effort often involves a combination of the knowledge of *fiqh* and ḥadīth. If two ḥadīths cannot be reconciled by recourse to the rules of interpretation, then one may be given preference over the other and in this way at least one of them will be upheld, if not both.

Mukhtalif al-ḥadīth is concerned exclusively with valid ḥadīth of the *Ṣaḥīḥ* and *Ḥasan* varieties but not with ḥadīth that is spurious and weak, which would not merit serious attention anyway. This branch of the ḥadīth studies is concerned, in other words, with ḥadīth that commands acceptance but is difficult to understand owing to conflict with other equally persuasive evidence either within or outside the ḥadīth. Moreover, *Mukhtalif al-ḥadīth* is concerned with two types of conflicting *aḥādīth*: firstly when they can be reconciled, and secondly when they cannot. The first of these may be illustrated in the two *aḥādīth* which follow:

- When the water reaches (the height of) two *qullas*, it does not carry dirt.[2]

  إذا بلغ الماء قلتين لم يحمل الخبث.

- God created water clean and will not make it unclean unless there is a change in its taste, colour or smell.[3]

  خلق الله الماء طهورا لاينجسه إلا ما غير طعمه أو لونه أو ريحه.

There is an apparent conflict here which can be resolved by recourse to particularisation of the general. The first ḥadīth declares water clean when it reaches a certain height (regardless of any change in its colour and taste). The second ḥadīth declares that water is clean (below the level of two *qullas*) so long as there is no change in its attributes of cleanliness. Each of the two ḥadīths operates as a specifier over the other and the conflict therein is resolved.

The second of the two possibilities envisaged of conflicting *aḥādīth* is when they cannot be reconciled with one another, and this also occurs in one or the other of the following two varieties. (a) When it is possible to identify a chronological order between the two ḥadīths, in which case the rules of abrogation (*naskh*) will apply to them and the one will abrogate the other. Some examples of this are found in our discussion of abrogation in ḥadīth in a separate section below.

(b) When a chronological order between the two conflicting ḥadīths cannot be ascertained, in which case recourse will be made to the rules of preference (*al-tarjīḥ*) to determine which of the two is stronger and therefore preferable. There are numerous grounds of *tarjīḥ*, most of which refer, in the context of ḥadīth, to the strength and reliability of its narrator, and to the clarity and strength of the wording of ḥadīth. In his *Tadrīb al-Rāwī*, al-Suyūṭī has discussed the grounds of *tarjīḥ* under seven main headings which are then subdivided into numerous sub-varieties that reach altogether to one hundred and nine grounds on which *al-tarjīḥ* may be attempted. I do not propose to discuss all of these here but will refer to some aspects thereof.

The principal grounds of preference that al-Suyūṭī has discussed are:

1. Conditions of the narrators, which refer to a variety of factors such as the knowledge of the narrators, their ages, their retentiveness, and their number (if there be many), proximity or otherwise to the source, and the manner in which the narrator received the information himself and then transmitted it to others and so forth. If one of the two conflicting ḥadīths is proven to be stronger on any of these grounds, it may be given preference.
2. The actual words and expressions (whether *samiʿtu, ḥaddathanī, ḥaddathanā,* etc.) and clarity of the language that the narrator has used which might indicate preferability and strength.
3. Whether the narration is verbatim or conceptual, and whether the ḥadīth actually refers to its own rationale and *ʿilla*.
4. Preference by reference to time and place – the Madīnese ḥadīth is given preference to the Makkī, and the ḥadīth itself may sometimes indicate the time and place of its origin.
5. Preference by reference to the wording of the ḥadīth: the specific is preferable to the general, the literal to the metaphorical, the one that expounds its cause to the one that does not, the explicit to the implicit, the verbal (*qawlī*) to the actual (*fiʿlī*), the longer text to the shorter and so forth.
6. Preference by reference to the ruling: prohibition takes preference over permissibility, and one that omits punishment or liability to the one that imposes it.

7. Preference by reference to external factors: ḥadīth which complies with the Qur'ān or other *aḥādīth* is preferred to the one that does not. The practice of the Companions is also a point of consideration, and so is the extraction of ḥadīth by al-Bukhārī and Muslim and so forth.

In the event where preference is totally unfeasible, then the *ʿulamāʾ* advise suspension (*al-tawaqquf*) which means that the conflict prevails and no action is taken in either direction. The four courses of action that are thus envisaged consist of (1) reconciliation and retention (*al-jamʿ*) whenever possible; (2) abrogation when this is ascertained; (3) preference; and (4) suspension. There is some disagreement as to whether abrogation should be the second or the last recourse, but al-ʿAsqalānī and al-Suyūṭī have opted for the order that is here presented.[4]

Ever since the time of the Companions, the *ʿulamāʾ* throughout the ages have tried to remove difficulties and conflicts in ḥadīth by recourse to interpretation and *ijtihād*. The scholars of ḥadīth were particularly challenged by the doubts and controversies expressed by sectarian movements, such as the Muʿtazila and the Kharijites, concerning the import and meaning of some *aḥādīth*. Imām Shāfiʿī (d. 204) was the first to write a book, entitled *Ikhtilāf al-Ḥadīth,* which appeared on the margin of the seventh volume of his *Kitāb al-Umm*. It is not an exhaustive work on the subject, but it provided a set of guidelines on methods of reconciliation and preference of conflicting ḥadīth. A more extensive work on the subject is *Ta'wīl Makhtalif al-Ḥadīth* by Muḥammad b. ʿAbd Allāh b. Muslim b. Qutayba al-Daynūrī (d. 271). The author has, in this work, engaged in disputation with those who were over-critical of the *Ahl al-Ḥadīth* and sought to widen the scope of conflict in ḥadīth by highlighting spurious conflicts and aspects of conflict that were more apparent rather than real. Ibn Qutayba addressed the alleged conflicts in ḥadīth, attempted reconciliation between them, and succeeded in providing effective responses to many of the Muʿtazilite claims. Many others have written on the subject and some *ʿulamāʾ* have considered this branch of the ḥadīth studies as "one of the most important, such that no learned scholar or *ʿālim*, whichever group he may belong to, can afford to neglect... It involves development of special acumen attained by scholars who are learned in ḥadīth, *fiqh* and *uṣūl al-fiqh*."[5] Another authoritative work on the subject is *Mushkil al-Āthār* by Abū Jaʿfar Aḥmad b. Muḥammad al-Ṭaḥḥāwī (d. 321 H) in four volumes, a later edition of which was published in India in 1333 H. Abū Bakr Muḥammad b. al-Ḥasan al-Isfahānī's (d. 406), *Mushkil al-Ḥadīth wa Bayānuh* is also well known.

Some of the early partisan movements such as the Kharijites, the Shīʿa, the Qadariyya and the Murji'a have quoted ḥadīth in support of their views and doctrines often at the expense of other often divergent evidence in the ḥadīth. When two *aḥādīth* are quoted by the two sides, there is often an apparent conflict which may take a great deal of explanation to reach an understanding over issues. I do not propose to engage the reader in minute details of this but will merely give the general outline of an example as follows:

The Kharijites have quoted in support of their viewpoints the following two *aḥādīth*:

1. A group of my *umma* will continue to be defenders of the truth and will not be harmed by the opposition of those who oppose them.

   لاتزال طائفة من أمتي على الحق ظاهرين لايضرهم خلاف من خالفهم.

2. Put your swords on your shoulders and then let your strength be shown in your number.

   ضعوا سيوفكم على عواتقكم ثم أبيدوا خضراءهم.

The first ḥadīth evidently envisages defence of truth through rational evidence and persuasion, whereas the second speaks of recourse to military methods.

Those who argued against this militant posture advised adherence to the community and quoted in support the following *aḥādīth*:

- You are to follow the community, for God Almighty's (protective) hand is with them.

  عليكم بالجماعة فإن يد الله مع الجماعة.

- One who boycotts the community even by the measure of a span truly severs his bond with Islam.

من فارق الجماعة قيد شبر فقد مات ميتة جاهلية.

The explanation to justify peaceful methods of defence or recourse to militarism and war may thus be sought in the true merit and value of the cause which is pursued. The question to ask may be whether the cause or principle for which one fights merits such a course of action in the first place.

Controversy has also arisen over the correct meaning of the ḥadīth which Ibn Māja has recorded on the authority of Abū Saʿīd al-Khudrī, and al-Ṭabarānī from ʿUbāda b. al-Ṣāmit, wherein the Prophet has said in a supplication.

> O My Lord! Help me live as a pauper, let me die as a pauper, and resurrect me among the paupers.[6]

اللهم أحيني مسكينا وأمتني مسكينا واحشرني في زمرة المساكين.

This ḥadīth is considered to be in apparent conflict with the Prophet's frequent denunciation of poverty, and also his other supplications in which he sought refuge from God against the evils of poverty. A ḥadīth has thus been recorded on the authority of ʿA'isha wherein "the Prophet, peace be on him, prayed to God against the evil of poverty (*fitnat al-faqr*),"[7] and said on another occasion that "God loves His servant who is affluent, pious, and modest."[8]

إن الله يحب العبد الغني التقي النقي.

These and similar other sayings of the Prophet have led some to reject his earlier quoted ḥadīth which apparently presented a conflict situation. Al-Qaraḍāwī who has referred to many of these instances has observed, and also quoted other commentators, to the effect that the correct meaning of poverty in the first ḥadīth is modesty and humility and not poverty in its literal sense. How can the literal meaning be upheld in the face of the Qur'ānic address wherein God Most High shows His favour to the Prophet Muḥammad by saying "... and He found you poor and made you affluent" (al-Ḍuḥā, 93:8)?

وَوَجَدَكَ عَآئِلًا فَأَغْنَىٰ

Noted here is also the ḥadīth wherein the Prophet drew a parallel between poverty of disbelief: "O Lord, I seek Thy refuge from disbelief and poverty."[9]

اللهم إني أعوذ بك من الكفر و الفقر.

The reality of all this is reflected in the fact that the Prophet lived a lifestyle of humility and shunned arrogance and pomp that was in vogue in Persian and Roman courts of his time.

Moreover, there is a ḥadīth that Abū Dāwūd has recorded on the authority of Umm Salama which prohibits women from looking at men, but the ḥadīth has been rejected due to conflict of evidence. The ḥadīth in question provides:

> Umm Salama, may God be pleased with her, said: I was with the Messenger of God when Maymūna was also present, at which time Ibn Maktūm turned up, and this was after we were ordered to practice veiling. So the Prophet told us to "hide from him". We said, O Messenger of God! Is he not blind? He can neither see nor recognise us! Then the Prophet said "Are you blind too then? Can you not see him?"[10]

Notwithstanding this being graded as a *Ṣaḥīḥ* ḥadīth, it is noted that one person in its chain of *isnād*, namely Nabhān the *mawlā* (freed slave) of Umm Salama is obscure and has been classified as among the weak (*al-ḍuʿafā'*). Besides, this ḥadīth is in conflict with the evidence recorded by both al-Bukhārī and Muslim which implies permissibility of a woman looking at a stranger.[11]

Thus according to a ḥadīth, which al-Bukhārī has recorded: The Prophet told Fāṭima bint Qays after her divorce became final, to "observe your waiting period in the house of Ibn Umm Maktūm, for he is a blind man, you may be changing your clothes but he would not be able to see you."[12]

اعتدي في بيت أم مكتوم، فإنــه رجل أعمى، تضعين ثيــابك ولا يراك.

According to another ḥadīth which both al-Bukhārī and Muslim have recorded, ʿĀ'isha has said that "The Prophet was screening me with his mantle on me while I was watching the Abyssinians playing in the courtyard of the mosque."[13]

رأيت النبي يسترني بردائـــه وأنا أنظـــر إلى الحبشـــة يلعبون في المسجد.

Al-Bukhārī has also placed this ḥadīth under the heading "Chapter on a woman's looking at the Ḥabash and the like of them without suspicion."[14] While speaking in support of this latter position, al-Qaraḍāwī has also quoted the views of the author of *Tafsīr al-Qurṭubī* and Qāḍī ʿIyāḍ al-Yaḥṣubī to the effect that it is permissible for a woman to look at a stranger or inspect what a man is doing; what is not permitted however, is when viewing takes place in a lacivious context.[15]

As already noted, a part of the disagreement that has arisen concerning the meaning of some *aḥādīth* is due to a tendency among the scholars and jurists to stick to the literal meaning of words and expressions even on occasions when a metaphorical meaning would seem preferable. There are numerous instances of departure from the literal to metaphorical meanings of words in the Qur'ān and the position is no different in the *Sunna*.[16] Some differences of opinion have arisen on this especially with reference to the attributes of God Most High and the precise meaning of activities or references that God has occasionally recorded of His own illustrious self. Some of these difficulties, but not all, can be removed in the understanding of such expressions in the Qur'ān and the *Sunna* by recourse to allegorical interpretation and metaphorical readings of the relevant words and sentences. We shall give more examples of this later, but it will be noted here that disagreement concerning the meaning of ḥadīth is known to have arisen between the Companions themselves. An example of this is the ḥadīth (of the cat) which Imām Aḥmad b. Ḥanbal and others have recorded on the authority of ʿAlqama.

> We were with ʿĀ'isha when Abū Hurayra arrived and ʿĀ'isha told him: Are you the one who reported the ḥadīth that 'a woman was tortured concerning a cat that she had kept in captivity and refused to feed or water the cat?' To this he said "I heard it from the Prophet". Then she said: Did you know who that woman was?

> The woman who did so was a disbeliever. For a believer is much too honoured by God Most High to let him be tortured for the sake of a cat. When you speak concerning the Prophet, you must be careful as to what you are saying.[17]

Al-Qaraḍāwī has quoted this episode and noted that in her critique of Abū Hurayra, ʿĀ'isha, may God be pleased with them both, did not give due credit to Abū Hurayra's ḥadīth and her analysis of it was also somewhat questionable: "May God bless ʿĀ'isha for her neglect of something that lies at the very heart of Islam." The punishment due to that woman was because of her callousness to let a weak animal die of hunger and thus her failure to show mercy. The principle that is upheld in the ḥadīth is of utmost importance "so much so that it makes Muslims proud to subscribe to a high standard of humanitarian value, one that demands care and compassion for all animals." Al-Qaraḍāwī went on to refer to another ḥadīth which confirms the one that Abū Hurayra had narrated. According to this additional ḥadīth God Most High granted forgiveness to an otherwise unruly woman for her act of compassion in giving water to a dog that was suffering from thirst.[18]

Moreover, Abū Hurayra's ḥadīth concerning the cat has also been narrated by another Companion, ʿAbd Allāh b. ʿUmar, which both al-Bukhārī and Muslim have recorded as follows:

> A woman was punished concerning a cat, which she kept in captivity until the cat died of hunger. So she was sent to Hell. God Most High said to her, "You did not feed the cat nor watered her while you tied her, nor did you send her out so that she could feed herself from the cast over of the earth."[19]

عذبت امرأة في هرة، حبستها حتى ماتت جوعا فدخلت في النار. قال الله: لا أنت أطعمتيها ولا سقيتيها، ولا أنت أرسلتيها فأكلت من خشاش الأرض.

To further illustrate the metaphorical in ḥadīth and difficulty that it may entail, we refer to a ḥadīth, recorded by both al-Bukhārī and Muslim, on the authority of ʿAbd Allāh b. ʿUmar that the Prophet, peace be on him, said:

> When the people of Paradise reside in Paradise, and those of Hell in Hell, then death is brought forward until it stands between Paradise

> and Hell, and then it is slaughtered. A caller will then call out: O people of Paradise! there shall be no death anymore; O people of Hell! there shall be no death anymore. The people of Paradise will exceedingly rejoice whereas the people of Hell will be saddened further.[20]

It is reported in another ḥadīth on the authority of Abū Saʿīd al-Khudrī that "death will, on the Day of Resurrection, be brought in the form of a pretty sheep ...."[21]

How is the former ḥadīth to be understood? How is death slaughtered or killed; and how does death itself, in other words, die? Some Muʿtazila commentators have underscored the difficulty here by saying that death is an attribute (*ʿaraḍ*) which has no physical existence or *corpus* (*jism*) and the one does not change into the other. How can an attribute be slaughtered? Others have doubted the authenticity of this ḥadīth and sidelined it altogether, and still others have said that the reference here is to the custodian (*mutawalī*) of death. There is also an opinion that denounces all of this as unwarranted extrapolation that seems to question God's unbounded power over all things. Then it is noted that all of this disagreement is caused by a refusal to read a simple metaphorical meaning in the ḥadīth which is that God will bring death to an end.[22] But even this view is questioned by Aḥmad Muḥammad Shākir who says that in the matter of the unseen (*ghaybiyyāt*) it is superfluous to resort to metaphorical interpretation; one should retain the literal meaning and leave it at that, and that nothing is beyond God's ability and power.[23]

For another example of the metaphorical we may review the following ḥadīth:

> God Most High created the creation and when He finished it, the womb rose and said: this is (or I am) the place of refuge for one who avoids severing the ties of kinship. God Most High said "Yes. Are you not pleased that I get close to one who gets close to you, and I sever ties with one who severs you?" The womb said yes, and God confirmed: It (this favour) is granted to you ..."[24]

إن الله عزّ وجل خلق الخلق حتى إذا فرغ منهم قامت الرحم فقالت: هذا مقام العائذ من القطيعة، قال: نعم، أما ترضين أن أصل من وصلك وأقطع من قطعك؟ قالت: بلى، قال: فذاك لك.

Is the reference to 'womb' here figurative or literal? – is a question over which commentators have differed, and there is evidence to the effect that the literal meaning is not meant.

Al-Qaraḍāwī has quoted Qāḍī ʿIyāḍ and *Tafsīr al-Qurṭubī* to this effect and has himself observed that this type of shift from the literal to metaphorical (*Majāzī*) meaning poses no issue, despite the somewhat more involved debate that has arisen over the place of the figurative in the Qur'ān and the *Sunna*. Ibn Taymiyya has gone on record to deny the occurrence of the metaphorical in the Qur'ān and ḥadīth. Al-Qaraḍāwī has referred to Ibn Taymiyya but added that what Ibn Taymiyya had meant was to close the door on the excesses of allegories in the essence and attributes of God Most High. This may be justified to some extent but not the totally negative attitude that Ibn Taymiyya has taken over the issue of the *Majāzī* in the Qur'ān.[25]

Even Ibn Ḥazm al-Ẓāhirī, whose literalist approach to the reading of the text has earned him the name 'Ẓāhirī', has not denied the occurrence of the metaphorical in the Qur'ān and the *Sunna*. Ibn Ḥazm went on to give the following two examples in support of his views: one of these is the ḥadīth which reads that "The Nile, Euphrates, Sayḥūn and Jayḥūn are the rivers of Paradise," and the other where the Prophet said that "There is a garden from the gardens of Paradise between my house and my pulpit."

النيل والفرات وسيحون وجيجون من أنهار الجنة. بين بيتي ومنبري روضة من رياض الجنة.

Ibn Ḥazm then comments that only the ignorant would hold on to the literal meaning of these, and it should be obvious in each case that metaphorical language has been used. "Rivers from Paradise" underscore the benefit that is derived from these rivers, and "a garden from Paradise" is meant to underscore the superiority of that particular place in that praying therein rewards one with Paradise.[26]

Yet the *ʿulamā'* have warned against indulgence in figurative interpretations and advised that only when the literal approach fails, one may resort to the metaphorical. Instances have been noted of unwarranted departure from the literal to the metaphorical reading of ḥadīth, including the ḥadīth, for example, which instructed the believer to:

> Wake up for *suḥūr* (pre-dawn meal in Ramaḍān), for there is blessing in the *suḥūr*.[27]
>
> تسحروا فإن في السحور بركة.

It is then said metaphorically that '*suḥūr*' in this ḥadīth means prayer and asking for forgiveness (i.e. *al-istighfār*) at that time rather then eating a meal as such. This is unnecessary and represents an unwarranted departure from the literal meaning as there are several other *aḥādīth* in support of the same.

Another and even more remote interpretation of ḥadīth may be said to be the one that some modern commentators have given concerning the references to "*al-Masīḥ al-Dajjāl*" who will appear before the return to earth of Jesus Christ. Muslims are advised to seek God's protection and help against the evil (*fitna*) of *Dajjāl*. Some people have advanced the view that references to *Dajjāl*, in the many *aḥādīth* where such references are found, imply western culture and its influence, which is blind (in one eye, just like the *Dajjāl*!) to the idea of spirituality and religion and sees life, the universe, and man as purely physical realities.

Al-Qaraḍāwī has referred to this and has rightly observed that it is rather a forced reading of the text and should be avoided. There are a large number of *aḥādīth* on this subject and also on the return of Jesus Christ that bring light and peace to humanity, so much so that when put together they become *Mutawātir*, and it is hardly acceptable to escape from all of this into some metaphorical interpretation that simply fails to inspire credibility.[28]

Two other ḥadīths that appear to be in conflict are as follows:

1. What is watered by rain is liable to one-tenth portion (in *zakāh*).

   فيما سقت الماء العشر.

2. There is no *zakāh* in less than five *awsuq*.

   ليس فيما دون خمسة أوسق صدقة.

The first of these is said to be concerned with produce of dry farming land and the second with produce of irrigated land. This is one way of resolving the apparent conflict, and the method here is one of interpretation (*ta'wīl*). The other way is proposed by recourse to the rules of the general (*ʿāmm*) and the specific (*khāṣṣ*). The more specific or *khāṣṣ* ruling of the second ḥadīth thus makes an exception to the general or *ʿāmm* ruling of the first ḥadīth. This would mean that no *zakāh* is imposed on less than five *awsuq*.[29] The second ḥadīth thus acts as a specifier over the first and both remain applicable as a result.

Al-Qaraḍāwī has advanced the argument on the other hand, that both of the two *aḥādīth* above are in disharmony with the Qur'ān. For the general proclamation of the Qur'ān on the subject of *zakāh* on agricultural produce does not make exceptions of the sort that are found in these as well as some other *aḥādīth*. The *āya* in question thus provides:

> He it is who created gardens with trellises and without, and dates and tilth with produce of all kinds, and olives and pomegranates similar in kind and different. Eat of their fruits in their seasons, but render the dues that are proper on the day that the harvest is gathered. (al-Anʿām, 6:141)

وَهُوَ ٱلَّذِىٓ أَنشَأَ جَنَّٰتٍ مَّعْرُوشَٰتٍ وَغَيْرَ مَعْرُوشَٰتٍ وَٱلنَّخْلَ وَٱلزَّرْعَ مُخْتَلِفًا
أُكُلُهُۥ وَٱلزَّيْتُونَ وَٱلرُّمَّانَ مُتَشَٰبِهًا وَغَيْرَ مُتَشَٰبِهٍ ۚ كُلُوا۟ مِن ثَمَرِهِۦٓ
إِذَآ أَثْمَرَ وَءَاتُوا۟ حَقَّهُۥ يَوْمَ حَصَادِهِۦ

This verse evidently does not differentiate between foodgrains, fruits and other agricultural produce and makes all liable to the payment of *zakāh*. Even the ḥadīth which provides that "there is no *zakāh* on vegetables" – is considered to be weak.

According to al-Tirmidhī, "the *isnād* of this ḥadīth is not sound and nothing reliable on this subject has been proven from the Prophet."[30] Al-Qaraḍāwī who has written a voluminous work on *zakāh* discusses this subject and questions some of the juristic conclusions, such as the one that makes only four categories of foodgrains liable to *zakāh*, to be at odds with the Qur'ān. How can one say that other fruits and vegetables as well as apple gardens, tea plantations, cotton and so much more which involve enormous amounts of produce are not liable to *zakāh*? This very position, he adds, has led some observers to the conclusion that the Islamic taxation system only makes the small farmers who grow wheat and barley liable to tax. "It is right for a

Muslim," al-Qaraḍāwī wrote "to stand in the way of any ḥadīth which he finds to be in conflict with the clear injunction of the Qur'ān and finds no other suitable interpretation for it."[31]

There is also a ḥadīth that appears in Abū Dāwūd, on the authority of Ibn Masʿūd, which states, somewhat surprisingly, concerning the pre-Islamic practice of female infanticide, that "Both the perpetrator of infanticide and its victim are in Hell."[32] One can understand the verdict of this ḥadīth on the perpetrator of this heinous crime, but why is the child condemned to the same predicament? This ḥadīth also appears to be in conflict with the Qur'ānic *āya*: "and when the female child buried alive is questioned: for what crime was she killed?" (al-Takwīr, 81:8-9).

وَإِذَا ٱلْمَوْءُۥدَةُ سُئِلَتْ ﴿٨﴾ بِأَيِّ ذَنۢبٍ قُتِلَتْ ﴿٩﴾

The ḥadīth at issue is therefore unreliable, and there is no suitable interpretation that can actually remove this conflict.[33] To give another example, we refer to a ḥadīth which both Muslim and Abū Dāwūd have recorded on the authority of Anas b. Mālik that a man asked the Prophet concerning his deceased father "where is my father?" to which the Prophet replied "your father is in Hell," and when the man was walking away, the Prophet called him, to say to him "my father and your father are (both) in Hell."[34] To this we apply the same analysis that was earlier presented concerning a similar ḥadīth that referred to the mother of the Prophet. The Prophet's father ʿAbd Allāh and his mother Āmina died at a time when no message nor scripture had been communicated to the inhabitants of Arabia, which means that they were not accountable. The ḥadīth verdict that condemns them to Hell therefore appears to be unsustainable and in conflict with the Qur'ān. To give yet another example of a difficult situation we refer to a ḥadīth in which the Murji'a have advised a peaceful and pro-*status quo* attitude and quoted the following ḥadīth in support of their viewpoint:

> One who utters *lā ilāha illā-Allah* goes to Paradise. It was asked then: Even if he commits theft and adultery! And he (the Prophet) said: Even with theft and adultery.
>
> من قال لا إله إلا الله فهو في الجنة، قيل: وإن زنى وإن سرق، قال: وإن زنى وإن سرق.

The opponents rejected this and quoted the following ḥadīth to the contrary:

> The adulterer does not commit adultery while he is a believer and the thief does not commit theft while he is a believer.
>
> لايزني الزاني حين يزني وهو مؤمن، ولايسرق السارق حين يسرق وهو مؤمن.

The explanation may be in the figurative language of the ḥadīth in both cases – both accentuating the value of true faith. One who has it cannot commit such and such, so to speak, and God may still grant him success if he repents. The literal meaning is not intended perhaps. A certain conflict appears also to exist between the following two *aḥādīth* one of which provides to the effect that "no contagious infection of disease nor bad omen is conveyed without God's permission,"[35] and another ḥadīth which directs the believers to "run from the leper like you run from a lion."

> لا عدوى ولا طيرة.
>
> فر من المجذوم فرارك من الأسد.

Both *aḥādīth* are accepted and an explanation is provided in that diseases are not inherently contageous but when a healthy person mixes with one who is infected with the disease, he may catch it. Transmission of disease is thus caused by contact and intermingling, and causation remains the accepted norm of the laws of God.[36]

[12] Unfamiliar Expressions in Ḥadīth

Gharīb al-Ḥadīth

THIS branch of the ḥadīth studies is concerned with odd and unfamiliar expressions that are encountered in ḥadīth. When the ḥadīth contains rare and difficult expressions, it becomes naturally difficult to understand. The *ʿulamā'* have, in fact, encountered unusual expressions in the ḥadīth especially after the documentation of ḥadīth on a large scale and it is said that the *tābiʿī al-tābiʿūn,* that is, the third generation of Muslims, were the first to speak on the subject. Outlandish elements may be inherent in the meaning of a word or words, or it may be due to customary usage and differences in customs and dialects. A certain degree of ambiguity and confusion has also been caused by contact and literary influence from non-Arab sources, especially the Persian language and tradition after the mid-second century hijra when such influences began to affect the language and culture of the Arabian peninsula.

Noted in this context is also the nature of the Prophetic mission of Muḥammad concerning whom it is proclaimed in the Qur'ān: "We did not send you but as a conveyer of good news and warnings to the whole of mankind" (Sabā', 34:28).

وَمَآ أَرْسَلْنَٰكَ إِلَّا كَآفَّةً لِّلنَّاسِ بَشِيرًا وَنَذِيرًا

The mission of the Prophet Muḥammad was not confined to the Qurayshites of Makka; he had to address and communicate with all the tribes of Arabia. Arab tribes had different dialects some of which were easy and light whereas others were unfamiliar even to the nearby tribes and were not well-known at all. The Bedouins among the Arabs were particularly noted for the use of unfamiliar words and expressions. They used to convert, for example, the definite particle *"al"* to a single letter *"mīm"* and this often sounded unfamiliar and confusing to others. This feature of the spoken Arabic in the Arabian peninsula was also noted in regard to the text of the Qur'ān. As is well-known, the Qur'ān was compiled into a single volume during the time of the first Caliph Abū Bakr, but then it was variously rendered and pronounced in the "seven dialects of the Arabs". These variations became a cause for concern strong enough to impress upon the third Caliph ʿUthmān to verify the text of the Qur'ān once again and then to order the variant versions to be destroyed.

With the arrival of non-Arab people into the Arabian peninsula in large numbers following the period of the Companions and the Followers, words of non-Arabic origin infiltrated into Arabic and were absorbed into the Arabic language, some of which then sounded less than familiar to the Arab speakers themselves. The newcomers and foreigners on the other hand themselves had difficulty in mastering the language of the Qur'ān and ḥadīth. Then there came a time when the *ʿulamā'* and scholars of ḥadīth were prompted to address the issue of unfamiliar words and expressions which had crept into the corpus of ḥadīth. For the vast bulk of ḥadīth was articulated and narrated in the words and expressions of the narrators and included among them were Arabs and non-Arabs from almost every corner of the Islamic domain. The early scholars of ḥadīth took a meticulous attitude toward such unfamiliar and difficult words and expressions as they encountered in the text of the ḥadīth. It is thus reported that Imām Aḥmad b. Ḥanbal was once asked about the precise meaning of a letter of an unfamiliar description in a ḥadīth to which he replied: "Ask those who are expert in *al-gharīb,* for I am reluctant to speculate concerning the sayings of the Messenger of God".[1] One of the experts of Arabic language, ʿAbd al-Malik b. Qurayb al-Aṣmaʿī (d. 216 H) was once asked about the meaning of the ḥadīth which simply read "*al-jāru aḥaqqu bi-saqabihi,*"[2] to which he replied "I do not wish to interpret the ḥadīth of the Messenger of God, but the Arabs tend to use '*al-saqab*' in the sense of "immediately adjacent" (*inna al-saqab al-lāziq*).

The ḥadīth would thus mean that "the neighbour has a greater claim to what is immediately adjoining his property."

The first work that addressed the *gharīb al-ḥadīth* was that of Abū ʿUbayd Maʿmar b. al-Muthannā al-Taymī (d. 209 H), a small book in which he explained unfamiliar expressions in ḥadīth by reference to Islamic or pre-Islamic origins of the words and how they might have been used in poetry and prose and the meaning they coveyed in the particular ḥadīth in which they occurred. Several works carrying the title *Gharīb al-Ḥadīth* were written, including a highly acclaimed one by Abū ʿUbayd al-Qāsim b. Sallām (d. 224) entitled *Gharīb al-Ḥadīth wa'l-Āthār,* and another by Muḥammad b. al-Qāsim al-Anbārī (d. 328).[3]

Some of these works are better organised than others and deal with words and expressions in alphabetical order which makes them easier to use. Abū ʿUbayd's work is comprehensive as it is said that it is the result of forty years of scholarship. Ibn Qutayba ad-Daynūrī (d. 276 H) subsequently wrote his work on *Gharīb al-Ḥadīth* in which he supplemented Abū ʿUbayd's work and filled in what was left out of Abū ʿUbayd's collection. One other work that acquired fame bears the title *Al-Nihāya fī Gharīb al-Ḥadīth wa'l-Āthār,* by Majd al-Dīn Abī'l-Saʿādāt b. al-Athīr (d. 606 H). Since this was written at a much later date, it has combined and consolidated preceding works on the subject and is accepted as a work of reference on *gharīb al-ḥadīth*. Many others wrote glosses and commentaries on it. Al-Suyūṭī (d. 911) summarised it in his *Al-Durr al-Nathīr Talkhīs Nihāyat Ibn al-Athīr,* and there is even one which bears the title *Al-Kifāya fī Naẓm al-Nihāya* by Abū'l-Fidā' Ismāʿīl b. Muḥammad al-Baʿlabakī al-Ḥanbalī (d. 785) which has turned the *Nihāya* of Ibn al-Athīr into a book of poetry. Arabic words such as *bahā'* (to take pride), *abhā'* (houses), *labata* (to fall, also to enjoy), *bughaysh* (rainfall), *ḥudhayyā* (tiding, good news) and many more such expressions that occur in *aḥādīth* are unfamiliar even to native speakers of Arabic and the *ʿulamā'* have elaborated on their precise meaning.[4]

There are basically two ways to explain the unfamiliar expressions in ḥadīth, one of which is to look into other *aḥādīth* or works of ḥadīth by different persons and on different subjects which may help to explain the problematic terms. This is the preferable of the two methods. The second method is, of course, through recourse to dictionaries, both general and specialised, as well as works on the subject of *gharīb al-*

ḥadīth. One of the most commonly used works of reference on the subject is that of Jār Allah Maḥmūd al-Zamakhsharī, *Al-Fā'iq li-Gharīb al-Ḥadīth.*[5] Al-Ḥākim al-Nīsābūrī has recounted what many *ʿulamā'* before him have said, that God Most High has favoured the Muslim *umma* with four people: with al-Shāfiʿī who advanced the understanding, or *fiqh*, of the ḥadīth of the Messenger of God; with Abū ʿUbayd (Qāsim b. Sallām) who explained the *gharā'ib* (pl. of *gharīb*) of the ḥadīth; with Yaḥyā b. Maʿin who cleared the ḥadīth of the Messenger of God from fabrication and lies; and with Aḥmad b. Ḥanbal who remained firm against adversity and hardship (*miḥna*) in serving the Messenger of God, peace be on him; without their services, Islam would have dissipated. Al-Nīsābūrī has also spoken in praise of similar distinguished services of ʿAlī b. al-Madīnī and other prominent figures in the field.[6]

Al-Nīsābūrī has quoted a number of *aḥādīth* in which words and phrases of an unfamiliar type occur and he then attempted to explain their meaning; he also tried to verify a particular meaning as the preferred meaning of the words in question. One such ḥadīth he quoted is in reference to a common expression of the Arabs who would say "*Khabuthat nafsī*" (my soul indulged in filth), and the Prophet said concerning it "Let none of you say *khabuthat nafsī,* but say rather *laqisat nafsī.*" This last word is somewhat unfamiliar and it is said to be synonymous to "*ḍāqat nafsī*" (my soul/heart suffocated) apparently in reference to a kind of pain or ailment to which it applied. Al-Nīsābūrī has also quoted some words that the Prophet spoke affectionately while playing with his grandson al-Ḥusayn, which have been subsequently explained by experts in the language. Quoted also is a poem cited by ʿAlī b. Abī Ṭālib which contains unfamiliar words. These too have been explained.[7] Since these are somewhat technical, quoting them here would not serve any good purpose for English readers.

[13] The Abrogator and Abrogated in Ḥadīth

al-Nāsikh wa'l-Mansūkh fi'l-Ḥadīth

THIS is an important yet little understood area of the ḥadīth. According to al-Zuhrī, even the learned jurists are often unaware of the abrogator and abrogated in ḥadīth. Al-Shāfiʿī's understanding of this subject and his contribution to it invoked compliments from subsequent scholars including the Imām Aḥmad b. Ḥanbal who went on record to say that al-Shāfiʿī was the one who "taught us the *mujmal* and *mufassar* (ambiguous and clarified) and the abrogator and abrogated in the ḥadīth of the Messenger of God, peace be on him."[1] Other prominent scholars who wrote on the subject include Aḥmad b. Isḥāq al-Tanūkhī (d. 318/930), Muḥammad b. Baḥr al-Isfahānī (d. 332/934), ʿUmar b. Shāhīn al-Baghdādī (d. 385/995) and Abū Bakr Muḥammad b. Mūsā al-Ḥamdānī (d. 584 H), who wrote *Al-Iʿtibār fi'l-Nāsikh wa'l-Mansūkh min al-Āthār*.[2]

Abrogation is defined as the removal or suspension of one *Sharīʿa* ruling by another, provided that the latter is of a subsequent origin and the two rulings are enacted separately from one another. The occasion for *naskh* arises only when there is a clear conflict between two *aḥādīth* and the conflict between their respective rulings cannot be reconciled nor can the one be distinguished from the other in regard to its subject matter, time or circumstance. *Naskh* occurs not only between one ḥadīth and another but also between the rulings of the Qur'ān and those of the ḥadīth. Abrogation, whether in the ḥadīth itself or between the Qur'ān and ḥadīth, is of relevance mainly to definitive rulings especially in the area of the *aḥkām*, as cases of clear conflict in this area would have to be resolved prior to enforcement. Since cases of conflict and abrogation between the Qur'ān and ḥadīth extend beyond the scope strictly of ḥadīth, *naskh* in its wider sense falls within the ambit more of *uṣūl al-fiqh* than ḥadīth. *Naskh* is a controversial subject and many of the conclusions that have been upheld on it in the works of some *ʿulamā'* have been questioned by others. The leading schools of Islamic law are also in disagreement over the scope of *naskh*. Among the four leading schools, only the Shāfiʿīs have attempted to narrow down the scope of *naskh* by holding the view that the Qur'ān and the *Sunna* can only abrogate themselves but that they do not abrogate one another. More recent research on the subject has on the whole shown that the scope of *naskh* may not be as wide as it was shown in some earlier writings on the subject.[3]

As already noted, *naskh* can occur only in the case of a clear conflict between two *aḥādīth*. Another prerequisite of *naskh* is to establish a chronological order between the two ḥadīths and verify that the abrogating ḥadīth is of a later origin than the one that it abrogates. The subject matter of ḥadīth must also be one that is amenable to abrogation: *Naskh* mainly applies to the *aḥkām* and even here the two rulings must be decisive and not open to interpretation. *Naskh* does not apply to purely rational subjects nor does it apply to factual statements that are in the nature of news and reports. To say that justice is a virtue cannot really be abrogated. Similarly one can deny a report but cannot abrogate it. These are some of the prerequisites of *naskh* which must be fulfilled before *naskh* is implemented.

There are four types of abrogation in ḥadīth. The first of these is one that is explicitly known from the saying of the Prophet himself. An example of this is the ḥadīth of Burayda which is recorded in *Muslim* that the Prophet, peace be on him, said: "I had forbidden you from visiting the graves. You may now visit them."[4]

كنت نهيتكم عن زيارة القبور، ألا فزوروها.

The facts of abrogation and the two rulings, one permissive and the other prohibitive, as well as the fact that these were separately enacted are all clear in the ḥadīth itself, which is why this type of abrogation is known as explicit abrogation (*al-naskh al-ṣarīḥ*).

Another example of this is the ḥadīth reported by Jābir b. ʿAbd Allāh that the Prophet said: "You may eat what is taken from the sea (below the surface) but do not eat that which moves about above the water."

ما حسر عنه البحر فكل، وما وجدته طافيا فوق الماء فلا تأكله.

This ḥadīth stands abrogated by another ḥadīth reported by Abū Hurayra that a man asked the Prophet:

> O Messenger of God! We go out in the sea and carry with us a little water; if we use that water for ablution we would not have enough for drinking. Can we make ablution by sea water? The Prophet, peace be on him, said to him: "The sea is clean, its water is clean and so is the dead of the sea."[5]

يا رسول الله، إنا نركب البحر ونحمل معنا القليل من الماء، فإن توضأنا به عطشنا، أفنتوضأ من ماء البحر؟ فقال رسول الله صلاّ الله عليه وسلم: هو الطهور ماؤه حل ميتته.

Second, abrogation in ḥadīth may also be known from the saying of a Companion rather than the text of the ḥadīth itself. An example of this is the ḥadīth reported by Abū Ayyūb al-Anṣārī that the Prophet said: "Refresh your ablution after consuming what is changed (cooked) by fire".

توضؤوا مما غيرت النار.

The ḥadīth stands abrogated, however, by what the Companion Jābir b. ʿAbd Allāh has said that: The last of the two rulings that is known from the Messenger of God, peace be on him, is that ablution is not vitiated by consuming food that is changed by fire (or cooked by fire).[6]

كان آخر الأمرين من رسول الله صلى الله عليه وسلم ترك الوضوء مما غيرت النار.

Another example of this is the ḥadīth narrated by ʿAbd Allāh b. ʿUmar that the Prophet, peace be on him, said "The deceased is tortured by the weeping of his relatives over his death".

This ḥadīth stands abrogated, however, by what the Prophet's widow, ʿĀ'isha, is reported to have said: "May God bless Abū ʿAbd al-Raḥmān (i.e. Ibn ʿUmar) who has not lied but has forgotten or mistaken that when the Messenger of God passed by a (deceased) Jewish woman whose relatives were crying over her, he said: They are crying while she is being tortured in her grave" (stating thus two separate things, i.e. not that the one had caused the other).[7]

Third, abrogation in ḥadīth may also be known through an historical or chronological sequence of events. An example of this is the ḥadīth that Shaddād b. Aws narrated from the Prophet to the effect that "cupping breaks the fast of both the cupper and the cupped"; and another ḥadīth reported by Ibn ʿAbbās that "The Prophet, peace be on him, cupped while he was fasting". The former ḥadīth is recorded by Abū Dāwūd and al-Nasā'ī and the latter by al-Bukhārī and Muslim.[8]

أفطر الحاجم والمحجوم.

إن النبي صلى الله عليه وسلم احتجم وهو صائم.

Imām Shāfiʿī has explained that the second ḥadīth has abrogated the first. This is because the first ḥadīth is known to have been uttered at the time of the conquest of Makka in the year 8 Hijra whereas the second was pronounced later in the Farewell Pilgrimage in the year 10. The *ʿulamā'* are consequently in agreement on the conclusion that cupping does not vitiate the fast.[9]

And lastly, abrogation in ḥadīth may be known through general consensus (*ijmāʿ*) such as the ḥadīth "one who drinks liquor shall be lashed, but if he repeated it four times, he shall be killed".

من شرب الخمر فاجلدوه، فإن عاد في الرابع فاقتلوه.

This ḥadīth is recorded by Abū Dāwūd and al-Tirmidhī, but it stands abrogated as consensus has made known that action is not taken on it, and it is abrogated. Ibn Ḥazm al-Ẓāhirī has taken an exception here but al-Nawawī wrote concerning it that "the Ẓāhiriyya disagreement does not detract anything from the said *ijmāʿ*. In addition, it is known that after pronouncing the ḥadīth in question, there was an occasion when the Prophet punished a man for drinking on a fourth occasion by beating but did not kill him.[10] Although *ijmāʿ* itself cannot abrogate ḥadīth it can nevertheless verify whether abrogation has or has not occurred.[11]

An area of the ḥadīth literature which is especially helpful and relevant to the occurrence or otherwise of abrogation in ḥadīth is the *asbāb wurūd al-ḥadīth*, that is, the phenomenology of ḥadīth which explain and specify occasions of the occurrence, or pronouncement of ḥadīth. One useful work on this subject is that of the Damascene Traditionist Ibrāhīm Muḥammad b. Kamāl al-Dīn, also known as Ibn Ḥamza al-Ḥusaynī's (d. 1120 H), *Al-Bayān wa'l-Taʿrīf fī Asbāb Wurūd al-Ḥadīth al-Sharīf*, which is alphabetically arranged in reference to persons and events. A Syrian edition of this work was published in Aleppo in 1329 H and it appears in two volumes. Many works have also been written on abrogation generally and on abrogation in ḥadīth in particular. An early work on the latter was *Nāsikh al-Ḥadīth wa Mansūkhuh* authored by al-Ḥāfiẓ Abū Bakr Muḥammad b. al-Athram (d. 261) who was a friend of the renowned Imām Aḥmad b. Ḥanbal. The work was written in three small booklets and it has survived. Another monographic work on the subject that bore the same title was *Nāsikh al-Ḥadīth wa Mansūkhuh* authored by al-Ḥāfiẓ Abī Ḥafṣ ʿUmar b. Aḥmad al-Baghdādī, known as Ibn Shāhīn (d. 385 H). A more comprehensive work was later written by al-Ḥāfiẓ Abū Bakr Muḥammad b. Mūsā al-Ḥāzimī (d. 584) entitled *Al-Iʿtibār fi'l-Nāsikh wa'l-Mansūkh min al-Āthār*.[12]

[14] Additional Segments to Ḥadīth by Reliable Narrators

Ziyādāt al-Thiqāt

TWO different versions of a ḥadīth are sometimes reported by two different but reliable narrators, or even by the same narrator at different points of time, one of which adds a segment to the shorter version or records some kind of variation to the words. The question then arises as to the admissibility or otherwise of the additional data to the ḥadīth in question. The additional part is more often than not reported by one narrator who is reliable and also knowledgeable on the subject.

Two situations are envisaged here, one of which is that the additional part to a ḥadīth either opposes the substance of the shorter version and stands in conflict with it or that it merely reiterates and endorses it. There is basically no problem when the additional information confirms totally the existing part, but there are often cases where the additional segment, although confirming the shorter version, nevertheless, contains a juristic addition or an element which may present a minor interference of some kind.

In the event where the additional part conflicts directly with the existing portion of the ḥadīth, the issue will be treated as one of conflict and preference (*al-taʿāruḍ wa'l-tarjīḥ*) to which the rules that apply to this subject will apply. This would necessitate looking into the circumstances and occasions of the two reports, the cause, if any, of the addition, and retentiveness of the narrators involved. If the addition is by a narrator or narrators who command a greater degree of reliability and are known for their care and accuracy in transmission compared to those who are associated with the shorter ḥadīth, then the longer version will be upheld and the shorter version will be treated as a *shādhdh* (stray) ḥadīth. If on the other hand, the additional elements, whether in the text of the ḥadīth or in its chain of transmission, are manifestly odd and isolated and are not supported by the much larger number of reported cases of the same ḥadīth, then the addition itself will be struck out and ignored. Attention will also be due to the occasion or circumstances in which the two versions originated. Were the two *aḥādīth* uttered at one and the same meeting or occasion when the Prophet actually pronounced them or on different occasions? If the latter be the case, then a conflict may be less likely to arise and both versions may be accepted as they are. But if it is established that the different versions originated at one and the same meeting or occasion, then the version that is transmitted by more narrators will prevail over that which is variantly transmitted by one, provided that the former are not known for error and oversight. Consequently the additional part of the ḥadīth which is transmitted by a single narrator is isolated and rejected for the simple reason that error by one person is more likely than by a multitude. But if the single narrator who has reported the addition is an eminently reliable person, who is also more knowledgeable on the subject, then his version, as noted above, will be preferred over the variant report of many who are known for careless reporting, although some ḥadīth scholars do not agree with this. However, on occasions, the preference of one over the other version may be determined on juridical grounds and the greater proximity that might be exhibited by one or the other with the Qur'ān and the relevant principles of *Sharīʿa*.[1]

As for the situation where the longer version of the same ḥadīth confirms and reiterates the shorter version, two possibilities can arise, one of which is where both versions are reported by the same narrator who has merely quoted the same ḥadīth but has elaborated it further on the subsequent occasion by adding something to it. This situation does not present a problem and the longer version is merely regarded as an elaboration and does not affect the original ḥadīth. But if the longer version of the ḥadīth adds a new point that does not exist in the shorter ḥadīth, then the longer ḥadīth is considered as a separate ḥadīth that is reported by a reliable narrator, and each part may be separately quoted. When the two parts of a ḥadīth are concerned with two different subjects, it is also permissible to quote only the relevant part in a context where the other part is left out. This also applies to a ḥadīth that may consist of more than two subjects or points.[2] A different scenario obtains, however, in the event where the same narrator is known to have cited the longer version of his ḥadīth first and then a shorter version on a subsequent occasion. The longer version is to be upheld as it is likely that he summarised it later with the assurance that he has already delivered the fuller version of the ḥadīth.[3]

An example of ḥadīth wherein the additional segment adds something which is however not in conflict with its shorter version is the one reported by Muslim through Abū Mālik al-Ashjaʿī, from Rubʿī, from Ḥudhayfa that the Prophet, peace be on him, said "... the earth has all of it been made into a mosque for us, and its soil has been purified for us."

وجعلت لنا الأرض كلها مسجدا وتربتها طهورا.

Abū Mālik b. Ṭāriq al-Ashjaʿī is the only one who has narrated this ḥadīth with the additional elements at the end, especially the reference to the soil "*turbatuhā*" which is absent in other reports. For other narrators including ʿUbayd Allah b. ʿUmar and Ayyūb who have reported it from Nāfiʿ from Ibn ʿUmar have reported the same ḥadīth without this additional element and reported it simply as "and the earth has been made into a mosque for us and purified."

As it appears here the additional version does not oppose the shorter version of the ḥadīth; both are therefore accepted and this is what Imām Mālik and Abū Ḥanīfa have also held, and it is the correct position. The Shāfiʿīs and Ḥanbalīs have held on the other hand that the additional element brings in an adjective (*waṣf*) which tends to introduce a change and the rules of *tarjīḥ* or preference would therefore apply. The Ḥanafīs and Mālikīs maintain that addition of the word "*turbatuhā*" (its soil, or dust) merely confirms that the ḥadīth refers to the earth "*al-arḍ*", whereas Imām Shāfiʿī and Ibn Ḥanbal read into this addition that it is the soil of the earth rather than all of the rest of the earth such as stones, trees and the like that is the focus of ḥadīth. Thus it would include 'soil' that is carried to a different surface, for example. Dry ablution, or *tayammum*, according to the Shāfiʿīs and Ḥanbalīs is thus valid only with clean soil. But if the shorter version of the ḥadīth is followed, *tayammum* would be valid on all clean surfaces of the earth.[4]

Another example to note here is the ḥadīth, recorded by both al-Bukhārī and Muslim from ʿAbd Allāh b. Masʿūd, which is as follows:

Abū ʿAmr ʿUthmān b. Aḥmad b. al-Sammāk reported from Ḥasan b. Mukarram from ʿUthmān b. ʿUmar from Mālik b. Mighwal from al-Walīd b. al-ʿAyzār, from Abū ʿAmr al-Shaybānī from ʿAbd Allāh b. Masʿūd who said that "I asked the Prophet, peace be on him: what is the best of all deeds? And he said "prayer when performed at the beginning of its time segment." Then I asked "then what?" and the Prophet, peace be on him, said "struggle in the way of God"; then I said "what else?" to which the Prophet replied "being good to one's parents".

سألت رسول الله صلى الله عليه وسلم: أي العمل أفضل؟ قال: الصلاة في أول وقتها، قلت: ثم أي؟ قال الجهاد في سبيل الله. قلت: ثم أي؟ قال: بر الوالدين.

Al-Ḥākim al-Nīsābūrī who recorded this ḥadīth wrote that this is a well-preserved ḥadīth which a group of leading figures have reported from Mālik b. Mighwal and also from ʿUthman b. ʿUmar, but they do not mention the phrase "at the beginning of its time segment". It is only Ḥasan b. Mukarram (and Bindār b. Bashshār), both of whom are trustworthy and knowledgeable (*thiqatān, faqīhān*) who have reported it with the added elements. Since the additional segment does not interfere with the substance of the ḥadīth, it is accepted.[5]

In another illustration that also appears in al-Ḥākim al-Nīsābūrī's chapter on *ziyādāt*, Abū ʿAlī al-Ḥāfiẓ narrated from Isḥāq b. Aḥmad, from Abū Yūsuf Muḥammad b. Aḥmad al-Ḥajjāj, from ʿIsā b. Yūnus from Ibn Jurayj from Sulaymān b. Mūsā, from al-Zuhrī from ʿUrwa from ʿĀ'isha, that the Prophet, peace be on him, said: "when a woman is married without the permission of her guardian (*walī*) and two upright witnesses, her marriage is null and void; if the marriage is consummated, she is entitled to the dower, and if there is a dispute, then the ruler is the *walī* of one who has no *walī*."

أيما امرأة نكحت بغير إذن وليها وشاهدي عدل فنكاحها باطل، فإن دخل بها فلها المهر وإن اشتجروا فالسلطان ولي من لا ولي له.

Al-Nīsābūrī then wrote that this is a well-preserved (*maḥfūẓ*) ḥadīth from Ibn Jurayj, from Sulaymān b. Mūsā al-Ashdaq from al-Zuhrī, but the phrase "and two upright witnesses" is not reported by anyone else except by Abū ʿAlī al-Ḥāfiẓ.[6] It is thus implied that the version of ḥadīth without this additional phrase is the verified and correct version.

Addition (*ziyāda*) can also occur in the *isnād* of a ḥadīth and the nature of the scrutiny that is involved here is similar to one that is noted of addition to the text. Credibility is thus given to that version which is narrated by a larger number of narrators, and the other version is consequently considered odd or isolated. An example of this is the ḥadīth, recorded by Muslim, which ʿAbd Allāh b. al-Mubārak has narrated from Sufyān, from ʿAbd al-Raḥmān b. Yazīd b. Jābir, from Busr b. ʿUbayd Allah, from Abū Idrīs, from Abū Wāthila b. al-Asqaʿ from Abū Murthād al-Ghanawī, that "I heard the Prophet, peace be on him, saying: "Do not sit by the graves nor perform prayers toward them."[7]

لا تجلسوا على القبور ولا تصلوا إليها.

Ibn al-Ṣalāḥ wrote that the reference to Sufyān in the *isnād* of this ḥadīth is an addition which is a mistake, and so is the reference to Abū Idrīs. As for the former, it appears that a number of reliable narrators have quoted this ḥadīth from ʿAbd al-Rahmān b. Yazīd b. Jābir directly and some of them have reported it in words that imply direct contact. As for the reference to Abū Idrīs, it also appears that the same group of reliable narrators who reported it from Ibn Jābir made no mention of Abū Idrīs coming in between Busr and Wāthila, but reported it such that Busr had received it directly from Wāthila in words that implied direct hearing. Having said this, Ibn al-Ṣalāḥ then quotes Abū Ḥātim al-Rāzī to the same effect, namely that Ibn al-Mubārak has imagined these additional names in the *isnād*, and his addition is therefore isolated and considered incorrect.[8]

Additions and discrepancies that are observed in the *isnād*, might amount to the same ḥadīth having been reported as a *Mursal* by a group of narrators whereas only one narrator has rendered is as a *Musnad*, that is ḥadīth with an unbroken *isnād*. Discrepancies in the *isnād* are, broadly speaking, determined by reference to the same methods which apply to discrepancies in the text. The rules of validation and impugnment (*al-jarḥ wa'l-taʿdīl*) and those which apply to the veracity and retentiveness of the narrators would thus be applicable.

Al-Khaṭīb al-Baghdādī (d. 463 H) has authored a book on the subject of additions to ḥadīth bearing the title *Kitāb al-Tamyīz al-Mazīd fī Muttaṣil al-Asānīd* (Book on distinguishing the additions to connected chains of transmission) in which he has identified many *isnāds* of this kind. But Ibn al-Ṣalāḥ who has also mentioned this work has expressed reservations about some of its conclusions. It is thus said that certain *isnāds* which should have been identified as *Mursal* have not been so identified and references to such ḥadīth therefore remained inconclusive. Similarly when there is evidence to show that direct hearing occurred between the two links in the *isnād*, but this has not been clearly and consistently stated as such.[9]

In his larger work, *Al-Kifāya fī ʿIlm al-Riwāya*, al-Baghdādī has quoted several prominent figures including ʿAbd Allāh b. al-Mubārak (d. 181) and Yaḥyā b. Maʿīn (d. 233) who have recommended that in the event of doubt as to the accuracy of a longer or a shorter version of ḥadīth, one should opt for the shorter version as this would also reduce the possibility of error and doubt in rendering the ḥadīth. This is then supported by the purport of a ḥadīth which al-Baghdādī and others have quoted. It is thus reported that the Prophet said in his Farewell pilgrimage: "May God gladden one who heard my speech and did not add anything to it and conveyed it to others. May the conveyer then deliver it to one who is even more attentive in preserving it."[10]

نضر الله من سمع مقالتي فلم يزد فيها فرب حامل كلمة إلى من هو أوعى لها منه.

Some ḥadīth scholars have held it permissible to shorten a ḥadīth which the narrator has narrated in full on a previous occasion but then condensed it or recapitulated its purpose and meaning at a reduced length. Having quoted these various views, al-Baghdādī then observes that it is not permissible to reduce a ḥadīth or omit a part of it if by doing so one is likely to truncate the ḥadīth or leave out a ruling, condition or provision therein that would undermine the integrity of the ḥadīth, especially when it is concerned with religious observances and *ʿibādāt*. When such is the case it becomes obligatory to quote the ḥadīth in full, without any omission or change whatsoever. But if the ḥadīth contains two separate parts one of which is not dependent on the other, nor is it a condition nor exception thereto, then it is permissible for the narrator to cite only the part that is relevant to his purpose. When this is the case, the other portion of the ḥadīth would to all intents and purposes be treated as a separate ḥadīth. Once the complete version of ḥadīth is verified, it becomes permissible to summarise it for purposes of brevity. In fact it is reported that Sufyān al-Thawrī (d. 161) used to do this and summarised a ḥadīth which he knew had already been narrated in its entirety. But he did so in such a manner that stayed clear of alteration in the purpose and meaning of ḥadīth.[11] As for addition of elements to ḥadīth by a reliable narrator, al-Baghdādī wrote categorically that it is acceptable regardless of the nature of its subject matter, be it concerned with legal rulings (*aḥkām*) or outside this sphere, provided that the narrator is "upright, retentive, careful and accurate," and that there is general agreement among ḥadīth scholars on this.[12] It is perfectly understandable, al-Baghdādī added, that two or three persons have heard the same ḥadīth and at the point of reporting, two of them forgot a certain point in the ḥadīth, which the third listener, who happened to be more attentive, remembered and reported it with the added elements. It is also possible that of the three persons, two suffered loss of concentration due to the late hour or fatigue and the like, and only one of them heard the complete version; then it is also possible that the other two have missed out on a word or a phrase in the same ḥadīth. Some ḥadīth transmitters who are reliable have actually gone on record to say that "I heard and retained what the rest of us did not," in which case their version of the report is admissible subject to verification.[13] It is also possible, al-Baghdādī added, that the one and the same narrator had narrated a ḥadīth once and then remembered about a word or phrase that he forgot in his earlier report, which he then added on a subsequent occasion, when he had time to refresh his memory on relevant details.

[15] Ḥadīth Classification I

Ṣaḥīḥ, *Ḥasan* and *Ḍaʿīf*

THE grading of ḥadīth transmitters, as noted in the previous section on impugnment and validation, enabled the *ʿulamāʾ* to classify the ḥadīth, from the viewpoint of acceptability or otherwise, into the three broad categories of *Ṣaḥīḥ* (sound), *Ḥasan* (fair) and *Ḍaʿīf* (weak). It may be noted at the outset, however, that these categories are less than exclusive and sometimes tend to be overlapping in that a particular ḥadīth may qualify for some of the conditions of *Ṣaḥīḥ* and some also of *Ḥasan*, which is why some scholars have actually introduced intervening categories of ḥadīth so that the name reflects the overlapping character of the *aḥādīth* that fall in between these classifications.

Ḥadīth is classified as *Ṣaḥīḥ* when its narrators belong to the first three classes of narrators. It is defined as a ḥadīth with a continuous *isnād* all the way back to the Prophet, or a Companion, consisting of upright persons who also possess retentive memories and whose narration is not outlandish (*shādhdh*) while it is, in the meantime, free of both obvious and subtle defects (*ʿilal*). The last two requirements here are concerned mainly with the text (*matn*) and what it all means is that both the *isnād* and *matn* of the ḥadīth are clear of apparent uncertainty and doubt. A *Ṣaḥīḥ* ḥadīth must not be outlandish in the sense that it does not contradict a reliable ḥadīth that is reported by a larger number of transmitters, or even by one transmitter of higher authority and ranking.[1] Abū Muḥammad Ḥusayn al-Baghawī (d. 516 H) has suggested a more simplified method of identifying *Ṣaḥīḥ* and *Ḥasan aḥādīth*. It is thus stated that a ḥadīth is *Ṣaḥīḥ* if it is recorded by both al-Bukhārī and Muslim or by one of them, and it is *Ḥasan* if it is recorded by Abū Dāwūd, al-Tirmidhī and others. It is further suggested that the best of *Ṣaḥīḥ aḥādīth* are those that are transmitted by the people of Madīna.[2] *Ṣaḥīḥ al-Bukhārī* was the first collection of ḥadīth that was exclusively devoted to *Ṣaḥīḥ* ḥadīth. Imām Mālik's *Muwaṭṭa'*, although earlier in time, is not given the same ranking as it contains *Mursal* and *Maqṭū*ʿ. Imām Mālik has also mixed the sayings of Companions with ḥadīth and does not therefore clearly distinguish between the *Marfū*ʿ and *Mawqūf*, whereas al-Bukhārī has distinguished and isolated the sayings of Companions and Successors and records only *Marfū*ʿ ḥadīth under the *Ṣaḥīḥ* category. As for Imām Shafiʿī's comment who said "I do not know of any book of knowledge greater in merit than the book of Mālik" – Ibn al-Ṣalāḥ wrote that this was said before al-Bukhārī and Muslim came into being.[3]

Ṣaḥīḥ is also not a monolithic category of ḥadīth as it has been divided into several sub-varieties. There are *Ṣaḥīḥ* on which there is general agreement (*muttafaq ʿalayh*) and *Ṣaḥīḥ* on which there is disagreement as to whether they should be classified as such. One of the well-known classifications of *Ṣaḥīḥ*, as already noted, is focused on al-Bukhārī and Muslim. The most authoritative of all *Ṣaḥīḥ* is that which are recorded by both al-Bukhārī and Muslim, followed by those which are recorded by al-Bukhārī, or by Muslim, alone, then ḥadīth which fulfil all of their conditions even if they do not appear in either. This is followed by *Ṣaḥīḥ* which fulfils the conditions respectively of either al-Bukhārī, or of Muslim but which, however, do not appear in either. The last of these seven varieties is *Ṣaḥīḥ* that is authenticated by other prominent *ʿulamā'*, independently, that is, of al-Bukhārī and Muslim. Geography is also a factor that is considered in determining the relative strength of *Ṣaḥīḥ*: *Ṣaḥīḥ* that originates in Madīna generally ranks highest, then comes Baṣra, then al-Shām (Syria) and then Kūfa.[4]

Ṣaḥīḥ has been further sub-divided into *Ṣaḥīḥ li-dhātih*, that is *Ṣaḥīḥ* in itself, and *Ṣaḥīḥ li-ghayrih*, or *Ṣaḥīḥ* because of some extraneous evidence. The former is a ḥadīth which fulfils all the requirements of *Ṣaḥīḥ* in that it has an unbroken chain of transmitters all of whom are reliable and retentive (*ḍābiṭūn*) and it is clear of hidden defects and outlandish content. *Ṣaḥīḥ li-ghayrih* also fulfils these requirements, except for one, which is that not all of its transmitters are known for retentiveness as occasional errors have been detected in some of their reports. It is then possible that the point of weakness on account of retentiveness of the narrator is made up for by some other evidence that may fall under one or the other of the following three types:

First, when the same ḥadīth is reported by another chain of transmitters wherein all the transmitters are fully qualified. An example of this is the ḥadīth transmitted by Muḥammad b. ʿAmr from Abū Salama from Abū Hurayra from the Prophet, peace be on him, who said: "Had it not been for fear of imposing hardship on my *umma*, I would have ordered them to brush their teeth before every (obligatory) prayer."

لولا أن أشق على أمتي لأمرتهم بالسواك عند كل صلاة.

Muḥammad b. ʿAmr b. ʿAlqama is well-known for truth and piety but not for retentiveness, according to some commentators, whereas others have approved of him in every respect. The above ḥadīth thus fails to qualify as *Ṣaḥīḥ* in itself and may have been qualified as *Ḥasan*, had it not been for the fact that it has also been reported by Muḥammad b. ʿAmr's teacher, and the latter's teacher consisting of al-Aʿraj, Saʿīd al-Muqbirī, al-Muqbirī's father from Abū Hurayra. It is on this basis that al-Tirmidhī has recorded this as a *Ṣaḥīḥ* as he has also found an additional *isnād* for it through another Companion, namely Zayd b. Khālid and the various chains of *isnād* thus reinforce one another.[5]

Second, when the ḥadīth in question is generally accepted by the *ʿulamā'*, which would, in turn, make up for the point of weakness in the transmission and it is elevated to *Ṣaḥīḥ* (*li-ghayrih*). This is because the *ʿulamā'* have known of the point of weakness in its transmission, on account of some compromise on retentiveness, but have nevertheless accepted it. An example of this is the ḥadīth which proclaims concerning the open sea that "Its water is clean and so is its (unslaughtered) corpse."

هو الطهور ماؤه الحل ميتته.

Notwithstanding some weakness in the *isnād* of this ḥadīth, al-Bukhārī has qualified it as *Ṣaḥīḥ*, and so has al-Tirmidhī. Ibn ʿAbd al-Barr has also commented in *Al-Istidhkār* that the *ʿulamā'* of ḥadīth have accepted this as a *Ṣaḥīḥ* ḥadīth.

Third, when the ḥadīth in question is in harmony with the Qur'ān or a principle of *Sharīʿa*, in which case it is elevated to the rank of *Ṣaḥīḥ*. This is because the *Sunna* generally supplements the Qur'ān and the ḥadīth in question would fit in with the general pattern of the relationship of the *Sunna* with the Qur'ān.

The *Ṣaḥīḥ* collections signify a later stage in the compilation of ḥadīth. In its early stages, the ḥadīth compilers simply collected ḥadīth of the Prophet without drawing a clear distinction between the *Ṣaḥīḥ* and other *aḥādīth*, and it was the Imām of ḥadīth, Ismāʿīl al-Bukhārī (194–256 H) who devoted his renowned collection to the compilation entirely of *Ṣaḥīḥ* ḥadīth. Of the six well-known collections of ḥadīth, known as *al-Ṣiḥāḥ al-Sitta*, only the first two, that is, *Ṣaḥīḥ al-Bukhārī* and *Ṣaḥīḥ Muslim*, are, in principle, devoted to the compilation only of *Ṣaḥīḥ* ḥadīth whereas the other four collections are not confined to *Ṣaḥīḥ* and also contain the *Ḥasan* and *Ḍaʿīf* varieties.

Ḥadīth experts have identified the most reliable chain of transmission (*aṣaḥḥ al-asānīd*) on the basis of their own understanding and *ijtihād*, which is why they tend to differ in their assessments. Al-Ḥakīm al-Nīsābūrī thus wrote that it is therefore not possible to say that the best *isnād* is from certain individuals among the Companions, or that which may be related by people from a certain town or a certain group of narrators. The Companions have transmitted ḥadīth which are quoted and passed on by certain individuals among the Successors, most of whom are trustworthy and it is difficult to be certain in giving absolute preference to some over the others.[6] But the ḥadīth scholars have attempted nevertheless to mention what they considered to be the most reliable of all *isnād*. Ibn al-Ṣalāḥ agreed with al-Nīsābūrī and goes on even to quote examples of discrepancies in such assessments.

Isḥāq b. Rāhawayh and Aḥmad b. Ḥanbal are quoted to have said that the most reliable of all *isnād* is al-Zuhrī from ʿAlī b. al-Ḥusayn from his father al-Ḥusayn from ʿAlī b. Abī Ṭālib. Yaḥyā b. Maʿīn considered the best of all *isnāds* to be Sulaymān al-Aʿmash from Ibrāhīm b. Yazīd al-Nakhaʿī, from ʿAlqama b. Qays from ʿAbd Allāh b. Masʿūd. Al-Bukhārī himself considered the best *isnād* to be Mālik from Nāfiʿ, from ʿAbd Allāh b. ʿUmar. Abū Manṣūr ʿAbd al-Qāhir al-Tamīmī also went on record to say that the best of all *isnād* is Shāfiʿī, from Mālik, from Nāfiʿ from Ibn ʿUmar. ʿAlī b. al-Madīnī and ʿAmr

b. ʿAlī al-Fallās considered the best *isnād* to be that of ʿAbd Allāh b. Ibn ʿAwn from Muḥammad b. Sīrīn from ʿĀbida al-Salmānī from ʿAlī b. Abī Ṭālib.

Ḥadīth scholars have generally held that no one more reliable than al-Shāfiʿī has ever narrated ḥadīth from Imām Mālik, and many of the *ʿulamā'* of later generations (*muta'akhkhirūn*) have considered as a "golden chain – *silsilat al-dhahab*," narration by Aḥmad b. Ḥanbal from al-Shāfiʿī from Mālik – Nāfiʿ – ʿAbd Allāh b. ʿUmar. Yet there is only one ḥadīth with this *isnād* in the *Musnad* of Aḥmad b. Ḥanbal, despite its voluminous content; but it is said that the ḥadīth in question actually consists of four *aḥādīth*, which the Imām has brought together under one *isnād*.[7]

Ḥasan ḥadīth is defined as a ḥadīth that falls between the *Ṣaḥīḥ* and *Ḍaʿīf*, and although its narrators are known for truthfulness, they have not attained the highest degree of reliability and prominence.[8] When the transmitters of ḥadīth have, in other words, reached the highest degree of reliability on grounds of *ʿadāla*, accuracy and retentiveness, the ḥadīth is ranked as *Ṣaḥīḥ*. Should there be any point of weakness in the records of the transmitters, especially with reference to retention (*al-ḍabṭ*) and accuracy, the ḥadīth is likely to be classified as *Ḥasan*. The transmitter of *Ḥasan*, in other words, qualifies as *ʿadl* and the ḥadīth is clear of hidden defect (*ʿilla*) and outlandish content (*shudhūdh*), but there is some doubt on grounds of accuracy and *ḍabṭ*. The *ḍabṭ* of a transmitter is usually tested and evaluated by comparing the reports of a particular transmitter with similar reports by other more reliable transmitters. When there is substantial correspondence, the *ḍabṭ* of the transmitter under review is established, but if there is wide discrepancy in the accuracy of his reports the person is likely to fail the test of accuracy on the ground of *ḍabṭ*. Retention (*ḍabṭ*) is also of two kinds, one of which is retention by memory (*ḍabṭ al-ṣadr*) and the other through documentation (*ḍabṭ al-kitāb*). Both of them are valid and *ḍabṭ* through accurate documentation may under the present circumstances be said to be the principal form of *ḍabṭ*. This is because the volume and scope of ḥadīth have grown so much that *ḍabṭ* without documentation has almost become unfeasible. Abū ʿĪsā al-Tirmidhī, the author of *Sunan al-Tirmidhī*, is said to have introduced this intermediate category of *Ḥasan* for the first time, as no one else seems to have used it before then. A *Ḥasan* ḥadīth may be elevated to the level of *Ṣaḥīḥ* if it is endorsed by another ḥadīth with a stronger *isnād*, in which case it would be called *Ḥasan li-ghayrih*, that is, *Ḥasan* because of that (extraneous) evidence. This is in contradistinction to *Ḥasan li-dhātih*, which is *Ḥasan* for its own sake. As noted above, this dual classification of *li-dhātih* and *li-ghayrih* also obtains on similar grounds for *Ṣaḥīḥ* and *Ḍaʿīf.*

Ḥasan is an intermediate category between *Ṣaḥīḥ* and *Ḍaʿīf* and it seems that most of the *ʿulamāʾ* of *ḥadīth* did not even recognise it as a separate category for some time. It seems that until it was generally recognised as a separate category, *Ḥasan* was generally subsumed under *Ṣaḥīḥ*. This is implied in the nomenclature of al-Tirmidhī's book as *al-Jāmiʿ al-Ṣaḥīḥ* despite the fact that it contained *Ḥasan* ḥadīth which the author himself had acknowledged. In earlier times, inconsistency of terms existed even with regard to *Ṣaḥīḥ* which writers and ḥadīth scholars have variously identified as *al-jayyid* (very good), *al-qawī* (strong), *al-thābit* (well-established, proven). The Imāms al-Shāfiʿī, Aḥmad b. Ḥanbal and al-Tirmidhī sometimes even used phrases such as *ḥasan jayyid*, *ajwad al-asānīd* and the like.[9]

A *Ḍaʿīf* ḥadīth is generally defined as one which fails to qualify the conditions of *Ṣaḥīḥ* and *Ḥasan*. More specifically a ḥadīth is classified weak or *Ḍaʿīf* if its narrators include a person or persons of lower grades than those accepted for *Ḥasan* on a scale of gradation that appears in our discussion of *al-jarḥ wa'l-taʿdīl* in chapter eight above. The weakness in *Ḍaʿīf* may be in the *isnād* or in the text (*matn*) or in both. There are many varieties of *Ḍaʿīf*; *Mursal* is one of them, and it is ḥadīth with a broken link in its *isnād* at the level of a Companion. A Follower (*tābiʿī*) has, in other words, reported it directly from the Prophet. The leading Imāms, Abū Ḥanīfa, Mālik and Shāfiʿī, have accepted the *Mursal,* not only of the Companion, in which one Companion might have reported a ḥadīth from a fellow Companion and not directly from the Prophet, but also of prominent scholars of the *tābiʿūn* such as Saʿīd Ibn al-Musayyib, Qatāda, and al-Zuhrī. Imām Shāfiʿī has also accepted *Mursal* if it was supported by another ḥadīth with an unbroken *isnād*, or when it was in harmony with the precedent of the Companions and also when the *ʿulamāʾ* generally accepted it. The Ḥanafīs, who accept *Mursal* of the first three generations, have justified their stance by saying that when an upright and learned person is convinced about the truth and reliability of a ḥadīth, he tends to link it directly to the Prophet, saying that the Prophet said such and such. Imām Aḥmad Ibn Ḥanbal does not rely on *Mursal* and the majority of *ʿulamāʾ* of ḥadīth and jurisprudence are of the view that acting upon the *Mursal* is not obligatory. Both *al-Bukhārī* and *Muslim*, however, contain the *Mursal* of Companions. It is noted, for instance, that much of the ḥadīth narrated by Ibn ʿAbbās falls under this category, due mainly to his young age: he was only thirteen at the time of the Prophet's demise, and has evidently narrated ḥadīth which he had subsequently learned from fellow Companions.[10] The *ʿulamāʾ* have generally accepted *Mursal* of the Companions, which is somewhat different from *Mursal* proper, since the latter involves direct report by a Follower or *tābiʿī*. In *Mursal* of the Companion (*Mursal al-Ṣaḥābī*), the Companion often reports a ḥadīth from the Prophet without having actually heard it from the Prophet but heard it from another Companion and attributes the ḥadīth directly to the Prophet. This may be due to the lower age of the Companion in question or due to his belated embrace of Islam; in either case it is not considered a serious weakness in the ḥadīth. Al-Suyūṭī has stated that "the two *Ṣaḥīḥ* collections (*al-Ṣaḥīḥayan*) contain countless numbers of *Mursal al-Ṣaḥābī*, for most of what they have reported is from other Companions and they are all deemed to be upright."[11] The younger Companions have often reported ḥadīth from the senior Companions and when they have reported ḥadīth from the Followers, they have usually explained why. *Mursal* of the Companion is generally held to be as good as a *muttaṣil*, or connected ḥadīth. This is because the missing link therein is, in all probability, another and probably a more senior Companion and that is not a serious defect although some have expressed reservations on this point as it is possible, although not very likely, that the Companion has actually relied on a Follower (*tābiʿī*).

Mursal is also sub-divided into several types beginning with the *Mursal* of a Companion who has seen the Prophet, as noted above, but his direct hearing of ḥadīth from the Prophet is not proven. This is followed by *Mursal* of the Follower (*tābiʿī*) who embraced Islam while the Prophet was alive but did not actually meet the Prophet. This is also known as *mukhaḍram* such as Saʿd b. Iyās al-Shaybānī,

Suwayd b. Ghafla and others; twenty of them have been mentioned altogether. Then comes the *Mursal* of prominent *tābiʿī* such as Saʿīd Ibn al-Musayyib and ʿUbayd Allah b. ʿAdī b. al-Khiyār. Many have considered this as the principal variety of *Mursal*; this being a ḥadīth that a leading Follower has attributed to the Prophet. And lastly *Mursal* of the minor figures among the Followers such as Qatāda, Ḥamīd al-Ṭawīl, Ibn Shihāb al-Zuhrī, Yaḥyā b. Saʿīd al-Anṣarī and others. One who has heard from the Prophet when a disbeliever and then embraced Islam after the Prophet's demise is a *tābiʿī* and there is no disagreement on this.

Only the *Mursal* of Companions is generally accepted, but the other types of *Mursal* are not. Even with regard to the *Mursal* of Companions, some scholars, such as Abū Isḥāq al-Isfarā'īnī have expressed reservations by saying that unless it becomes known that the Companion in question has heard it from the Prophet or a fellow Companion, it is possible he may have received it from a non-Companion, that is a Follower, in which case it becomes unreliable. It has, however, been said in response that the case where a Companion might transmit ḥadīth from a *tābiʿī* is rather unlikely and rare, and the *Mursal* of a Companion most likely refers to another Companion.[12] Al-Nawawī has been quoted to have said that "the *Mursal* ḥadīth is a weak ḥadīth according to the vast majority of ḥadīth scholars, al-Shāfiʿī, and most of the *fuqahā'* and jurisprudents of *uṣūl*."[13] This is because of ignorance of the condition of the missing link which may possibly be weak or may be a person other than a Companion even when it is known that the transmitter in question is one who only narrated ḥadīth from reliable persons.

Munqaṭiʿ is another type of *Ḍaʿīf*. This is a ḥadīth in which there is a broken link in the *isnād* somewhere below the level of Companion or that it consists of a link that is ambiguous and vague. A hypothetical example of this might be when it is said that Mālik reported from Ibn ʿUmar, or that 'a man' reported from Ibn ʿUmar. This is because Mālik has not seen ʿAbd Allāh Ibn ʿUmar and there must have been an intervening link, which is unknown, although one might guess that it was Nāfiʿ, but that guess is of no value. But if that link is clearly identified to be Nāfiʿ, then it would be one of the strongest chains of *isnād*, which is known, among the *ʿulamā'* of ḥadīth, as the Golden

Chain. *Munqaṭiʿ* is also a general term, especially to the *ʿulamāʾ* of *uṣūl al-fiqh* who tend to apply it to any ḥadīth with a broken *isnād*.

Muʿḍal is another variety of *Ḍaʿīf* in which the chain of *isnād* consists of two broken links, one after the other. When it is said, for example, that Shāfiʿī reported from Ibn ʿUmar, the link jumps over two generations consisting possibly of Mālik and Nāfiʿ. This is even worse than *Munqaṭiʿ* simply because two links are missing in the *isnād*. An example of *Muʿḍal* is the ḥadīth that Imām Mālik has reported from Abū Hurayra that the Prophet, peace be on him, said "a slave is entitled to food and clothes in a decent manner, and may not be asked to do work that is beyond his capacity" (*Al-Muwaṭṭaʾ*, *Kitāb al-Istiʾdhān, bāb al-amr biʾl-rifq biʾl-mamlūk*).

للمملوك طعامه وكسوته ولا يكلف من العمل إلا ما يطيق.

This is a *Muʿḍal* as Imām Mālik narrated it directly from Abū Hurayra, but it has elsewhere been reported as a *Muttaṣil* (connected) ḥadīth wherein Mālik reported it from Muḥammad b. ʿAjlān, from his father from Abū Hurayra (al-Ḥākim al-Nīsābūrī, *Maʿrifat ʿUlūm al-Ḥadīth*, p. 37).

Matrūk, or abandoned, is yet another variation of *Ḍaʿīf* wherein the *isnād* consists of a transmitter who is suspected of lying, be it concerning the ḥadīth of the Prophet or lying in any other context. An example of *Matrūk* is the ḥadīth of al-Jārūd b. Yazīd al-Nīsābūrī, from Bahz from his father, from his grandfather that the Prophet said "when anyone tells his wife: you are divorced as from next year, God willing, it is of no effect."

إذا قال لأسرته: أنت طالق إلى سنة إن شاء الله فلا حنث عليه.

This is a *Matrūk* ḥadīth as al-Jārūd is suspected of lying and many scholars, including al-Dhahabī, have identified him as such.

Maqlūb (reversed) is also a weak ḥadīth and it consists of a reverse order of reading in its *isnād* or its text. An example of reversal in the text is the ḥadīth of Abū Hurayra which both al-Bukhārī and Muslim have recorded that the Prophet, peace be on him, said "what I have prohibited to you – avoid it, and what I have commanded you to do – do it to the extent of your ability."

Al-Ṭabarānī has reported this ḥadīth from Abū Hurayra in the reverse order, which brings the latter portion of the ḥadīth first so as to read "what I have commanded you to do – do it ...". Reversal in the *isnād*, on the other hand, may involve the whole of the *isnād*, such as attaching the *isnād* of one ḥadīth to another ḥadīth, or it may involve reversal in names, such as Murra b. Kaʿb, when rendered as Kaʿb b. Murra.

Al-Mudraj (inserted) is another variety of *Ḍaʿīf* which consists of inadvertently inserting the speech of a Companion, a Follower, or a ḥadīth transmitter into the text or *isnād* of the ḥadīth of the Prophet. Insertion in the text may occur at the beginning, middle, or end of the text. An example of insertion at the end is the ḥadīth reported by ʿAbd Allāh b. Masʿūd who said that the Prophet, peace be on him, took him by his hand and taught him the *tashahhud* and said: "say: *at-taḥiyyātu li-Allāhi waṣ-Ṣalawātu*, then the *tashahhud*, and said when you have cited this you have completed your *ṣalāh*; if you wish to stand up (and go) stand, or sit if you wish."

قل: التحيات لله والصلوات، فذكر التشهد، قال: فإذا تلوت هذا فقد قضيت صلاتك، إن شئت تقوم تقم وإن شئت تقعد فاقعد.

Al-Ḥākim al-Nīsābūrī wrote concerning this ḥadīth that the latter portion of it (i.e. when you have cited this ...) is ʿAbd Allāh b. Masʿūd's own statement which the narrator has mistakenly added to the ḥadīth.[14]

Munkar, which is another variety of *Ḍaʿīf*, is a ḥadīth whose narrator cannot be confirmed to have fulfilled the prerequisites of *ʿadāla* and retentiveness of memory and his ḥadīth is also contrary to one narrated by a more reliable narrator on the same subject. *Munkar* is similar to *shādhdh* with one difference, which is that in *shādhdh* the ḥadīth of a reliable narrator is contrary to one reported by many reliable narrators whereas reliability of the narrator of *Munkar* is doubtful.

Muḍṭarib (confounded) is also another variety of *Ḍaʿīf*, and it refers to a ḥadīth the contents of which are inconsistent with a number of other *aḥādīth*, none of which can be preferred over the others.[15] The confusion sometimes originates in conflicting reports from the same narrator. An example of this is the ḥadīth of Anas b. Mālik who said that he prayed behind the Prophet, as well as Abū Bakr and ʿUthmān, and heard them opening the *ṣalāh* directly with the Sūra al-Fātiḥa without citing the *bismala* first. Elsewhere it has been reported from Anas that Anas was questioned concerning the *basmala* where he said that he had not known anything on this from the Prophet. Sometimes the confusion relates to a portion of the *isnād* such as when two narrators report a ḥadīth with the same *isnād* but they differ with regard to one link therein. An example of the *Muḍṭarib* occurs in the *matn* of the following two ḥadīths, both of which are supported by acceptable *isnāds*. Fāṭima bt. Qays said that the Prophet was asked concerning the *zakāh* and he said: "property is liable to rights other than the *zakāh*." The same ḥadīth has been reported in conflicting words wherein it is stated that "property is liable to no rights other than *zakāh*."

في المال حق سوى الزكاة.
ليس في المال حق سوى الزكاة.

Neither of these can be preferred, nor can they be reconciled, hence a *Muḍṭarib*.[16] Sometimes the confusion arises when the same ḥadīth is reported as a *Mursal* by one and as *Muttaṣil* by another. It may be possible to ascertain grounds by which one of the ḥadīths in question is given preference whereas this may not be feasible if the two reports are about equal in all respects and the confusion would therefore remain unresolved.[17]

Ḍaʿīf has once again been divided into two types, namely *Ḍaʿīf*, acting on which is not objectionable and this resembles the *Ḥasan* in the terminology of al-Tirmidhī. The second type of *Ḍaʿīf* is that which is totally spurious, acting on which is not recommended, but there is some difference of opinion on this.

The *ʿulamāʾ* have held three different views with regard to acting on *Ḍaʿīf* ḥadīth. The first view is that it is of absolutely no value and should not be followed whether in reference to moral virtues (*faḍāʾil wa mawāʿiẓ*) or to legal rules (*aḥkām*). This is the view of the leading *ʿulamāʾ*, including al-Bukhārī and Muslim, Yaḥyā b. Maʿīn, Abū Bakrā Ibn al-ʿArabī and that of the Ẓāhirī school. The proponents of this view have referred to the Qurʾānic directive to "take not a stand over something which you do not know" (al-Isrāʾ, 17:36).

وَلَا تَقْفُ مَا لَيْسَ لَكَ بِهِۦ عِلْمٌ

Since *Ḍaʿīf* fails to impart positive knowledge, it does not provide an adequate basis on which to determine a ruling of *Sharīʿa*. It is better to act, in such cases, on the basis of personal reason (*ra'y*) rather than a weak ḥadīth.

The second view validates *Ḍaʿīf* ḥadīth generally and considers that acting upon a weak ḥadīth is preferable to acting on personal opinion and *ra'y*. Imām Aḥmad b. Ḥanbal and Abū Dāwūd al-Sijistānī, among others, are associated with this view, but they rank such ḥadīth below the *fatwā* of Companion. It is noted, however, that the distinction between *Ḍaʿīf* and *Ṣaḥīḥ* may not have been so clear-cut in Imām Ibn Ḥanbal's time, and it seems likely that Imām Aḥmad counted the *Ḥasan* as a variety of *Ḍaʿīf*. The *Ḍaʿīf* must, however, fulfil three conditions, one of which is that the weakness in it is slight and not dominant, and there is consensus on this. The second is that it is in harmony with the accepted norms and principles of Islam and there is nothing strange in it. Thirdly, it is not made the basis of belief as the possibility is not overruled that it may not be genuine.[18]

The third view which is preferred by the *fuqahā'* and many *ʿulamā'* of ḥadīth has it that a *Ḍaʿīf* ḥadīth may be followed in moral virtues but not in legal injunctions (*aḥkām*), provided that it fulfils certain conditions, namely that none of its narrators are implicated in lying and distortion of ḥadīth, nor known as *matrūk al-ḥadīth*, that its message is in conformity with the valid norms and principles of Islam, and that acting on it is not accompanied by dogmatic belief.

Ibn al-Ṣalāḥ al-Shahrazūrī (d. 643 H) advises that whenever one speaks of a *Ḍaʿīf* ḥadīth, one should identify it as such and also specify if the weakness is only in the transmission (*ḍaʿīf al-isnād*). For it is possible that another chain of transmission may be found concerning the same ḥadīth that is free of defect and would help to strengthen the *isnād* and elevate the ḥadīth to the rank of *Ṣaḥīḥ*. Ibn al-Ṣalāḥ further advised that when one recites or transmits a *Ḍaʿīf* ḥadīth without its *isnād*, one should avoid saying that "the Prophet, peace be on him, said such and such" in a definite tone of voice but should say instead that "it is reported from the Prophet, peace be on him," or that a ḥadīth in such and such terms has been transmitted to us and so forth. Ibn al-Ṣalāḥ has, moreover, noted the tendency among the scholars of ḥadīth that they tend to ignore weakness in the *isnād* of *Ḍaʿīf aḥādīth* when they refer to such *aḥādīth* in the context of moral virtues and encouragement (*al-targhīb wa'l tarhīb*), narratives and preaching outside the scope of the *aḥkām*. It is then recommended that one should not confuse the *Ḍaʿīf* with the *Ṣaḥīḥ* ḥadīth and should clearly identify them for what they are.[19]

Ibn al-Ṣalāḥ has also stated: "when they say that this ḥadīth is *Ṣaḥīḥ*," it means that it has a continuous *isnād* and a text that is free of defects and, as such, it fulfils all the requirements of a *Ṣaḥīḥ* ḥadīth, but it does not necessarily mean that it is true and authentic as a matter of certainty. For even in the *Ṣaḥīḥ* category there are *aḥādīth* that are narrated by one upright narrator, and as such, the possibility of error and forgetfulness cannot be eliminated altogether. But for practical purposes this possibility is not given much attention in that a *Ṣaḥīḥ* ḥadīth does provide a valid basis of judgement and acting on it becomes obligatory. In a similar vein when "they say concerning a ḥadīth that it is not *Ṣaḥīḥ* – *ghayr Ṣaḥīḥ*," it does not mean decisively that it is a lie, for it is still possible that it is a true ḥadīth but has failed to have a valid *isnād* that fulfils all of its necessary requirements.[20] Sometimes ḥadīth scholars use the expression *Ṣaḥīḥ al-isnād* (sound of *isnād*) with regard to a *Ṣaḥīḥ* ḥadīth, which implies doubt in the accuracy of the text thereof. Another expression that is sometimes used is that a ḥadīth expert may identify a ḥadīth as *aṣaḥḥ shay' fi'l-bāb* (the best that there is on the subject). This expression does not imply that the ḥadīth is *Ṣaḥīḥ*, let alone the best of *Ṣaḥīḥ*; it may indeed mean that the ḥadīth is weak, or that it is the least weak of the *aḥādīth* on the subject and that no stronger ḥadīth is available on that matter.[21]

The *ʿulamā'* are not entirely consistent in their evaluation of ḥadīth into the *Ṣaḥīḥ* category for reasons that relate both to the requirements of *Ṣaḥīḥ* as well as qualifying or disqualifying certain individuals as upright and retentive. The first level of disagreement (*ikhtilāf*) concerns the minimum requirements of *isnād*. Whereas some *ʿulamā'* have stipulated for a *Ṣaḥīḥ* ḥadīth that it should qualify as a *ʿAzīz*, which effectively means that it should have two separate *isnāds*, others have accepted into *Ṣaḥīḥ* ḥadīth which falls under the category of *Gharīb*. This last is a ḥadīth which is supported by a single narrator in at least some part of its chain of *isnād*. There thus arises a certain amount of *ikhtilāf* as to whether one or both of *ʿAzīz* and *Gharīb*, or only one but not the other is accepted into the category of *Ṣaḥīḥ*. This might explain the dual characterisation by al-Tirmidhī of some *aḥādīth* as *Ṣaḥīḥ Gharīb*. Disagreement could also arise over individual transmitters and *aḥādīth* as to whether a particular transmitter, or ḥadīth, as the case may be, has fulfilled all or only some of the requirements of *Ṣaḥīḥ*, with the consequence that the same ḥadīth is evaluated by some *ʿulamāʾ* as *Ṣaḥīḥ* whereas others may have placed it under *Ḥasan*. Moreover, al-Tirmidhī has identified certain *aḥādīth* with the somewhat unusual terminology of "*Ḥadīth Ḥasan Ṣaḥīḥ*". This has given rise to much debate among the scholars of ḥadīth. What it simply means, however, is that the ḥadīth is supported by two *isnāds*, one of which qualifies it as *Ṣaḥīḥ* and the other as *Ḥasan*, or else that there is only one *isnād* for the ḥadīth which is considered as *Ḥasan* by some and *Ṣaḥīḥ* by others.[22]

There is a tendency among the *ʿulamāʾ* of ḥadīth, when classifying a ḥadīth under a certain category, whether *Ṣaḥīḥ*, *Ḥasan*, or *Ḍaʿīf*, to speak in a language that often amounts to a probability such that does not overrule the possibility of a remaining doubt. In their classification of ḥadīth, the *ʿulamāʾ* often draw the conclusion that this or that ḥadīth has fulfilled the requirements of *Ṣaḥīḥ*, or that its text has fulfilled these requirements. This manner of expression usually conveys some hesitation and differs from unqualified expressions that describe a ḥadīth to be authentic beyond all doubt.[23]

As already noted, *Ḍaʿīf* is not a monolithic category but consists of degrees of weakness in both the text and the *isnād*. Ḥadīth experts have, in this connection, discussed the classes of weak narrators and have written monographic works on the subject. The very title, for example, of Muḥammad Ibn Ḥibbān al-Bustī's (d. 354 H) work, *Al-Majrūḥin min al-Muḥaddithīn wa'l-Ḍuʿāfāʾ wa'l-Matrūkīn* is indicative of this. Weakness can be attributed to character, to memory, and ignorance, etc., of the narrator and also to various aspects of the ḥadīth itself.

Just as the *ʿulamāʾ* were able to identify the most reliable *isnād* and its component names of transmitters, they have also identified and publicised the most spurious and unreliable *isnāds* in conjunction usually with the leading Companions or in reference to particular localities. The most spurious *isnād* (*awhāʾl-asānīd*) with reference to Abū Bakr al-Ṣiddīq is thus noted to consist of Ṣadaqa b. Mūsā al-

Daqīqī, from Farqad al-Subkhī, from Murra al-Ṭayyib from Abū Bakr al-Ṣiddīq. The weakest *isnād* with reference to ʿĀ'isha Ṣiddiqa is al-Ḥārith b. Shibl from Umm al-Nuʿmān al-Kindiyya from ʿĀ'isha. With reference to Ibn ʿAbbās the most spurious *isnād* is al-Suddī al-Ṣaghīr Muḥammad b. Marwān, from al-Kalbī, from Abū Ṣāliḥ, from Ibn ʿAbbās. Ibn Ḥajar al-ʿAsqalānī has called this a "string of lies – *silsilat al-kadhib*". The weakest of all *isnāds* concerning ʿAlī b. Abī Ṭālib is ʿAmr b. Shimr, from Jābir al-Juʿfī, from Ḥārith al-Aʿwar, from ʿAlī. Similar information has been compiled concerning Abū Hurayra and others, as well as concerning transmitters from various places such as the Yemen, Egypt, al-Shām and Kūfa, etc. The weakest of the Yemenite *isnād* is thus said to be Jaʿfar b. ʿUmar al-ʿAdanī, from al-Ḥakam b. Abān, from ʿIkrama from Ibn ʿAbbās. Ḥadīth that is transmitted through any of these so-called black-listed channels is classified as *Matrūk* (abandoned).

The *ʿulamā'* have often declared a ḥadīth as *Ḍaʿīf* even when only one link in its chain of *isnād* is known to be unreliable; for example, the ḥadīth that "one who performs six units of (supererogatory) prayers after the (obligatory) *Maghrib* prayer without engaging in conversation in between would have earned the equivalent of twelve years of worship."

The *isnād* of this ḥadīth consists of ʿUmar b. Rāshid, from Yaḥyā b. Kathīr, from Abū Salama, from Abū Hurayra, from the Prophet. The leading *ʿulamā'* of ḥadīth, including Aḥmad b. Ḥanbal, Yaḥyā b. Maʿīn, Dāraquṭnī, al-Bukhārī and Ibn Ḥibbān have all declared ʿUmar b. Rāshid as unreliable and weak, as one whose report counts for nothing, and so forth. The ḥadīth is thus identified as *Ḍaʿīf* because of ʿUmar b. Rāshid.[24]

Many prominent contemporary *ʿulamā'* including Aḥmad Muḥammad Shākir, Nāṣir al-Dīn al-Albānī, Yūsuf al-Qaraḍāwī, ʿAjjāj al-Khaṭīb and Mannāʿ al-Qaṭṭān have advocated the view that the *Ḍaʿīf* should be abandoned altogether.[25] I too believe that a restrictive approach to the admissibility of weak ḥadīth is safer and in greater harmony with the objective of preserving the purity of ḥadīth. To mix the weak with the general corpus of valid ḥadīth is likely to undermine the credibility of the latter and it should be avoided. This may also be said generally regardless of the subject matter of ḥadīth, whether it relates to moral virtue (*faḍā'il*), encouragement and warning (*al-targhīb wa'l-tarhīb*), or the legal rules (*aḥkām*) of *Sharīʿa*.

According to the general rule, the overall acceptability of a ḥadīth is determined on the weakest element in its proof. Thus the presence of a single weak narrator in an otherwise sound *isnād* would weaken the ḥadīth and take it out of the *Ṣaḥīḥ* category altogether. A weak ḥadīth does not constitute a *Sharʿī* proof (*ḥujja*) and is therefore rejected.[26] It will be noted, however, that the clear cases of rejection have already been largely identified and a ḥadīth that is so rejected is labelled either as *Matrūk* (also known as *Maṭrūḥ*) and *Mawḍūʿ*. A ḥadīth in the *Ḍaʿīf* category is not always of this type and one finds varying shades of weaknesses. To evaluate these, the rules of impugnment and validation (*al-jarḥ wa'l taʿdīl*) are employed. The *ʿulamā'* are inclined to be brief on validation (*taʿdīl*) but more specific on impugnment (*jarḥ*). The tendency here is conveyed in the Arabic phrase *al-ijmāl fī'l-taʿdīl wa'l-tafṣīl fī'l-tajrīḥ* (brevity on validation but elaboration on impugnment). When a narrator is declared as trustworthy and *ʿadl*, one usually does not find much elaboration of the grounds of such assessment, hence little detail as to whether the person in question was regular in the performance of prayer in congregation, fasting, etc. This is partly because the grounds of *taʿdīl* can be numerous and cumbersome to itemise. But when it comes to impugnment, the nature and ground of the defect in the narrator, such as inaccuracy in reporting, confusion, defect of memory, distortion and lying, etc., are specified. Even here, it may be added, the tendency is to avoid unnecessary detail, for it is often deemed sufficient to specify a single defect in order to impugn the probity of a narrator, and this is what the *ʿulamā'* were inclined to do. This attitude may be further explained by saying that impugnment partakes in necessity (*ḍarūra*) and invokes in turn the legal maxim that "necessity must be measured by its true proportions" (*al-ḍarūratu tuqaddaru bi-qadarihā*). This restrictive approach toward impugnment has often had the result that there is no need to mention two or three reasons to impugn someone if one is enough to achieve the same result.[27]

Ḥadīth has also been classified under several other categories which may, in turn, fall under any of the three classes of *Ṣaḥīḥ*, *Ḥasan* and *Ḍaʿīf*, or that its relevance to any of these may not be self-evident. This is the subject that is taken up next.

[16] Ḥadīth Classification II

Marfūʿ, Mawqūf, Muttaṣil, Maqṭūʿ Muʿanʿin, Mu'annan and *Muʿallaq*

THIS classification is predicated on the question as to who has actually uttered the ḥadīth, or to whom may it be attributed. The terms that are used for this classification are also descriptive of their purpose and consist of characterisations and adjectives (*ṣifāt*) that help a better understanding of ḥadīth, which are, however, not indicative of its placement on the three-point scale of *Ṣaḥīḥ – Ḥasan – Ḍaʿīf*. The classification we are about to review, in other words, does not look into the inner strength or weakness of ḥadīth but merely seeks to identify its origin and the likelihood or otherwise of it originating from the Prophet himself. There are several of these classifications, of which we only review the salient ones as follows.

Marfūʿ (Elevated) and *Mawqūf* (Suspended)

The underlying idea of this classification is that a ḥadīth may sometimes consist of the statement or conduct of one or more Companions, which is then elevated and attributed to the Prophet himself, due to a strong, even irrebuttable, assumption that no one else could have validated it in the first place, even though a direct saying of the Prophet on it is not available on record. This procedure of elevating the saying of a Companion and its attribution directly to the Prophet is called *rafʿ* (elevation) and the ḥadīth is then identified as elevated (*Marfūʿ*). For without this explanation, all ḥadīth are presumed to be originating from the Prophet and would all be considered *Marfūʿ*, in which case there would remain no basis for the classification. A *Marfuʿ* ḥadīth stands in contradistinction with *Mawqūf* (suspended); the latter refers to a ḥadīth that stops at the level of the Companion and does not reach the Prophet himself. This is because the Companion has not attributed it to the Prophet nor is the subject such that an attribution of that kind could be taken for granted.

Marfūʿ is a wide-ranging concept, much wider, one might say, than the *Mawqūf*, presumably because the underlying notion in all ḥadīth is that they must originate in one way or another in the person of the Prophet. Since this is a focal point of reference in all ḥadīth, the concept of *Marfūʿ* becomes a wide-ranging one and tends to arise in reference to all ḥadīth whose attribution to the Prophet is not self-evident and yet the subject is such that could not have escaped the attention of the Prophet.

Marfūʿ may consist of a saying, act or tacit approval and it may likewise be a continuous (*muttaṣil*) ḥadīth, or *ghayr muttaṣil*, that is, ḥadīth with a broken *isnād*, which might include a *Mursal*. The subject matter of *Marfūʿ* is such that it could only have been said or acted by the Prophet or that his approval can be taken for granted over it. The narrator may be a Companion, which would normally be the case, or it may be someone else, and often the narrator himself identifies it as *Marfūʿ*. The subject matter of ḥadīth often gives a better indication of it being a *Marfūʿ* ḥadīth. When a Companion says something concerning the text of the Qur'ān or the occasion of its revelation and the matter is such that he could not have said it entirely of his own opinion, it is classified as *Marfūʿ*. According to an alternative definition, attributed to al-Baghdādī, *Marfūʿ* consists of what a Companion has reported concerning a saying, act, tacit approval, or a personal attribute of the Prophet. The origin, in other words, is the Prophet, and the Companion also attributes it to the Prophet.[1] This would preclude *Mursal* from the purview of *Marfūʿ*. Ibn al-Ṣalāḥ has added that according to this definition, *Marfūʿ* is identical with *muttaṣil*, that is, ḥadīth with a continuous *isnād*.[2] This would also mean that *Marfūʿ* does not include a discontinued, or *ghayr muttaṣil*, ḥadīth.

When the saying of a Companion contains a reference such as "we were commanded to do such and such, or were forbidden from such and such, or we used to do such and such," – this is usually classified under *Marfuʿ* if it is attributed to the Prophet and the matter is such that could not have escaped the Prophet's attention, provided also that it is attributed to the time of the Prophet. If the saying of the Companion is not so attributed to a general practice of the Companions or to the time of the Prophet, then it would fall under *Mawqūf*. An example of the former is the saying of the Companion, al-Mughīra b. Shuʿba, that "the Companions of the Messenger of God used to knock at his door with their finger nails."

كان أصحاب رسول الله صلى الله عليه وسلم يقرعون بابه بالأظافر.

Although this is not a *Musnad* (ḥadīth with a continuous *isnād* all the way back to the Prophet), it is very likely, nevertheless, to have come to the knowledge of the Prophet. *Marfūʿ* in this sense also includes the saying of a Companion concerning the personal attributes of the Prophet.[3] Another typical example of *Marfūʿ* is the saying of the Companion, Jābir b. ʿAbd Allāh, concerning the rituals of the regular prayer (*ṣalāh*): "we used to say *takbīr* when we rose and *tasbīḥ* when we descended."[4]

كنا إذا صعدنا كبرنا وإذا نزلنا سبحنا.

Thus it is very likely that the Prophet had known of this and authorised it himself. Similarly the statement of Anas b. Mālik falls under *Marfūʿ* when he said that "Bilāl was ordered to read the *adhān* in even (numbers) and the *iqāma* in odd".[5]

أمر بلال أن يشفع الآذان ويوتر الإقامة.

Mawqūf (suspended) is ḥadīth that is attributed to the Companion; it may consist of words, action or tacit approval, but its *isnād* stops at that level and falls short of reaching the Prophet himself. *Mawqūf* may have a continuous chain of *isnād* up to the level of the Companion, in which case it would be a connected *Mawqūf* (*al-Mawqūf al-mawṣūl*). Should there be disruption in its *isnād*, however, it would be a disconnected *Mawqūf* (*al-Mawqūf ghayr al-mawṣūl*).[6] This distinction is also true of *Marfūʿ* in that a *Marfūʿ* may be either connected (*muttaṣil*), or disconnected (*ghayr muttaṣil*). *Mawqūf* can also include suspended ḥadīth below the level of the Companion, in which case the narrator would specify exactly where the suspension occurred (e.g.

Mawqūf upon Ṭāwūs, or ʿAṭā' or al-Zuhrī). In the absence of such qualification, a *Mawqūf* normally means suspended at the level of the Companion only. The jurists of Khurāsān have drawn a parallel between *Mawqūf* and *Athar* as they equate the one with the other. A similar equation is drawn between *Marfūʿ* and *Khabar*. The *ʿulamā'* of ḥadīth, on the other hand, tend to use *Athar* as a general term that includes all of these.

As for a commentary on the Qur'ān that a Companion might have attempted, if it can be based on the opinion of the Companion, which he has also not attributed to the Prophet, it would fall under the *Mawqūf*. This also applies to commentaries that cannot be based on the personal opinion of the Companion, yet it is known that the Companion in question has been influenced by the *ahl al-kitāb*, especially the Jews, in advancing it. Thus the commentaries that some Companions have advanced with regard to the chapters of the Qur'ān and the hidden mysteries of creation and stories of bygone Prophets that were based on *Isrā'īliyāt* – these are all classified under *Mawqūf* and further weakened if they sound contrary to reason and their attribution to the Prophet is unlikely and remote. Even if they were known to have attempted such due to pious motives, this will not add to the credibility of their comments. But if the Companion is known to have avoided *Isrā'īliyāt* and says something which is not likely to be his own opinion, then it would qualify as *Marfūʿ*. An example of this is the statement of the renowned Companion, ʿAbd Allāh b. Masʿūd, that "one who declares as true a sorcerer (*al-sāḥir*) or one who forecasts the future by employing the fortune teller (*al-kāhin*), he denies what is revealed to the Prophet Muḥammad, peace be on him." However, when a Companion advances an opinion that consists of his own thought and he does not attribute it to the Prophet either, it would be considered as his personal *ijtihād* which would not be binding on anyone, unless it is adopted by general consensus, in which case it would be binding.

Included in the *Mawqūf* are also the sayings of Followers (*tābiʿūn*) such as "we were ordered to do such and such or were forbidden from such and such." This is also the case with regard to such statements of a *tābiʿī* that in his time, or in earlier times "the *Sunna* was such and such." There is some disagreement as to whether some such statements would qualify as *Marfūʿ*, *Mursal* or *Mawqūf*, but the correct position is that they are *Mawqūf*. An example of this is the saying of the *tābiʿī*, ʿUbayd Allah b. ʿAbd Allāh b. ʿUtba that "according to *Sunna*, the prayer leader on the day of *Fiṭr* and the day of (Eid) *al-Aḍḥā* is to sit on the pulpit and read the *takbīr* seven times prior to the sermon (*khuṭba*)." Al-Shāfiʿī, al-Nawawī, and al-Bayhaqī among others have held this to be *Mawqūf*, although it is reported that initially al-Shāfiʿī had said it was *Marfūʿ* but later changed his view over it and considered it to be *Mawqūf*.[7]

As for the question whether *Mawqūf* (of the Companion) is a weak ḥadīth because its attribution to the Prophet is uncertain, it is suggested that there is weakness among the *Mawqūf* and much of the *Isrāʾīliyāt* tend to creep into it, just as there is also sound and fair (*Ṣaḥīḥ* and *Ḥasan*) in the *Mawqūf*. Thus it may be said that *Mawqūf* qua *Mawqūf* is not necessarily all weak. This is true especially of that variety of *Mawqūf* wherein the Companion does not speak of his own opinion and *ra'y* but of something that can be presumed to have been authorised by the Prophet. This type of *Mawqūf* may even qualify as *Ṣaḥīḥ* or *Ḥasan* that can provide a valid proof and basis of judgement. What needs to be stated is that the rules of *uṣūl al-ḥadīth*, be it related to *Ṣaḥīḥ*, *Ḥasan*, or *Ḍaʿīf*, should be applied to *Mawqūf* in order to determine strength and weakness therein and not to dismiss it all simply because it is *Mawqūf*.[8]

Muttaṣil (connected) and *Maqṭūʿ* (broken)

Muttaṣil, or *Mawṣūl* is defined as ḥadīth with a continuous *isnād* in which every narrator has received the ḥadīth from his immediate link above. The *isnād* may be continuous all the way back to the Prophet himself, in which case it would also be *Marfūʿ* and *Musnad* or it may reach up to the level of the Companion and thus qualify as a *Mawqūf*. Al-Khaṭīb al-Baghdādī has equated *Muttaṣil* with *Musnad* which would evidently confine the *Muttaṣil* to *Marfūʿ*, but this equation tends to amount to what Ṣubḥī al-Ṣāliḥ has described as the dominant usage (*ghalabat al-istiʿmāl*). It is, in other words, very likely that *Muttaṣil* would also be *Marfūʿ*, but not always. The equation is somewhat similar to al-Baghdādī's other equation which he drew between *Mursal* and

Munqāṭiʿ. This too contemplates the most likely situation which may not always be the case.[9] Ibn al-Ṣalāḥ has also noted that the *Muttaṣil* may include not only the *Marfūʿ* but also the *Mawqūf* ḥadīth.

As for the question whether the saying of the Followers (*tābiʿūn*) which are transmitted through a continuous *isnād* can also be included under *Muttaṣil* – it is suggested that *Muttaṣil* in its unqualified usage does not include this, but the term *Muttaṣil* may be used if it is qualified with the name of the *tābiʿī* in question. Thus it may be said that "this is *Muttaṣil* up to Saʿīd b. al-Musayyib," otherwise it would be classified as *Maqṭūʿ*. Ibn al-Ṣalāḥ prefers to confine *Muttaṣil* to *Marfūʿ* and *Mawqūf* only.[10]

And lastly *Maqṭūʿ* is a ḥadīth that is suspended at the level of a leading figure among the Followers (*tābiʿūn*) such as Saʿīd b. al-Musayyib, Ibrāhīm b. Yazīd al-Nakhaʿī (d. 96), Masrūq b. al-Ajdaʿ (d. 62), Ḥasan al-Baṣrī (d. 111) and others.[11] This is different from *Munqaṭiʿ*, which is elsewhere explained under the general category of *Ḍaʿīf*, although it is said that al-Shāfiʿī and also al-Ṭabarānī have used the two interchangeably. This was, however, as al-Suyūṭī explained, before the terminology was firmly established.[12] *Maqṭūʿ* may also consist of saying, action or tacit approval that is attributed to a *tābiʿī*. Imām Abū Ḥanīfa considers it weak, so much so that it fails to provide a valid basis of judgement, and he prefers acting on analogy (*qiyās*) over *Maqṭūʿ*. It is said that only the *Maqṭūʿ* which is attributed to leading figures among the Followers who met with the leading Companions may be taken as evidence. The leading Followers include Saʿīd b. al-Musayyib, al-Shaʿbī, al-Nakhaʿī and Masrūq.

Muʿanʿin (from from), *Mu'annan* (that that), and *Muʿallaq* (hanging)

Muʿanʿin is ḥadīth with an *isnād* in which "so and so narrates from so and so (i.e. *fulān ʿan fulān*)" is used without actually specifying the manner of its reception between the two links whether by direct hearing or other methods. The *isnād* of such ḥadīth is considered unbroken and continuous (*muttaṣil*), nevertheless, if it fulfils the following three conditions: firstly that the narrator is an upright person (*ʿadl*), secondly that he actually met with his immediate source, and lastly that the ḥadīth is clear of *tadlīs*.[13] The mere possibility of a meeting between the narrator and his source is not enough to fulfil these requirements.

Muʿanʿin is very frequent in both *al-Bukhārī* and *Muslim* and most other collections of ḥadīth, but compared to *al-Bukhārī*, it is more frequent in *Muslim* for the simple reason that Muslim did not require that his narrators should have actually met one another. Muslim went on record to explain his position on this in the introduction to his *Ṣaḥīḥ Muslim* and how he omitted the condition of actual encounter despite the fact that many of his senior colleagues and predecessors, including al-Bukhārī and ʿAlī al-Madīnī had stipulated and applied it. Muslim maintained instead that narration by way of *ʿanʿana* and *muʿanʿin* is normal and must be held to mean that the narrator has actually heard his teacher if they are contemporaries and trustworthy individuals.[14]

Many of the leading *ʿulamā'* of ḥadīth have expressed reservations over Muslim's position on this. Thus according to Ibn al-Ṣalāḥ "what Muslim has said is debatable. It is also noted that Muslim actually went against the leading Imāms of ḥadīth, namely ʿAlī b. al-Madīnī and al-Bukhārī on this."[15] Ibn al-Ṣalāḥ is not alone as many others have held similar views, some of whom have actually equated *Muʿanʿin* ḥadīth to *Mursal*, which they do not consider to amount to valid evidence unless it is proven to be *muttaṣil*. It is thus stated, and rightly so, that in the event where direct hearing (*samāʿ*) is established between the narrator and his teacher or, the use of words whether in the form of *Muʿanʿin* or other similar expressions should matter little and the ḥadīth that is consequently reported will be considered as *Muttaṣil*. This can also be said if the narrator and his *shaykh* are known to have actually met, provided that there is no ambiguity and *tadlīs* is overruled.[16] Ṣubḥī al-Ṣāliḥ has referred to Ibn Ḥajar al-ʿAsqalānī's view on this and considered it authoritative. Al-ʿAsqalānī has distinguished the following three different positions concerning *ʿanʿana*: Firstly, that *ʿanʿana* is normally equivalent to *haddathanā* (so and so spoke to us) and *akhbaranā* (so and so informed us); secondly, that it does not imply these when uttered by a *mudallis* (concealer); and thirdly, that it is equivalent to *akhbaranā* that is used to imply grant of permission (*ijāza*). There is continuity (*ittiṣāl*) in all of these but some fall short of direct hearing (*samāʿ*) which is the most reliable method of reception and transmission.[17] *Muʿanʿin* is thus considered a *Muttaṣil* (connected) ḥadīth unless there is evidence to suggest that this is not the case.

Similar doubts have been voiced concerning the *Mu'annan*. This is a ḥadīth with an *isnād* wherein the particle *ʿan* (that) occurs and tends to introduce an element of ambiguity as to the actual method of communication between the narrator and his immediate source. For example "so and so narrated to us *that* so and so said" (*haddathanā fulān anna fulānan yaqūl...*). Imām Mālik has considered this to be equivalent to *Muʿanʿin*. Thus when the narrator says "*ʿan fulān*" (from so and so) or "*anna fulanan qāla*" (that so and so said) - the two phrases are about the same. According to Abū Bakr Aḥmad b. Hārūn al-Bardījī, a scholar from Azerbaijan, the *Mu'annan* is different from *Muʿanʿin* as the former implies discontinuity (*inqiṭāʿ*) unless direct hearing is proven with regard to the ḥadīth in question, even if it be through a different source. Al-Suyūṭī who has referred to al-Bardījī then concluded that the correct position is what Imām Mālik has held in that *an* is equivalent to *ʿan* and both imply continuity (*ittiṣāl*) provided that actual meeting (*al-liqā'*) has occurred and the ḥadīth is clear of *tadlīs*, in which case both indicate direct hearing (*samāʿ*). It is then stated that in cases where *isnād* reaches a Companion, it matters little whether the Companion uses one or the other of these expressions, or any equivalent thereof – all would indicate *ittiṣāl*. Thus when a Companion narrates in such words "the Prophet, peace be on him, said – *qāla Rasūl Allāh*," or "*anna Rasūl Allāh qāla*," or "*ʿan Rasūl Allāh annahu qāla*," or "*samiʿtu Rasūl Allāh annahu yaqūl*" – all of these are equivalent expressions. But then again, it is said that this is the privilege of the Companions. So the debate continues, but even so the general position that is stated by Imām Mālik, Ibn al-Ṣalāḥ, al-Suyūṭī and others still remains.[18] I do not, however, propose to engage in further detail here due to the subtleties of Arabic expressions.

The *Muʿallaq* (lit. hung) is a ḥadīth in which one or more links are omitted from the beginning of *isnād* at the lower end, or any other part thereof. Sometimes the entire *isnād* is omitted where the person quoting a ḥadīth simply says "the Prophet, peace be on him, said ...," or when it is said in reference to a Companion that "Ibn ʿAbbās said such and such" or "Abū Hurayra narrated such and such," or "Saʿīd b. al-Musayyib said while quoting Abū Hurayra ...".

This manner of reference to ḥadīth became increasingly widespread after the documentation of the bulk of ḥadīth and proliferation of scholarly writings on it. Writers often did not mention the whole of the *isnād* but merely referred to the two ends of its chain of transmission such as "al-Bukhārī reported on the authority of Abū Bakr" or similar other expressions that merely attempted to identify the *isnād* without giving any of its details. Works compiled after the fourth century hijra, such as al-Khaṭīb al-Tabrīzī's *Mishkāt al-Maṣābīḥ*, for example, quoted the ḥadīth from the six major collections and frequently employed this manner of reference to the *isnād* of the ḥadīth. Even in *Ṣaḥīḥ al-Bukhārī* itself numerous ḥadīth cited are of *Muʿallaq* variety, so much so that Ḥāfiẓ Ibn Kathīr wrote a book on al-Bukhārī entitled *Taghlīq al-Taʿlīq* (closure of the suspended) in which he filled in the missing parts of al-Bukhārī's *taʿlīqāt* as they were already known. *Ṣaḥīḥ Muslim* is also said to contain 14 *aḥādīth* of this type. Ibn al-Ṣalāḥ has observed in this connection that al-Bukhārī employed *taʿlīq* usually with reference to a very well-known ḥadīth, or that he did so because he had elsewhere given the full *isnād*.

According to the rules that the *ʿulamā'* of ḥadīth have generally upheld, the *Muʿallaq aḥādīth* of al-Bukhārī are considered as *Ṣaḥīḥ* if the suspension is made in decisive words, such as *qāla* (said), *faʿala* (did), *amara* (commanded), *nahā* (prohibited), *dhakara* (mentioned) *rawā* (narrated) and so on. Suspension (*taʿlīq*) would not convey validity and soundness (*ṣiḥḥa*) if it occurs in a defective form or expression (*sighat al-tamrīḍ*) such as "it is narrated from so and so" (*yurwā ʿan kadhā wa kadhā*), "it is said of him" (*yuqālu ʿanhu*), "it is mentioned, or narrated" (*yudhkaru, yuḥkā*) and the like, which are in any case usually not employed in the typical cases of *taʿlīq*.[19]

It is inadvisable to consider that the three ḥadīth varieties of *Muʿanʿin*, *Mu'annan* and *Muʿallaq* are necessarily weak. They may qualify as *Ṣaḥīḥ*, or *Ḥasan* or *Ḍaʿīf* depending on the specifications of their respective *isnād*s and the individual narrators therein.

[17] Ḥadīth Classification III

Fard, *Gharīb*, *ʿAzīz*, *Mashhūr*, *Mutawātir*, and *Āḥād*

ḤADĪTH classifications that are reviewed in this chapter are also premised on the number of narrators in their *isnād* without any reference to the placement of ḥadīth on the three-point scale of *Ṣaḥīḥ* – *Ḥasan* – *Ḍaʿīf*. The classification thus begins with ḥadīth that is narrated by one person (*Fard*) or a single chain of *isnād*, and the *ʿAzīz*, which is narrated by two persons at every level, and then *Mashhūr* and so forth. These are separately addressed as follows.

Fard (single) and *Gharīb* (strange)

Fard is described as a ḥadīth that only one Companion has narrated from the Prophet, even if the ḥadīth has become well-known and reported by many at the lower levels of the *isnād*. An example of this is the ḥadīth which proclaims that "Acts are to be judged/evaluated by their intentions."[1] Only one Companion, namely ʿUmar b. al-Khaṭṭāb, has narrated it from the Prophet although it has subsequently become so well-known that it has found its way into almost all the six major ḥadīth collections. *Fard* is subdivided into two types, namely absolute, that is, *al-Fard al-Muṭlaq*, and relative, *al-Fard al-Nisbī*.

Absolute *Fard* is a ḥadīth that is narrated by literally a single Companion, as was the case with the above example. Relative *Fard* refers to a ḥadīth that narrators from only a single place, or a single teacher or group have reported. The application of *Fard* to this type of ḥadīth is relative in the sense that it may have actually been narrated by many but they all belong to the same locality or group – such as the people of Kūfa, or Baṣra or Madīna, etc. When *Fard* is used without further qualification, it usually means absolute *Fard*, and this is not synonymous with *Shādhdh*. For *Shādhdh* is basically a *Fard* which also opposes another more reliable ḥadīth that is reported by many, and it is on this ground that *Shādhdh* and *Fard* differ from each other.[2]

An example of *Fard Nisbī* which is narrated by the people of one locality from a single person is the ḥadīth of Ibn Burayda who said that he never held a judicial post after he heard the following ḥadīth from his father: "Judges are of three types, two of whom are in Hell and one in Paradise. The two include a judge who knowingly renders a wrong judgement, and one who renders a wrong judgement unknowingly. The judge who is in Paradise is one who renders a right judgement."[3]

القضاء ثلاثة، فإثنان في النار وواحد في الجنة: فأما الإثنان فقاض قضى بغير الحق وهو يعلم فهو في النار، وقاض قضى بغير الحق وهو لا يعلم فهو في النار. وأما الواحد الذي في الجنة فقاض بالحق فهو في الجنة.

Al-Ḥākim al-Nīsābūrī wrote that this ḥadīth has only been reported by the people of Khurāsān (*khurāsāniyyūn*) and its narrators are all from Marw (in Bukhārā).

Gharīb is similar to *Fard* to begin with, but it may differ with it at the lower levels of the *isnād*. *Gharīb* is defined as a ḥadīth which is narrated by only one narrator at any one link of its *isnād*, be it the middle, lower or upper end. So long as there is a link in the *isnād* which consists of a single narrator, this would qualify the ḥadīth as *Gharīb*. It may thus be said that every *Fard* is also a *Gharīb* but not vice versa. An example of *Gharīb* is the ḥadīth narrated by Muḥammad b. Sūqah, from Muḥammad b. al-Munkadir, from Jābir b. ʿAbd Allāh that the Prophet, peace be on him, said concerning Islam: "This religion is firm so penetrate into it gently without causing yourself repulsion in the worship of God. For a camel rider who does not take rest breaks the animal's back without traversing the earth."

إن هذا الدين متين فأوغل فيه برفق ولا تبغض إلى نفسك عبادة الله فإن المنبت لا أرضا قطع ولا ظهرا أبقى.

Al-Ḥākim al-Nīsābūrī wrote concerning this ḥadīth that no one except Muḥammad b. Sūqah reported it from Muḥammad b. al-Munkadir.[4] Another example of *Gharīb* is the ḥadīth that ʿAbd Allāh b. Dinār narrated from ʿAbd Allāh b. ʿUmar that "The Prophet, peace be on him, prohibited sale and gift of clientage (*al-walāʾ*)."[5]

إن النبي صلى الله عليه وسلم نهى عن بيع الولاء وهبته.

To classify a ḥadīth either as *Gharīb* or *Fard* does not necessarily imply its strength or weakness on the *Ṣaḥīḥ* – *Ḥasan* – *Ḍaʿīf* scale of evaluation. For placing a ḥadīth on this scale would all depend on the conditions of its narrators and reliability of its *isnād*. Having said this, however, most of the *Gharīb* ḥadīth are likely to be weak. Ibn al-Ṣalāḥ has given many examples of *Gharīb* and has stated that al-Zuhrī has recorded no less than ninety *aḥādīth* of this type and some of them have also found their way into the *Ṣaḥīḥayn*.[6]

ʿAzīz (strong) and *Mashhūr* (well-known)

Al-ʿAzīz is a ḥadīth in which at least one link in its *isnād* consists of two narrators, even if the other links include more than two provided that none of the links in the *isnād* consists of less than two narrators. It is called *ʿAzīz* (a derivative of *ʿizza*) as it is said to be strong and consequently infrequent (*qalīlan*). The strength here refers to the minimum of two narrators in every link of the *isnād*. An example of *ʿAzīz* is the ḥadīth wherein the Prophet declared that "None of you believes (truly) unless he loves me more than his father and son."[7]

لا يؤمن أحدكم حتى أكون أحب إليه من والده وولده.

This ḥadīth has been narrated by two Companions, Anas b. Mālik and Abū Hurayra. Then Qatāda b. Diʿāma and ʿAbd al-ʿAzīz b. Ṣuhayb narrated it from Anas, and then Shuʿba and Ḥusayn al-Muʿallim narrated it from Qatāda, and Ismāʿīl b. ʿAliyya and ʿAbd al-Wārith narrated it from ʿAbd al-ʿAzīz b. Ṣuhayb, then many more narrated it afterwards.

ʿAzīz may be a sound/*Ṣaḥīḥ* ḥadīth due to the reliability of its narrators or it may qualify as *Ḥasan* or even *Ḍaʿīf*, notwithstanding the number of its narrators. To qualify a ḥadīth as such is a question, once again, of the conditions of its narrators in the *isnād*, and not necessarily of their number.

When the number of narrators at every link of the *isnād* is no less than three, the ḥadīth would be classified as *Mashhūr*. It is called *Mashhūr* (widespread, well-known) because of the larger number of narrators that are involved in its *isnād*. It is important to note that *Mashhūr* must have become well-known and widespread during the first three generations of the advent of Islam, as following that period, most *aḥādīth* are believed to have become widespread and well-known. An example of *Mashhūr* is the following ḥadīth which declares the basic attribute of a Muslim: "A Muslim is one from whose tongue and hand other Muslims are safe."[8]

المسلم من سلم المسلون من لسانه ويده.

It is to be noted once again that a well-known or *Mashhūr* ḥadīth is not necessarily a *Ṣaḥīḥ*/Sound ḥadīth, as it may well fall under the *Ḥasan* or even *Ḍaʿīf* categories depending on the condition of its narrators in the *isnād*. Authenticity and soundness according to ḥadīth experts is not determined on the quantitative factor of the number of transmitters, nor indeed on how well-known, or less well-known, a ḥadīth might be. Attention is paid instead to the reliability of the narrators, whether one, two or more, and the strength and weakness of ḥadīth is evaluated on that basis. A *Ṣaḥīḥ* ḥadīth is not defined, for example, as ḥadīth which is reported by a certain number of narrators. This is the basic position, but al-Ḥākim al-Nīsābūrī has suggested nevertheless that a *Ṣaḥīḥ* ḥadīth must be no less than *ʿAzīz* and that *Fard* and *Gharīb* may not be evaluated as *Ṣaḥīḥ*. Yet he also pointed out that a *Mashhūr* ḥadīth does not necessarily qualify as *Ṣaḥīḥ*.[9] It thus remains to be said that al-Ḥākim al-Nīsābūrī does not actually lay down conditions but says what would seem to be the most likely situation – when he says, for example, that *Fard* and *Gharīb* do not measure up to the level of *Ṣaḥīḥ*.

Al-Ḥākim has actually given many examples of *Mashhūr* which fail to qualify as *Ṣaḥīḥ*, and this includes the following: "pursuit of knowledge is an obligation of every Muslim"; "There is no *nikāḥ* without the *walī*"; "May God gladden a person who hears my speech and retains it ...".[10]

طلب العلم فريضة على كل مسلم.
لا نكاح إلا بولي.
نضّر الله امرءاً سمع مقالتي فوعاها...

The following are some examples of the *Mashhūr* ḥadīth which are also included in the *Ṣaḥīḥ* category: "I have been commanded to prostrate on seven organs (of the body)"; "every good deed partakes in charity"; "one who comes to the Friday prayer, let him take a bath."[11] Al-Ḥākim has also given examples of ḥadīth that have become well-known and widespread but which are weak/*Ḍaʿīf* and even worthless.

أمرت أن أسجد على سبعة أعضاء.
كل معروف صدقة.
من أتى الجمعة فاغتسل.

The diffusion (*ishtihār*) of a ḥadīth is also a relative concept to some extent in that a ḥadīth may be well-known in certain quarters but not in others. An example of this is the ḥadīth, that "Divorce is the most detested of all permissible things in the eyes of God."

أبغض الحلال إلى الله الطلاق.

This is said to be well-known among the jurists/*fuqahā'*, whereas the ḥadīth "My community will not be taken to task for mistake, forgetfulness, and duress" is well-known among the *ʿulamā'* of *uṣūl* (jurisprudence).

رفع عن أمتي الخطأ والنسيان وما استكرهوا عليه.

There are also *aḥādīth* which are better known among the grammarians and the general public, but not so among the scholars of ḥadīth and so on.[12] Well-known as some *aḥādīth* are in some quarters, this factor of relativity by itself is not taken into account in the definition of *Mashhūr*, which is basically a ḥadīth that is narrated by a minimum of three narrators in every link of its *isnād*. One might also add here in passing that what al-Ḥākim al-Nīsābūrī has written about the relative fame of a certain ḥadīth in some quarters but not in others is also relative and liable to change. Some of the statements that he made then may not be applicable in the same way at the present time.

Mutawātir (recurrent), *Āḥād* (solitary)

This is basically an extension of the previous classification as it is also premised on the number of transmitters involved in the *isnād* of ḥadīth. The *Āḥād* and *Mutawātir* classification tends to acquire greater significance in *uṣūl al-fiqh* than it does in *uṣūl al-ḥadīth*. This may partly be due to the fact that *uṣūl al-fiqh* is basically a science of the proofs and sources of *Sharīʿa* and the number of ḥadīth transmitters in an *isnād* consequently becomes the focus of attention more so in *uṣūl al-fiqh* than the *uṣūl al-ḥadīth*. For the latter is basically concerned, not so much with numbers, but with the qualifications of ḥadīth transmitters. Thus the *Āḥād – Mashhūr – Mutawātir* trio of the *uṣūl al-fiqh* leaves its centre stage and tends to give way, in the context of *usul al-ḥadīth*, to the *Ṣaḥīḥ – Ḥasan – Ḍaʿīf* classification, which is more focused on merit, uprightness, knowledge, retentiveness and so on of individual narrators of ḥadīth. A ḥadīth may be identified as *Ṣaḥīḥ* even if it is transmitted by a single but strong and reliable narrator as the criterion here is not the number but the credentials of individual narrators. A *Ṣaḥīḥ* ḥadīth may also be one that is transmitted by two, three, or a much larger number throughout its chain of *isnād* or only in some of its parts. Thus it would follow that a *Ṣaḥīḥ* ḥadīth may be an *Āḥād*, *Mashhūr* or *Mutawātir*. The number of transmitters in the *isnād* is not entirely irrelevant to qualifying a ḥadīth as a *Ṣaḥīḥ* ḥadīth but it is not the defining element, so to speak, of a *Ṣaḥīḥ* ḥadīth.

Mutawātir is defined as a ḥadīth narrated by a large number of people, so much so that it is inconceivable that they could have all collaborated in order to perpetuate a lie. That possibility is precluded owing to the large number, diversity of residence, locality and time of the narrators. A *Mutawātir* report must by definition be based on sense perception and not on any other ground such as the rationality of its message or because it merely conveys what is a matter of axiomatic knowledge. To say that the world has a creator or that telling the truth is a virtue need not be supported by *Mutawātir* as these are rational and axiomatic.

The narrators of *Mutawātir* are not required to meet the qualifications of *ʿadāla* and retentiveness in the same way as is required in *Āḥād* ḥadīth. This is because in *Mutawātir* credibility is given solely to the multitude and number and not to personal qualifications. Thus the narrator of *Mutawātir* can include anyone, including children. They need not even be Muslims. Thus if the entire population of a town, who are non-Muslims, report that they witnessed a huge fire, or explosion in their town, this would engender certainty and knowledge beyond dispute.

A ḥadīth is classified as *Mutawātir* only when the number of its reporters in every generation is large enough to preclude the possibility of collusion to propagate a lie. Ḥadīth would thus fail to qualify as *Mutawātir* if its reporters are found to be biased or associated with one another through a political or sectarian movement. There is no specified minimum nor a maximum for the number of reporters of *Mutawātir*, although various figures from as low as four to as high as several hundred have been mentioned. To inspire certainty and conviction is the basic purpose, and this can hardly be linked to a particular number. Certainty can sometimes be inspired by a relatively small number if it is also endorsed by corroborative evidence. The number of reporters in a *Mutawātir* must, however, remain large from the start to the end of the *isnād*. A ḥadīth would therefore fail to qualify as *Mutawātir* if the number of its narrators are reduced at any point in its *isnād*. There is no objection to an increase in the number of narrators. Thus if the number of narrators in one generation is thirty and it is increased to forty, this would be seen as a positive rather than a negative factor.

Mutawātir ḥadīth is of two types, namely verbal *Mutawātir*, or *Mutawātir lafẓī*, which consists of the verbatim transmission of the sayings of the Prophet, of which there are very few in existence, and *Mutawātir* in meaning, or *Mutawātir Maʿnawī*, which are quite frequent. *Mutawātir* in meaning may consist of several reports through different channels which tend to support a common theme and meaning between them. An example of the verbal *Mutawātir* is the ḥadīth that "one who lies about me deliberately must prepare himself for a seat in Hell fire."[13]

من كذب علي متعمدا فليتبوأ مقعده من النار.

This ḥadīth has been narrated by a number of Companions including ʿAlī b. Abī Ṭālib, al-Zubayr b. al-ʿAwwām, Anas b. Mālik, Salama b. al-Akwaʿ, and Abū Hurayra; many more have narrated it from each of them in the same as well as in the next generation, and the number of its narrators has thus multiplied manyfold further down the line of its chain of transmission.

An example of the *Mutawātir Maʿnawī* is the sum total of the various ḥadīth reports that have been known on the raising of hands (*rafʿ al-yadayn*) at the time of supplication (*duʿā'*).[14] There are numerous reports that confirm this, and although each one of these, if taken individually, would only count as an *Āḥād* ḥadīth, the common theme and purport of them amounts to *Mutawātir*. A theoretical example of this is the generosity of the legendary Ḥātim, who may have given small or large amounts of gifts, hospitality and help to various people, but when all of these are put together they support a common theme which is the generosity of Ḥātim. This may also be said with regard to so many other things, such as the manner in which the *wuḍū'* is performed, or the way the prayer leader leads the *ṣalāh*, the manner that the *ḥajj* is performed and so on.

Mutawātir conveys certainty (*al-ʿilm al-yaqīn*) which may not be open to challenge or doubt and the ruling that is established by it is also decisive in respect of proof. Critics have, however, maintained that *Mutawātir* is in effect a large number of solitary (*Āḥād*) reports put together. If the component parts of *Mutawātir* can be open to doubt, then *Mutawātir* also does not eliminate doubt. There may be an element of truth in this, especially in our own time when we witness unprecedented developments in media and communications. A news report can become widespread overnight and everyone who is exposed to it may also accept it but that by itself does not guarantee its certainty and truth. But this response need not be projected backwards in the context of ḥadīth. It is just that the notion of *Mutawātir* may need to be adjusted in the context of recent developments and news reports. The conventional response to the critique that is discussed here is that the individual components of *Mutawātir* may be open to doubt but that the sum total of the *Āḥād* reports is not the same as the individual *Āḥād* components thereof. On the contrary *Mutawātir* does engender positive knowledge when it fulfils all of its requirements.

The *ʿulamāʾ* have also differed as to the existence and scope of the first type, that is, the verbatim *Mutawātir* in ḥadīth. Some like Ibn Ḥibbān al-Bustī have denied the existence of this type of *Mutawātir* altogether, whereas Ibn al-Ṣalāḥ has held it to be rare. Ibn Ḥajar al-ʿAsqalānī, Ibn Ḥazm al-Ẓāhirī, Qāḍī ʿIyāḍ, Jalāl al-Dīn al-Suyūṭī and others have held that they are not rare. Ibn Ḥajar even criticised Ibn al-Ṣalāḥ for having said that *Mutawātir Lafẓi* is rare. Al-Suyūṭī has also authored a book bearing the title *Al-Azhār al-Mutanāthira fī'l-Akhbār al-Mutawātira* (scattered flowers in *Mutawātir* reports), which he later summarised in his *Qaṭf al-Azhār* (plucking the flowers) where the author compiled a collection of such *aḥādīth*. Included in this collection are the following *aḥādīth*: (1) "Every intoxicant is wine and all wine is forbidden"; (2) "May Allah felicitate the person who heard my speech ..."; (3) "Everyone will find easy that for which he has been created"; and "Islam began as a stranger ..." and so forth.

كل مسكر خمر وكل خمر حرام.

نضر الله امرءا سمع مقالتي.

كل ميسر لما خلق له.

بدأ الإسلام غريبا.

Al-Bukhārī and Muslim have also recorded a number of *aḥādīth*, one of which is that "The Prophet, peace be on him, wiped over his boots (or long leather socks)".[15]

Many scholars, including Ibn Ḥajar, have held that this is a *Mutawātir* narrated by seventy to eighty narrators in every generation, including the *ʿashara mubashshara* (the ten whom the Prophet greeted as dwellers of Paradise) among the Companions.

Al-Bukhārī and Muslim have also recorded the ḥadīth on the "visual sight of God Most High" on the Day of Resurrection (*ru'yat Allah fī'l-ākhira*), and also the *ḥadīth al-ḥawḍ* wherein the Prophet described his *ḥawḍ* (water basin, pool) in the Hereafter and so on.

The *Āḥād* (solitary), also known as *khabar al-wāḥid*, implies a ḥadīth that is narrated by one transmitter, but this understanding is not always accurate. *Āḥād* is actually defined as a ḥadīth that does not fulfil the requirements of *Mutawātir*. It may have been narrated by one, two or three persons at every level or the number may vary, but their number does not reach that of the *Mutawātir*. This is why *Āḥād* according to the majority of ḥadīth scholars and jurists includes the *Gharīb*, *ʿAzīz* and *Mashhūr*.

Only the Ḥanafīs have interposed the last of these, namely the *Mashhūr*, in between the *Āḥād* and *Mutawātir*. The Ḥanafīs have thus defined *Āḥād* as a ḥadīth the number of whose narrators are less than that of *Mutawātir*, and it has not become widespread to the extent of the *Mashhūr* during the first three generations. As such the *Āḥād* is neither confined to a single narrator nor is it necessarily a weak ḥadīth, but it can include the weak ḥadīth in the category of *Fard* and *Gharīb*. The *ʿulamāʾ* of *uṣūl al-fiqh* and ḥadīth have laid down a number of requirements that the transmitter of *Āḥād* ḥadīth must fulfil before it can form valid *Sharʿī* evidence. These are roughly the same requirements as the narrator of *Ṣaḥīḥ* must fulfil, namely competence, *ʿadāla*, retentiveness and so on. The narrator of *Āḥād* must be a competent person and also a Muslim at the time of transmitting the ḥadīth, but not necessarily at the time of receiving it. When these requirements are met and the ḥadīth is free from obvious and hidden defects, it is decisive evidence according to the Ẓāhirīs and Ḥanbalīs but it is less than decisive (i.e. *ẓannī*) according to the majority of the *madhāhib*. The leading *madhāhib* such as the Ḥanafīs and Mālikīs have also proposed some of their own conditions to verify reliability and strength of the *Āḥād* ḥadīth.[16]

Imām Mālik has thus considered the *ʿamal ahl al-Madīna*, or the Madīnese practice, to be preferable to *Āḥād* ḥadīth in the event of a conflict arising between the two. This the Imām justified on the analysis that the Madīnese practice is the true reflection of the teachings and *Sunna* of the Prophet and as such it is more reliable than the reports of odd individuals. One case of such conflict arose between the Madīnese practice and the ruling of the *Āḥād* ḥadīth concerning *khiyār al-majlis*, or the option of contractual session. The ḥadīth in question provided that "the parties to a sale have the option (to revoke their contract) until they part company."[17] The ḥadīth thus entitled the parties to *khiyār al-majlis*, which meant they could revoke their contract during the continuation of the session or meeting of contract, but not afterwards. Imām Mālik on the other hand upheld the Madīnese practice on this subject and disentitled the contracting parties to *khiyār al-majlis*. The Madīnese practice, according to the Imām, was that a contract became binding and enforceable as of the moment a valid offer and acceptance took place. This was effectively the moment when an agreement had come into being and from that point onwards the parties had no option to revoke it.[18]

The Ḥanafī *madhhab* also stipulated three conditions that the *Āḥād* ḥadīth must fulfil in order to constitute a proof and basis of judgement. One of these was that the narrator of *Āḥād* is not known to have acted against it himself. Should it be known that the narrator had actually acted contrary to his own report, this would mean the report is unreliable. It was on this ground that the Ḥanafīs did not rely on the *Āḥād* ḥadīth narrated by Abū Hurayra because it was known that he did not act on it himself. The ḥadīth stipulated that "when a dog licks a dish, wash it seven times, one of which must be with clean sand."

إذا ولغ الكلب في إنـاء أحدكم فليغسله سبعـا، إحداهـن بالتراب الطاهر.

The second condition that the Ḥanafīs have proposed is that the content of the *Āḥād* ḥadīth is not such that would necessitate the knowledge of a vast number of people. One would in that eventuality expect that more than one person would report such a ḥadīth, and the fact that only one has done so makes the ḥadīth doubtful. One such ḥadīth that the Ḥanafīs have not accepted is "Anyone of you who touches his sexual organ must refresh his ablution."[19]

إذا مس أحدكم ذكره فليتوضأ.

And lastly, in the event of a conflict between the *Āḥād* ḥadīth and the normal principles of *Sharīʿa*, the *Āḥād* ḥadīth would be followed if its narrator is a knowledgeable person, or *faqīh*, failing which the normal rules of *qiyās* would be preferred.

When the *Āḥād* ḥadīth has met all of these requirements, action upon it becomes obligatory even if all doubt as to its authenticity is not eliminated. This is because probability (*ẓann*) is acceptable as a basis of action in the practical rulings of *Sharīʿa*. But it is generally agreed that in the matter of belief and *ʿaqīda* where decisive evidence is normally required the *Āḥād* does not constitute a proof on its own.

As noted earlier, when a ḥadīth is transmitted by a group of narrators and their reports have become widely known during the first three generations of the advent of ḥadīth, it is known as *Mashhūr*. A *Mashhūr* ḥadīth often begins as an *Āḥād* in the first link and then becomes well-known afterwards. It thus appears that the *Ṣaḥīḥ* ḥadīth can be a *Mutawātir*, *Mashhūr* or *Āḥād*. A *Mutawātir* is unlikely to be other than *Ṣaḥīḥ*, but there are examples of *Mashhūr* ḥadīth that have become widely known and yet they do not appear in the *Ṣaḥīḥ* collections.

[18] Confirmation and Follow-Up

al-Mutābiʿ wa'l-Shāhid

THE basic idea of *mutābiʿ* and *shāhid* is to follow-up and confirm a ḥadīth which is narrated by only one transmitter in a single chain of *isnād*. The purpose is to find out whether additional support can be found for it by tracing its chain of transmission at various levels all the way back to the level of Companions. Confirmation and follow-up may also be located from similar other *aḥādīth* that might have been reported through alternative channels. The purpose is to ascertain whether the ḥadīth is credible and whether its transmitter is reliable. The enquiry that occurs here is basically concerned with ḥadīth in the category of *al-Fard*, that is, ḥadīth which is narrated only by a single narrator throughout its chain of *isnād*. When this kind of ḥadīth is encountered in the sphere especially of legal rulings (*aḥkām*), confirmation is often sought and the search that is undertaken as a result is governed by the rules of "confirmation and follow-up".

When the report of one narrator is confirmed by another, and the latter agrees with the former entirely through the same chain of transmission without any change in the ḥadīth, the original narrator (and his ḥadīth) are called *mutābaʿ* (followed), and the new narrator (and his ḥadīth) as *mutābiʿ* (follower). The process here is known as *mutābaʿa*. But when confirmation for a ḥadīth is found through an entirely different *isnād*, from a different Companion, that is, but the ḥadīth conveys the same meaning or a closely similar meaning, the lowest narrator in the chain of *isnād* (and his ḥadīth) is called *shāhid* (witness). The process is still known as *mutābaʿa*.

An illustration of *mutābaʿa* that appears in Ibn al-Ṣalāḥ is as follows: Supposing Ḥammād b. Salama narrated a ḥadīth from Ayyūb, from Ibn Sīrīn, from Abū Hurayra, from the Prophet. The ḥadīth is found to be somewhat doubtful and needs to be confirmed. Firstly we look if any other reliable narrator, that is, other than Ḥammād, has narrated the same ḥadīth from Ayyūb. The search here may take the researcher to the six collections and the *Muwaṭṭa'* etc. If someone else is found to have also transmitted the same ḥadīth from Ayyūb then a confirmation is found, and this is known as a complete follow-up (*mutābaʿa tāmma*). But if no one other than Ḥammād is found to have transmitted the same ḥadīth from Ayyūb, then one looks one level up to find if anyone other than Ayyūb might have reported it from Ibn Sīrīn. If a confirmation is found at this level, it would be less than complete as it does not descend all the way down but is located at a higher level, which is why it is called a deficient follow-up, or *mutābaʿa nāqiṣa*. But if the follow-up is unsuccessful at the level of Ayyūb, then one tries to ascertain whether anyone other than Ibn Sīrīn might have reported the same ḥadīth from Abū Hurayra, and if such a confirmation is found, it would still be known as a deficient follow-up. And lastly the search may be taken up to the highest level to find out whether any other Companion, that is other than Abū Hurayra, might have reported the same ḥadīth from the Prophet. This too falls under *mutābaʿa nāqiṣa*.

Shāhid (lit. witness) is sometimes used interchangeably with *mutābaʿa* but it is different to *mutābaʿa* in one respect, which is that if the follow-up backwards succeeds only in finding another ḥadīth which is found at any level of the enquiry, it would be called *shāhid*, which is the second best form of confirmation for the ḥadīth at issue.

There may be instances where all the three types of *mutābaʿa* combine together in respect of the one and same ḥadīth. An example of this is the ḥadīth which Imām Shāfiʿī has narrated in *Kitāb al-Umm* from his teacher Imām Mālik, from ʿAbd Allāh b. Dīnār, from ʿAbd Allāh b. ʿUmar that the Prophet, peace be on him, said:

> A month is twenty-nine days. So do not start fasting until you see the new moon (for Ramaḍān) and do not end the fast until you see

the new moon (for Shawwal). But if it became invisible to you then complete fasting for thirty days.

الشهر تسع وعشرون، فلا تصوموا حتى تروا الهلال، ولا تفطروا حتى تروه، فإن غم عليكم فأكملوا العدة ثلاثين.

This ḥadīth with its particular wording was somehow thought to be in need of confirmation as al-Shāfiʿī seemed to have been the only person to have narrated it from Imām Mālik, and it was consequently counted as one of the oddities (*al-gharā'ib*) of al-Shāfiʿī. The reason for this was that the disciples of Imām Mālik had narrated this ḥadīth with the same *isnād*, however, with the phrase "... if it became invisible to you, then measure it (by counting)" (*fa-in ghamma ʿalaykum fa'qdirū lahu*). But then a follow-up for al-Shāfiʿī's ḥadīth was found as ʿAbd Allāh b. Maslama al-Qaʿnabī had also reported it from Imām Mālik and it was recorded by al-Bukhārī.[1] This was a complete follow-up, or *mutābaʿa tāmma*.

An incomplete follow-up (*mutābaʿa nāqiṣa*) for the same ḥadīth was also found in the *Ṣaḥīḥ* of Ibn Khuzayma wherein one ʿĀṣim b. Muḥammad had narrated it from his father Muḥammad b. Zayd from his grandfather ʿAbd Allāh b. ʿUmar. Someone else had, in other words, reported the ḥadīth from the same Companion, but the ḥadīth ended with the phrase "... then complete thirty days – *fa-akmilu thalāthīn*". This ḥadīth was also recorded in *Ṣaḥīḥ Muslim* from ʿUbayd Allāh b. ʿUmar, from Nāfiʿ, from Ibn ʿUmar with the last phrase being "measure (by counting) upto thirty days" (*fa'qdirū thalāthīn*). Now we had in effect two incomplete follow-ups.

Then a similar ḥadīth in the nature of a *shāhid* was found in al-Nasā'ī from Muḥammad b. Ḥunayn from ʿAbd Allāh b. ʿAbbās, from the Prophet and it conveyed the same meaning as the one that was initially reported by ʿAbd Allāh b. Dīnār from ʿAbd Allāh b. ʿUmar. Al-Bukhārī had also recorded a closely resembling ḥadīth from Muḥammad b. Ziyād from Abū Hurayra with the latter part being worded: "... If it (the moon) became invisible to you then complete by counting thirty days for Shaʿbān (i.e. the preceding month to Ramaḍān)" (*fa-in ghamma ʿalaykum fa-akmilū ʿiddata Shaʿbān thalāthīn*). This is considered to be a *shāhid* in that it conveys a similar meaning, although in slightly different words to the original ḥadīth that was reported by al-Shāfiʿī. The original ḥadīth thus mentioned that the fasting month may be twenty-nine days, i.e. you can sight the moon to confirm it, but if you are unable to do so then count up to thirty days, both for the previous month and for Ramaḍān itself.

Another example of confirmation is the ḥadīth narrated by Sufyān b. ʿUyayna from ʿAmr b. Dīnār, from ʿAṭā' b. Abī Rabāḥ, from Ibn ʿAbbās that the Prophet, peace be on him, said with regard to the tanning of hides "If the hides of (animals) are taken and tanned, you may benefit by them".

لو أخذوا إهابها فدبغوها فانتفعوا به.

A similar ḥadīth was reported by Ibn Jurayj from ʿAmr b. Dīnār from ʿAṭā' without, however, mentioning the word 'tanning'. The ḥadīth simply validated taking benefit from animal skins. Confirmation was obviously needed here to verify one or the other of the two *aḥādīth*. Then upon enquiry al-Ḥāfiẓ Aḥmad al-Bayhaqī found such confirmation, when it was noted that Usāma b. Zayd had also narrated a ḥadīth with a similar meaning from ʿAṭā' from Ibn ʿAbbās, that the Prophet, peace be on him, said, "Did you not take off its skin, tan it and benefit by it?"

ألا نزعتم جلدها فدبغتموه فاستمتعتم بها.

This was a *mutābaʿa* in which Usāma b. Zayd followed and confirmed Sufyān b. ʿUyayna. The confirmation was complete in that Usāma was located at the same level in the chain of *isnād* as that of Sufyān. It was basically the same ḥadīth and the word 'tanning' occurred in both, even though the grammatical forms of words were slightly different. Then a *shāhid* was also found for the same ḥadīth through a report by ʿAbd al-Raḥmān b. Waʿla from Ibn ʿAbbās that the Prophet, peace be on him, said "When a hide is tanned it becomes clean."[2]

أيما إهاب دبغ فقد طهر.

This is a *shāhid* in that the wording of this ḥadīth is different and so is its chain of *isnād*, but it is still a *shāhid* in the sense of conveying the same message as the original ḥadīth of Sufyān.

In the event where the search for confirmation is unsuccessful and nothing either identical or similar is found to support the ḥadīth at issue, then a note is usually added such as "Ibn Sīrīn alone has reported it from Abū Hurayra" (*tafarrada bihi Ibn Sīrīn ʿan Abī Hurayra*," or that "Ayyūb alone has narrated it from Ibn Sīrīn," so as to show that the ḥadīth is not supported by any other report. When this is the case, then two possibilities tend to arise: either that the message of the ḥadīth stands alone and it is divergent from what is narrated by other more reliable sources, in which case it will be labelled as odd/strange (*shādhdh*) and rejected, or that the basic message of the ḥadīth, which is narrated by a reliable person, is not in disharmony with a divergent ḥadīth that is narrated by someone more reliable, then it would be known as accepted (*Maqbūl*). The opposite of the odd/*shādhdh* ḥadīth that is consequently upheld is known as retained (*Maḥfūz*).

It may be noted here in passing that in the search for *mutābaʿa* or confirmation in order to locate a *mutābiʿ* or a *shāhid*, a weak or *Ḍaʿīf* ḥadīth, which is not, however, a forgery nor totally discredited, may be taken into account. This is because confirmation here does not provide original information on ḥadīth, but something to reiterate or endorse an existing ḥadīth. More information on this and on distinguishing a relatively weak from a totally weak and discredited ḥadīth is found in the context of impugnment and validation (*al-jarḥ wa'l-taʿdīl*), which is the subject of a previous chapter of this work. Attention would in that context be paid to points of strength or weakness in both the wording of the ḥadīth as well as its chain of transmission and a detailed enquiry may follow as a result.[3]

[19] Prerequisites of Authenticity

A *Ṣaḥīḥ* (sound/authentic) ḥadīth basically means that it consists of words that the Prophet Muḥammad has truly said, and if it describes an action of the Prophet or a tacit approval on his part, that he actually did what is reported.[1] To prove the authenticity of a ḥadīth is thus largely a question of establishing that it has been accurately and reliably transmitted and recorded.

The *ʿulamāʾ* of ḥadīth and jurisprudence have laid down a variety of conditions for the authentification of ḥadīth, which may be summarised as follows:

1. The ḥadīth must be accompanied by an *isnād* in which the transmitter has given the name of the authority from whom he learned the ḥadīth; and that authority must give the name of his source or teacher from whom he received the same ḥadīth, and so on until it reaches the Prophet. This chain of transmitters constitutes the *isnād*, or *sanad* (support), simply because the authenticity of the ḥadīth rests on it.

There is some disagreement as to determining the origins of *isnād*. Some have said that *isnād* first appeared toward the end of the first century hijra while others have suggested the middle of that century as the starting point of *isnād*. The rudiments of *isnād* might have even started during the lifetime of the Prophet, but in this period, the need for *isnād* was naturally not very stressing. The civil war (*fitna*) that followed the assassination of the Caliph ʿUthmān is often seen as the main cause that prompted the development of *isnād*. This would confirm that *isnād* began during the time of the Companions. In this regard Muḥammad Ibn Sīrīn (d. 110) is quoted to have said that "no one asked about *isnād* before, but when the *fitna* broke out, they would say, name to us your men."[2]

It is a familiar feature of *isnād* that the names and number of transmitters therein increase in every successive generation. Sometimes a ḥadīth transmitted by one Companion is then transmitted by a number of persons in the next generation, who may happen to be residing in different localities. This gave rise to the question of how the particular transmitter obtained the information from his immediate source. Was it through direct hearing and personal contact or in some other way? The *ʿulamāʾ* of ḥadīth have identified the various ways in which ḥadīth is obtained from the source and then transmitted and delivered to the next link in the *isnād*, a subject that I have reviewed in chapter two of this work.

The number of transmitters in the *isnād* largely depends on the intervening period of time between the demise of the Prophet and the date of the compilation of ḥadīth, which could be as few as one or two, or as many as half a dozen or more. Some *aḥādīth* were compiled fairly early. Hammām Ibn Munabbih, for instance, recorded his *Ṣaḥīfa* around the year 50 AH, and reported ḥadīth on the authority of Abū Hurayra who related it from the Prophet. Here the *isnād* consists of one link, a Companion. Imām Mālik (d. 179 AH) related in his *Al-Muwaṭṭaʾ aḥādīth* on the authority of his teacher, Nāfiʿ, who related, in turn, from ʿAbd Allāh Ibn ʿUmar, who was a Companion relating directly from the Prophet. In this *isnād*, there are two intervening links in the *isnād*. The best *isnād* of Abū Hurayra is that of Ibn Shihāb al-Zuhrī, from Saʿīd b. al-Musayyib from Abū Hurayra, which also consists of three links. Two other chains of transmitters that are recorded concerning Abū Hurayra, both described as *aṣaḥḥ al-asānīd* are: Abū al-Zanād, from al-Aʿraj, from Abū Hurayra, and the other is Yaḥyā Ibn Abī Kathīr from Abū Salama from Abū Hurayra. Having recorded this al-Ḥākim al-Nīsābūrī then commented that identifying a certain *isnād* as the best or most reliable *isnād,* or a Golden Chain (*silsilat al-dhahab*), etc., is largely a matter of personal assessment and *ijtihād* and the *ʿulamāʾ* have differed in their assessments. Then al-Nīsābūrī goes on to identify some of these himself. The best *isnād* concerning Abū Bakr al-Ṣiddīq is thus Ismāʿīl Ibn Abī Khālid, from Qays Ibn Abī Ḥāzim, from Abū Bakr, and the best *isnād* concerning ʿUmar Ibn al-Khaṭṭāb is al-Zuhrī, from Sālim, from his father ʿAbd Allāh b. ʿUmar, from ʿUmar. The best *isnād* concerning ʿĀ'isha is ʿUbayd Allāh b. ʿUmar from al-Qāsim Muḥammad b. Abū Bakr from ʿĀ'isha. Al-Nīsābūrī has also listed the best-known *isnāds* concerning the various regions including Makka, Yemen, Egypt, al-Shām (Syria) and Khurāsān. Imām Shāfiʿī has related ḥadīth on the authority of Imām Mālik, and Imām Aḥmad b. Ḥanbal related from Imām Shāfiʿī. In this chain, which is often referred to as the Golden Chain, all the links were not only renowned scholars and *ʿulamā'* but also students and contemporaries of one another. As will be noted, most of the *isnāds* that are known as *aṣaḥḥ al-asānīd* consist of two intervening links. Two other similarly short *isnāds* are those of Muḥammad b. Sīrīn – ʿUbayda b. ʿAmr – ʿAlī b. Abī Ṭālib; and Ibrāhīm al-Nakhaʿī – ʿAlqama b. Qays – ʿAbd Allāh b. Masʿūd. *Isnāds* which consist of only three links are known as *al-thulāthiyāt*, and these have sometimes been placed in separate collections. Ibn Ḥajar al-ʿAsqalānī has thus compiled a volume entitled *Thulāthiyāt al-Bukhārī*, and al-Safārīnī has compiled a similar collection concerning the *Musnad* of Ibn Ḥanbal bearing the title *Thulāthiyāt Aḥmad b. Ḥanbal. Isnād* that consists of fewer links, known as *al-isnād al-ʿālī*, or upper *isnād*, is considered more reliable as the possibility of error and doubt increases with every additional link in the chain of *isnād*. To search for a shorter *isnād* in preference to one that is lower is an act of merit and highly recommended.[3]

As noted above, from the viewpoint of its proximity or otherwise to the Prophet, *isnād* is divided into two types, namely elevated *isnād* (*al-isnād al-ʿālī*) which consists of fewer links and transmitters, and descended *isnād* (*al-isnād al-nāzil*) which involves a larger number of links and transmitters. The former travels vertically down from a Companion to a Follower, then to a Successor and so on, not necessarily one person at each level, but there is no horizontal movement within the same generation or *ṭabaqa*. The descended *isnād* on the other hand contains more than one person sometimes reporting horizontally from one another before it moves downwards.

Proximity in *isnād* that is desirable must at all times mean proximity to the Prophet through a clean *isnād* that is devoid of weakness (*isnād naẓīf ghayr ḍaʿīf*). "Closeness of *isnād* indicates closeness to the Prophet. To be close to the Prophet means closeness to God Most High".[4] The second best step to take along this route is to find the closest *isnād* to one of the recognised Imāms of ḥadīth such as Imāms Mālik, al-Thawrī and al-Shāfiʿī, whose knowledge and trustworthiness is beyond reproach. Next in this order comes the *Ṣaḥīḥayn*, that is al-Bukhārī and Muslim, and the effort to find an elevated *isnād* that involves short and direct transmission from one of the teachers of al-Bukhārī or Muslim that involves the least number of intervening links. This also applies to other recognised and reliable collections of ḥadīth. So also is the effort to cut down on the time lag between the transmitters. If the time lag between the two levels or *ṭabaqa* is say fifty years, then an alternative *isnād* that shows this lag at thirty or forty years should be preferred. Lastly, to ascertain an elevated *isnād*, one also needs to look into the method of transmission and delivery between the various levels, and direct hearing (*samāʿ*) is naturally preferable to other methods. This would mean that one has tried not only to reduce the number of intervening links but also the overall time lag from the beginning to the end of the *isnād*.[5] The chain of transmitters in most of the *aḥādīth* that are recorded in the Six Major Collections (*al-Ṣiḥāḥ al-Sitta*) consists, more or less, of four to six links, including the Companion who witnessed the ḥadīth.[6] Many prominent *ʿulamā'* have gone on record to say that since *isnād* is the conveyer and vehicle of the *Sunna* of the Prophet, it is a part of religion, and that diligent and conscientious rendering of *isnād* is an act of merit and a means to gaining the pleasure of God Most High.

The *isnād* must be continuous and uninterrupted. A ḥadīth with a broken *isnād* does not qualify as a *Ṣaḥīḥ* ḥadīth. If the missing link is a Companion who is supposed to have received the ḥadīth in the first place and his name is not mentioned, the ḥadīth is then called *mursal*. *Mursal* is defined as a "ḥadīth transmitted by a Follower (*tābiʿī*), who has not met with the Prophet and yet has quoted the ḥadīth directly from the Prophet".[7] If the missing link is below the level of the Companion, that is, somewhere in the middle of the chain of *isnād*, the ḥadīth is called *munqaṭiʿ* (severed or broken). However, if the missing link is lower down at the very end, it is called *muʿallaq* (suspended). And then if more than one link is missing in the *isnād*, it is called *muʿḍal*. All of these are grouped under *Ḍaʿīf* (weak) and *Mardūd* (rejected) categories and they are not supposed to be included in either *Ṣaḥīḥ al-Bukhārī* or in *Ṣaḥīḥ Muslim*. However, if the missing link in *Munqaṭi*ʿ becomes known through another *isnād* and the necessary clarification is provided, the *Munqaṭi*ʿ may be accepted and acting upon it would be valid.

One of al-Bukhārī's pre-conditions of a *Ṣaḥīḥ* ḥadīth, which distinguishes his collection from that of *Ṣaḥīḥ Muslim*, was that al-Bukhārī only recorded ḥadīth in which the transmitter of ḥadīth had met with his immediate source. This has actually meant two conditions, one of which was that the two were contemporary, and the other that they actually met one another. Imām Muslim has only insisted on the first but not on the second of these conditions. It is suggested, however, that Muslim's condition often, if not always, fulfils that of al-Bukhārī, simply because a reliable narrator will normally not report a ḥadīth without verifying it with his source and would not, as it were, report through hearsay evidence.

Imām Muslim has categorically said that "*Mursal* is the type of ḥadīth which is not a proof (*laysa bi-ḥujja*) neither in our view nor in the view of the learned scholars of ḥadīth".[8] The *Muwaṭṭa'* of Imām Mālik, however, contains numerous *mursal aḥādīth* and it is also found in other works of ḥadīth. There are exclusive collections of the *mursal* ḥadīth, such as the *Kitāb al-Marāsīl* by Abū Dāwūd (d. 275 H) which has isolated the *mursal* from other *aḥādīth*. Another work to mention is the *Marāsīl* of Ibn Abī Ḥātim al-Rāzī (d. 277 H) which focuses on the chains of transmission (*al-asānīd*) of the *mursal* variety.[9]

Most of the *mursal* that originate in Madīna is transmitted by Saʿīd b. al-Musayyib (d. 99 H) and these are considered to be generally sound as Ibn al-Musayyib was the son of a prominent Companion, Musayyib Ibn Ḥuzn, who accompanied the Prophet on many important occasions. Saʿīd b. al-Musayyib's credentials also stand out for the fact that he met the leading Companions including ʿUmar, ʿUthmān, ʿAlī, Ṭalḥa and Zubayr, and he was also one of the seven outstanding jurists and *Muftīs* of Madīna. The *ʿulamā'* of ḥadīth have considered the *Mursal* of Ibn al-Musayyib as the best of all *mursal* (*aṣaḥḥ al-marāsīl*).[10]

2. Every link in the chain of *isnād* must be known to be an upright person (*ʿadl*) at the time of reporting the ḥadīth. The minimum requirement of *ʿadāla* is that the person has not committed a major

sin/crime and has not persisted in committing minor ones, nor is he known for committing degrading profanities such as association with persons of ill-repute and indulgence in humiliating jokes. Although the *ʿulamāʾ* are unanimous on the requirement of *ʿadāla*, they have differed somewhat on what it precisely means. *ʿAdāla* is often associated with piety and decorum (*murūʾa*). An *ʿadl* person, according to al-Khaṭīb al-Baghdādī, is one "who is known for his performance of obligatory religious duties, observance of what is prohibited, diligence in pursuit of righteousness in his conduct and in dealings with others, discipline in speech, and truthfulness". Yet al-Baghdādī has also noted that *ʿadāla* is something more than a simple exhibition of piety, and can only be known by consistent information concerning the conduct and activities of a person.[11] The sum total of *ʿadāla* is reflected in the confidence that is inspired by it in a particular individual. It is generally held that no one can be free of all sin or of some neglect in the performance of duties. A competent person who is known to be assiduous in the fulfilment of obligations, avoids prohibitions, and has integrity of character in speech and in conduct is presumed to be *ʿadl*.[12]

The *ʿadāla* of a transmitter must be established by positive evidence. When there is no evidence available as to the *ʿadāla* of a transmitter, his report is unacceptable. Similarly, a report by an anonymous person (*riwāyat al-majhūl*) such as when the *isnād* reads in part that "a man reported such and such" is unacceptable. Ignorance of a person's character may be inclusive of both the apparent and hidden (*ẓāhir wa bāṭin*) aspects of personality, in which case his report is unacceptable and there is general consensus on this. A person may on the other hand be known for what is apparent in him but unknown for his inner qualities. This is known as *al-mastūr* (concealed) and there is disagreement as to whether ḥadīth transmitted by a *mastūr* is admissible. Some have expressed doubt but the Shāfiʿīs, Ḥanafīs and many others have held that report by a *mastūr* is acceptable as in the matter of ḥadīth transmission it is preferable to proceed from the position of optimism (*ḥusn al-ẓann*) on the reliability of the transmitter. It is also difficult to verify the inner *ʿadāla* of a person and knowledge of the manifest aspect of one's character is therefore sufficient to make one's report admissible. This concession is not extended, however, to witnesses in judicial disputes as it is possible for the judge to verify the inner aspects of *ʿadāla* as well as the apparent manifestations thereof.[13] Al-Khaṭīb al-Baghdādī has to this effect quoted a ḥadīth on the authority of ʿAlī b. Abī Ṭālib that "a Muslim who deals with people justly and speaks to them while avoiding telling a lie and fulfils promises he makes, has accomplished just character and *murū'a*; backbiting him is forbidden and fraternising him a requirement".[14]

Al-Khaṭīb al-Baghdādī has stated that a *majhūl* according to the traditionists (*ahl al-ḥadīth*) is one who is unknown to the *ʿulamā'* of ḥadīth and his report is not recognised by anyone other than a single narrator. Examples of this are ʿAmr dhū Murr, Jabbār al-Ṭā'ī, and Saʿīd b. Dhī Huddān from whom no one other than Abū Isḥāq al-Subayʿī has transmitted any ḥadīth. Similarly Jurayd b. Kulayb is a *majhūl* as no one other than Qatāda b. Diʿāma has transmitted any ḥadīth from him. Al-Baghdādī has added that ignorance (*jāhala*) is removed if two knowledgeable persons have transmitted ḥadīth from a particular narrator. This removes the *jahāla* but does not necessarily establish the *ʿadāla* of the narrator in question. For *ʿadāla* is established by means of explicit affirmation of uprightness and not merely by means of identification.[15]

The *ʿadāla* of a narrator may be established by various means, including validation (*taʿdīl*),[16] that is, when at least one upright and knowledgeable person, and according to some jurists, two such persons, confirm it, or when the transmitter is known to have been admitted as a witness in the court, or when a learned scholar has relied on his report. But there must be positive evidence that the scholar did not do so for any particular reason, fear or favour, that might compromise the reliability of his position. It has been further suggested that the scholar in question must be known to have accepted the reports only of upright narrators.[17]

The qualification of *ʿadāla* is established for all the Companions of the Prophet regardless of their juristic or political views. This conclusion is based on the Qur'ān, which declares in a reference to the Companions that "God is well-pleased with them, as they are pleased with Him" (al-Tawba, 9:100). This is supported by a number of *aḥādīth* in which the Prophet has also spoken highly of his Companions, both in general terms and also by reference to particular individuals among them.[18]

A person's reputation for being upright and trustworthy also serves as a proof of his *ʿadāla*. According to some *ʿulamāʾ* of ḥadīth, such a reputation is even more credible than confirmation by one or two individuals. With regard to certain figures, such as Imām Mālik, Imām Aḥmad b. Ḥanbal, al-Awzāʿī, Sufyān al-Thawrī, Sufyān b. ʿUyayna, al-Layth b. Saʿd, ʿAlī b. al-Madīnī, Yaḥyā b. Maʿīn, etc., their reputation for *ʿadāla* is proof above the technicalities of *taʿdīl*. It is reported that Imām Aḥmad b. Ḥanbal was once asked concerning Isḥāq b. Rahawayh and his response was "The like of Isḥāq – you ask me about him?" A similar response has been recorded from Yaḥyā b. Maʿīn who was asked concerning Abū ʿUbayd al-Qāsim b. Sallām and he replied "you ask me concerning Abū ʿUbayd?" A person's reputation for corruption is also admitted as evidence to impugn his *ʿadāla*. In the event of conflicting information concerning the *ʿadāla* of a narrator, the majority maintain that he or she is disqualified.[19]

The requirement of *ʿadāla* applies to all varieties of ḥadīth, especially the solitary or *Āḥād* ḥadīth, which is reported usually by one or a few individuals. Only with regard to the *Mutawātir* ḥadīth which is proven by the report of a large number of individuals, the requirement of *ʿadāla* is not emphasised as much as in the case of *Āḥād* ḥadīth.

To ascertain the reliability of narrators of ḥadīth, the *ʿulamāʾ* of ḥadīth have compiled biographical data, on a massive scale, of the transmitters of ḥadīth, giving the place and date of the person's birth, his family connections, education and names of his teachers and students, his profession and financial condition and the date of his death. The biographical literature, especially relating to the *tārīkh al-ruwāt* and *ṭabaqāt* contains useful information and assessment of the degree of reliability of narrators, and a special terminology has been developed for this purpose, as I have already elaborated in chapter five.[20]

Murūʾa is a difficult word to translate but generally it implies decorum, integrity and qualities that are associated with a 'gentleman'. In the textbooks on ḥadīth *murūʾa* often features side by side with piety in the definition of *ʿadāla*. In the usage of Arabs, *murūʾa* is associated with manliness and courage as well as avoidance of demeaning behaviour that compromises personal honour and is socially humiliating. The works of *fiqh* and ḥadīth also mention avoidance of profanities such as urinating in a standing posture (one may now add, perhaps in a wrong place), stealing a slice of bread, association with lowly characters, even eating in public thoroughfares and walking bare headed. The correct position on this, however, refers such matters to the prevailing custom. Many of the things that were associated with *murū'a* in the past have evidently changed and current custom seems to have attributed certain other things with social decorum and *murū'a*. One who throws away litter carelessly in public places, or wears trendy clothes that are not appropriate with one's standing or circumstance, or one who spoils library books that one borrows, and the like, may now be seen to be more relevant to integrity and *murū'a*. A ḥadīth transmitter must possess *murū'a* as a part of his probity and *ʿadāla* but what *murū'a* actually means is often determined by reference to the prevailing custom.

There is a difference between the *ʿadāla* of a witness and of a ḥadīth transmitter in that some of the requirements in the former do not apply to the latter. The question of gender, whether male or female, that is relevant to testimony is not relevant to the narration of ḥadīth, nor is slavery of any relevance nowadays. A blind person is not qualified to be a witness but he or she is qualified to be a narrator of ḥadīth. Even a person who is punished for slander (*qadhf*) and is consequently disqualified to be a witness is still held to be qualified to transmit ḥadīth, according to the majority, excepting the Ḥanafīs, after repentance and show of remorse over his past behaviour.[21]

The *ʿadāla* of a person is, in principle, deemed to be monolithic and unchangeable, according to the majority, and it is, as such, not amenable to increase or decrease. It is also deemed to be indivisible in that a person either possesses it or not, and cannot therefore be said to be partially upright. *ʿAdāla* in this sense resembles the faith (*īmān*) which is also said to be monolithic and unchangeable.[22] The correct view, however, is that *ʿadāla*, like faith and retentiveness of memory, is capable of increase and decrease, although the pace and frequency of change therein is not expected to be either rapid or frequent. Minor changes in experience and outlook do not necessarily affect the attribute of *ʿadāla*, yet a succession of such changes or drastic turn of events may well lead to a significant change in the reliability and *ʿadāla* of a person. Yet for purposes of ḥadīth narration, it is the undiminished *ʿadāla* which qualifies a person to narrate ḥadīth, and not any reduced or compromised version thereof. The *ʿulamāʾ* of ḥadīth have thus maintained that a narrator of ḥadīth must be clear both of major defects of character as well as persistently recurring minor ones that compromise one's integrity and *murūʾa*.[23]

As for the narration of one who is charged with pernicious innovation (*bidʿa*) and propagation of dubious doctrines that are contrary to valid precedent, the *ʿulamāʾ* have held two different views. Many leading *ʿulamāʾ*, including Imām Mālik, have held that narration of an agent of *bidʿa* (*mubtadiʿ*) is unacceptable absolutely regardless of the nature of his *bidʿa*. The second view on this is one of stipulated acceptance, as it reflects on the nature of the *bidʿa*. This may either be such that invokes infidelity (*kufr*) on its propagator, in which case he is disqualified and there is general agreement on this – and it was on this basis that the heretics known as al-Zanādiqa were disqualified. A mere accusation of *kufr* or *bidʿa* amounting to *kufr* by one's opponents is not enough to disqualify the *mubtadiʿ*, as many opposing factions in history have actually accused one another of *bidʿa* and *kufr*. One must, in other words, determine the nature of *bidʿa* amounting to *kufr* on the basis of objective evidence. The *bidʿa* that disqualifies a narrator of ḥadīth must be such that denies an essential aspect of Islam and its *Sharīʿa* or a principle that is established as an essential part of the religion – such as denial of one of the five pillars of the faith, or denial of an attribute of God Most High that is clearly conveyed in the Qur'ān.[24] In the case of *bidʿa* of a lower order, if the *mubtadiʿ* has gone so far as to advocate a lie in order to promote his doctrine, and has invited others to embrace it, he is disqualified. Sufyān al-Thawrī is quoted as having said that he would admit the testimony of the agents of caprice (*ahl al-ahwāʾ*) when they are upright *ʿudūl* in other respects, that is, in matters other than their own doctrines. Imām Shāfiʿī has similarly stated that a simple advocacy of *hawā* and *bidʿa* is not a disqualification unless it is known that the *mubtadiʿ* has advocated a lie. Ibn al-Ṣalāḥ has noted an additional requirement which is that ḥadīth reported by a *mubtadiʿ*, who is not inviting others to his *bidʿa*, must also not endorse the *bidʿa* he has advocated. If it is relevant to the *bidʿa* in question, it is unacceptable.[25]

It is to be noted, however, that the *ʿulamāʾ* of ḥadīth have sometimes qualified as reliable persons those who are accused of deviation and *bidʿa*, yet truthful enough to be narrators of ḥadīth. Abū Dāwūd al-Sijistānī went on record to say that among the deviationists, no other faction has been more truthful in the narration of ḥadīth than the Kharijites. It is further noted that al-Bukhārī has relied on the narration of one ʿImrān b. Hattān who was a confirmed deviationist, and also that Yaḥyā b. Maʿīn and Aḥmad b. Ḥanbal validated one ʿAbd al-Ḥamīd b. ʿAbd al-Raḥmān al-Himmānī (d. 202) who was an active propagator of *irjāʾ* and *murji'a* (the belief that a grave sin does not necessarily amount to *kufr* and that the hope (*irjāʾ*) for forgiveness from God still remains valid). It is noted in this context that these great Imāms validated the ḥadīth of the individuals concerned on the basis of the personal knowledge of their character, which is the correct approach, unlike the approach that focuses on the narrator's association with a sect, faction or group often in disregard of the person's character as such. Al-Baghdādī has further noted that the Companions and the Followers have accepted report and testimony of the Kharijites especially those whom they considered to be trustworthy and pious. They have accepted narration, for example, from ʿImrān b. Haṭṭān who was a Kharijite and from Ibn Abī Najīḥ who was a Muʿtazilī and from numerous other individuals who were associated with Qadariyya, the Shiʿites and Murji'a. It thus became well-known and consensus is established to the effect that personal character rather than association with a sect or faction is the determining factor of a person's probity and *ʿadāla*.[26]

The majority of the *ʿulamāʾ* of ḥadīth have held that a *mubtadiʿ* is not disqualified and ḥadīth may be transmitted from him, if he is clear of *kufr* and knowingly advocating a lie, whether or not he is actively engaged in propagating *bidʿa*. Some have stipulated that he is qualified only if he has restrained himself from actively inviting others to his *bidʿa*.[27] One who has lied in his dealings with the people but is known to have subsequently repented and corrected himself is not disqualified, but he is disqualified regardless of repentance, if he has attributed a lie to the Prophet.[28]

3. None of the narrators in the *isnād* is known to be implicated in forgery, sectarian, political and theological disputes. A ḥadīth

is therefore suspect if it smacks of scholastic fanaticism or when it advocates a particular dogma and doctrine. The report for example that "There will be a man in my *umma* by the name of Muḥammad b. Idrīs (al-Shāfiʿī) who will be more harmful to my *umma* than the devil (*iblīs*), and there will be a man in my *umma* by the name Abū Ḥanīfa who will be the shining light (*sirāj*) of my community". There are numerous similar reports concerning ʿAlī and Muʿāwiya, one of which simply has it "When you see Muʿāwiya on my pulpit, kill him". In yet another report it is stated "Whoever says that the Qur'ān is the created speech of God becomes an infidel and his wife stands divorced from him as of that moment". All of these evidently indulge in corruption and crude fanaticism, and the *ʿulamā'* have isolated them in their works under the general heading of *Mawḍuʿāt* (forgeries).[29]

4. As noted above, the narrator of ḥadīth must be a contemporary of the teacher on whose authority he relates the ḥadīth. This means that he must have been born before the death of his teacher by a period long enough to enable him to acquire the knowledge of ḥadīth. Al-Bukhārī has further stipulated that there must be evidence to show that the narrator has met with his immediate source. It is consequently taken as a sign of forgery when a narrator reports a ḥadīth directly from his teacher and there is evidence to show that the former was born long after the latter's demise, or that the two never entered the same locality.[30] Both the teacher and disciple must be fit for delivery and reception of ḥadīth and neither is too forgetful, confused or disabled nor suffers from defects that render his *ʿadāla* and retentiveness questionable.

The *ʿulamā'* on the whole do not require evidence of actual encounter between teacher and disciple and take it for granted that words such as "I heard – *samiʿtu*", or "so and so spoke to me – *ḥaddathanī*" actually mean that the two have met. They are thus content with the possibility of a meeting and do not require actual proof. This is the position of Imām Muslim. But al-Bukhārī required evidence of an actual meeting, where, when and for how long, etc., was the Shaykh teaching in a *madrasa* or a mosque when the disciple met him – or any other such information to show actual encounter between the narrator and his immediate source.

5. The narrator of ḥadīth must possess a retentive memory so that his report can be trusted. If he is known for committing frequent errors and inconsistencies, his report would be unacceptable. The faculty of retention (*ḍabṭ*) is the ability of a person to listen to an utterance, to comprehend its meaning as it was originally intended, and then to retain it and take all necessary precautions to safeguard its accuracy. In cases of doubt in the retentiveness of a transmitter, if his report can be confirmed by comparison to the recognised works of authority on the subject, or by the action of his predecessors, it may be accepted. If someone has suffered weakness of memory due to illness or old age, only ḥadīth that he related prior to that event can be accepted. But in the absence of any verification, reports by persons who are totally obscure and whose retentiveness cannot be established are unacceptable. The retentive faculty of a narrator is established through his work or when a number of upright and trustworthy transmitters are known to have relied on his reports and have used it as evidence/reference in their own work.[31]

A narrator's forgetfulness does not necessarily invalidate his ḥadīth according to the majority of jurists and ḥadīth experts, except for the Ḥanafīs who maintain that ḥadīth is invalidated if the narrator cannot confirm nor recognise what he had narrated. Thus the Ḥanafīs rejected the ḥadīth of Sulaymān b. Mūsā from al-Zuhrī from ʿUrwa from ʿĀ'isha from the Prophet that "When a woman is married without the permission of her guardian, her marriage is null and void."

This is because of what Ibn Jurayj had said that "I met with al-Zuhrī and asked him about this ḥadīth but he did not recognise it".[32] Another example of this is the ḥadīth of Rabīʿat al-Ra'y, from Ṣuhayl b. Abī Ṣāliḥ from his father from Abū Hurayra that "the Prophet, peace be on him, adjudicated by one witness plus an oath." ʿAbd al-ʿAzīz b. Muḥammad al-Darāwardī then said "I met Ṣuhayl and asked him about it but he did not recognise the ḥadīth."[33]

Many of the leading scholars of ḥadīth are known to have forgotten what has been heard from them, but this should not invalidate the original report on account merely of forgetfulness. Humans are prone to forgetfulness and it is due partly to this that many, including Imām Shāfiʿī, have warned against narration from the living.

Retention with the aid of writing is acceptable but it is recommended that the writing is legible and does not omit the dots over or under the letters nor is it turned into abbreviation and sign language that no one other than the writer is able to read. Words and phrases should also not be split between the ending of one and the beginning of a new line so as to prevent distortion.[34]

One who is known for laxity (*al-tasāhul*) in the hearing of ḥadīth, such as falling asleep at meetings, or is willing to accept hearsay in ḥadīth, or one who makes frequent errors, fail to qualify as retentive of ḥadīth and their narration is therefore not accepted. Similarly, when the narrator is known to have made an error and this becomes clear to him yet he stubbornly persists in it, his narration is disqualified.

When the requirements of *ʿadāla* and *ḍabṭ* of the narrator are ascertained and established his report becomes acceptable and the possibility of error and doubt in it is considered remote and insignificant, although not impossible. The report is considered to provide a valid basis for action and judgement. *ʿAdāla* and *ḍabṭ* qualify the narrator to transmit ḥadīth that is then relied upon, but the ḥadīth itself must naturally be free of obvious and hidden defects and outlandish contents, or *shudhūdh*. The *isnād* of ḥadīth must also be free of defects such as broken links, suspension (*taʿlīq*), and ambiguities that are associated with the *isnād*.[35]

6. With regard to the text *matn* of ḥadīth it is noted that it must be in the familiar eloquent and dignified style of the prophetic language. If it is a report of an action of the Prophet, it should be such that can be expected of him. The presence of obscene and objectionable words, and statements that are particularly crude, ridiculous and unbecoming of the Prophet are usually taken as signs of forgery in ḥadīth and rejected. But even more important than words are the meaning and purpose, which is what the ḥadīth critics have pointed out. A certain poverty of style in the standards of expression is not given too much weight as *aḥādīth* are often in the words of the narrators themselves. But if the meaning is corrupt to an extent that it cannot bear harmony with the standards of prophetic speech, it would be taken as a sign of forgery.[36] The meaning is generally held to be corrupt when it engages in patently inreasonable assertions. Corruption of purpose and meaning

is also caused by unwarranted expatiation in the attributes of God Most High, His illustrious self, or negation of those of His attributes which are clearly established in the Qur'ān. Thus the so-called ḥadīth that "I saw my Lord in ʿArafāt riding a red camel," and the so-called ḥadīth of the Prophet that "I saw my Lord on the Night of Ascension in the heaven with a curtain of fire between us but I saw everything even the crown studded with pearls that He was wearing". Corruption in purpose is also noted when a so-called ḥadīth violates the basic positions of *Sharīʿa* such as by declaring permissible the lives and properties of people and validating attack on their personal dignity. The Prophet can similarly not be expected to take assertive positions and speak either for or against sectarian movements and factions that never existed in his lifetime nor was the subject of any relevance to his mission and purpose. There is so much forgery on this and similar other themes that are patently corrupt, partisan and incredible.

7. The text and message of the ḥadīth must be consistent with the Qur'ān. Should there be a clear case of conflict in such a way that no reasonable compromise and interpretation can remove it, the ḥadīth is rejected. The so-called ḥadīth, for example, that "The offspring of adultery (*zinā*) shall not enter Paradise down to seven generations" was rejected by the Prophet's widow, ʿĀ'isha, as it violated the clear text of the Qur'ān that "No soul shall carry the burden of another soul" (al-Anʿām, 6:164).

وَلَا تَزِرُ وَازِرَةٌ وِزْرَ أُخْرَىٰ

Similarly the report that "whoever begets a child and names him Muḥammad, he and his offspring shall go to Paradise" is clearly in conflict with the Qur'ānic principle that "Anyone who has done an atom's weight of good shall see its reward, and anyone who has done an atom's weight of evil shall see its recompense" (al-Zalzala, 99:7-8).

A clear conflict with the ruling of *ijmāʿ* is also taken as a sign of forgery in ḥadīth. The so-called ḥadīth, for example, that "One who performs the obligatory prayer (*ṣalāh*) on the last Friday of Ramaḍān would have made up for all the prayers he has missed throughout his life for seventy years" – is contrary to the ruling of *ijmāʿ* that no other form of worship replaces a *ṣalāh* that has been missed out. And lastly, when a ḥadīth conflicts with another well-known ḥadīth that is proven by a superior *isnād*, it is seen as a sign of forgery. This last instance of conflict is a wider subject that the *ʿulamā'* have looked into under the general heading of *Mukhtalif al-Ḥadīth* (also known as *Mushkil al-Ḥadīth*) which is the subject of a separate chapter in this work. This branch of the ḥadīth studies is concerned mainly with discrepancies and conflicts which are, however, reconcilable by recourse to the normal rules of interpretation, and it is in this respect where *Mukhtalif al-Ḥadīth* differs from the study of abrogation in ḥadīth. This latter branch of the ḥadīth studies, known as *al-Nāsikh wa'l-Mansūkh fi'l-Ḥadīth*, is on the other hand concerned exclusively with conflicts that cannot be reconciled on grounds of interpretation. *Mukhtalif al-Ḥadīth* was the subject of a particular work bearing the title *Ikhtilāf al-Ḥadīth* by Imām al-Shāfiʿī, who was the first to discuss this subject in the seventh volume of his *Kitāb al-Umm*. This was followed by *Ta'wīl Mukhtalif al-Ḥadīth* of Ibn Qutayba al-Daynūrī (213-267) and many other contributions ever since. The branch of ḥadīth studies which is concerned with abrogation in ḥadīth stipulate a number of requirements that must be met before abrogation can occur, but this too is the subject of a separate chapter of this book.[37]

8. Ḥadīth which is not historical and fails to qualify the test of historical evidence that was known during the time of the Prophet is rejected. The ḥadīth, for example, reported by Saʿd b. Muʿādh and Muʿāwiya b. Abū Sufyān that "the Prophet levied the *jizya* (poll tax) on the Jews of Khaybar and relieved them of hardship" is discredited on account of the historical fact that *jizya* was not known at that time, that is, the year of Khaybar, and that the Qur'ānic ruling on *jizya* was only revealed later in the year of Tabūk, and that Saʿd b. Muʿādh had also died before the year of Khaybar. In yet another report, Anas b. Mālik has stated that "I entered the public bath and saw the Messenger of God wearing a wrapper and said: O Anas, I have forbidden entry to a public bath without a wrapper". The facts of history show on the other hand, that the Prophet did not enter a public bath as they did not exist in Madīna at the time.[38] Some ḥadīth collections have also recorded

ḥadīth concerning the bygone Prophets, attributing exaggerated body size and height, such as sixty metres, to them, which is patently unhistorical and has never been proven by factual evidence.

9. The text must be in agreement with reason. If it is illogical in purpose and meaning, it is suspected of being a forgery. Anything that is totally superstitious, or in clear conflict with accepted norms, or contradictory in itself or totally incredible *vis-à-vis* the clear principles of the *nuṣūṣ* would come under suspicion. The so-called ḥadīth, for example, that "the ark of Noah circumambulated the Kaʿba seven times and then prayed two units of prayer at the end," is evidently irrational and therefore rejected. The report similarly that "God Most High revived from the dead the parents of the Prophet Muḥammad and they embraced Islam in his presence" is evidently unreasonable and contrary to familiar experience. Noted under this category are also ḥadīth which contain detailed prophecies of future events with their dates and places of occurrence.[39]

When the ḥadīth in question promises a disproportionate reward or warns of an exceedingly severe punishment for a trivial act, it would be suspected of being a forgery. Numerous reports are on record of spurious ḥadīth under the general heading of *al-targhīb wa'l-tarhīb* (encouragement and warning) that promises, for instance, permanent abode in Paradise for recitation of a verse of the Qur'ān, or for a simple act which may be *mandūb* (recommendable), or even omitting something in the nature of a *makrūh* (reprehensible).[40]

10. The narrator must not be totally unknown (*majhūl*). To eliminate obscurity and ignorance, the *ʿulamā'* of ḥadīth stipulate that at least two upright persons should have transmitted ḥadīth from the person in question. Only the Companions are exempted from this requirement. Examples of some of the *majhūl* narrators that are given include such names as ʿAmr dhū Murr, Jabbār al-Ṭāʿī and Saʿīd b. Huddān from whom no one else but Abū Isḥāq al-Subayʿī has narrated, which means that they are obscure.

Narration by two upright persons is, however, good enough to remove ignorance as to the identity of the person (*jahālat al-ʿayn*) but it does not establish uprightness (*ʿadāla*) of the narrator in question. Ḥadīth is not acceptable when it is transmitted by an unknown person.[41]

Majhūl (obscure) is sub-divided into three types, one of which is of unknown identity (*majhūl al-ʿayn*). This type of obscurity is removed by narration from the person concerned by two upright persons. If only one person has narrated ḥadīth from him, the obscurity still remains. *Majhūl* to the *ʿulamā'* of ḥadīth is one from whom no more than one person has reported. Al-Bukhārī and Muslim are noted in this connection for having narrated ḥadīth from Mirdās al-Aslamī, and Rabiʿa b. Kaʿb respectively. These are considered to be *majhūl* as only one person, namely Qays b. Ḥāzim has narrated ḥadīth from the former, and Abū Salama ʿAbd al-Raḥmān b. ʿAwf from the latter. Ibn al-Ṣalāḥ who initially made this observation was, however, refuted later by al-Nawawī who said that both al-Aslamī and Ibn Kaʿb were Companions and they cannot therefore be classified under the category of *majhūl*.[42]

The second type of *majhūl* is one who is not known for his uprightness (*ʿadāla*), and this also occurs in two types, namely one whose *ʿadāla* is unknown overtly and covertly (*min ḥayth al-ẓāhir wa'l-bāṭin*), and one who appears to be upright but no insight into his character is available. *ʿAdāla* in principle requires positive evidence on both of these, but questions tend to arise if a person is only known to be upright in appearance but his true character remains hidden (*mastūr*). There is a difference of opinion as to the admissibility of ḥadīth from the *mastūr*. Many consider it to be admissible as it is often difficult to verify the inner quality of *ʿadāla* in the individual narrators of ḥadīth. Ibn al-Ṣalāḥ has made the observation that works of authority on ḥadīth often accept and record ḥadīth from persons whose inner aspect of *ʿadāla* remains unknown.[43]

11. The narrator must also know the conditions of his *shaykh*/ teacher and ascertain his knowledge and character and only then should transmit ḥadīth from him. It will be noted in this connection that there is usually a process of selection involved in the teacher-disciple relationship. The *shaykh* of ḥadīth, like the teacher in most

other branches of knowledge in the traditional system, selected his disciple on the basis of the latter's ability and prospects. The disciple too tended to select as to whom he wanted to study with and acquire the knowledge of ḥadīth from; and he consequently investigated the ability and reputation of the individual teachers of ḥadīth. Hence the *shaykh* and his disciple are expected to have known one another and may well have developed a relationship that is taken into account in the context of ḥadīth transmission. The ḥadīth scholars have looked into this from the perspective of the classes of narrators, or *ṭabaqāt*, which enabled them to assess the extent of the disciple's closeness with his *shaykh*. The classes or *ṭabaqāt* that may be reviewed from this perspective are as follows:

a. The first class, or *ṭabaqa*, of narrators comprise those who have maintained a close association and companionship with their *shaykh*. These are disciples who have kept the company of their *shaykh* in his circles of teaching and during his journeys and both the *shaykh* and disciple are upright and retentive and combine absolutely the best qualities that ḥadīth narrators could be expected to have. An example of this would be the companionship of Nāfiʿ with ʿAbd Allāh b. ʿUmar and that of Imām Mālik with al-Zuhrī.

b. The second class, or *ṭabaqa*, of narrators comprise those who have kept regular but intermittent company of their *shaykh* that does not altogether amount to discontinuity of contact. They do not maintain the same level of companionship and association with their *shaykh* as those who belong to the first class above. Yet they know their teachers well enough to remain clear of doubt with regard to ḥadīth transmission from them. Examples of this *ṭabaqa* may be seen in the relationship of ʿAṭā' b. Abī Rabāḥ with ʿAbd Allāh Ibn ʿAbbās, and that of Abū ʿAmr al-Awzāʿī with al-Zuhrī.

c. The third class of narrators apply to those who have kept as close an association with their teachers as those of the first *ṭabaqa* above but who have not escaped doubt over their character and retentiveness, and their transmission of ḥadīth falls between acceptable and rejectable. Examples of this *ṭabaqa* are said to include the companionship with al-Zuhrī of Jaʿfar b. Burqān and ʿAbd Allāh b. Ḥafṣ al-ʿUmarī.

d. The fourth class includes those whose companionship with the *shaykh* is slight and they have also not escaped doubt over the likelihood of impugnment (*al-jarḥ*). An example of this would be Isḥāq b. Yaḥyā al-Kalbī in relationship to al-Zuhrī.

e. The fifth class comprises the weak and the obscure (*al-ḍuʿafā' wa'l-majhūlin*) who occasionally attended the teaching sessions of their teacher but with little regularity and commitment. The ḥadīth that they transmit from their *shaykh* is on the whole unacceptable and it would be advisable for them not to have attempted it in the first place. Examples of this class in relationship to al-Zuhrī would be ʿAbd al-Quddūs b. Ḥabīb al-Dimashqī and Muḥammad b. Saʿīd al-Maslūb.

With reference to the bulk of the *aḥādīth* that al-Bukhārī and Muslim have recorded, it is noted that they qualified the first two of these five classes and only occasionally qualified narrators that fell in the third, but they disqualified the fourth and fifth classes altogether. This is understood from the familiar expression "in accordance with the condition of the two *shaykhs* – *ʿalā sharṭ al-shaykhayn*."

It may be noted, however, that some ḥadīth transmitters tended to have a weak association with a particular *shaykh* of ḥadīth but they qualified better with another *shaykh*. This is taken into account by al-Bukhārī who has disqualified the reports of one Hāshīm from al-Zuhrī but has accepted his narration from persons other than al-Zuhrī.[44]

12. Both the text and *isnād* of the ḥadīth must be clear of subtle and hidden defects, or *ʿilla,* and also clear of concealment, *tadlīs*.[45] These two subjects, namely *ʿilal al-ḥadīth* and *tadlīs* have been separately addressed and need not therefore be elaborated here.

[20] Conclusion and Reform Proposals

IN my introductory remarks I commented on the strengths and weaknesses of methodology and methodological guidelines that the *ʿulamāʾ* have developed for the authentication of ḥadīth. I then expounded in the ensuing chapters the salient features of ḥadīth studies, methods of ḥadīth criticism, subtle defects in ḥadīth and prerequisites of authenticity, all of which are evidently designed to ensure the purity of both the *isnād* and text of the ḥadīth. What I have presented in this book in reality provides only a bird's-eye view account of the painstaking efforts that the *ʿulamāʾ* and scholars of ḥadīth have taken to verify the authenticity of the ḥadīth of the Prophet. The sheer wealth of the scholarly works on ḥadīth methodology and sciences and the effort that has gone into the compilation of countless numbers of valuable works on ḥadīth spanning the entire history of Islamic scholarship cannot fail to impress. The *ʿulamāʾ* have clearly seen the ḥadīth studies as an arena where they combined meticulous scholarship with a sacred purpose and the results they have achieved are clearly remarkable. The purpose was to render the ḥadīth as accurately as possible. The ḥadīth transmitters, compilers and critics "tried to reproduce exactly what they had learnt from their teachers ... They reproduced each word and letter, including the diacritical marks and the vowel points, without deviating in the least from what they had received." Zubayr Siddiqi who made these observations went on to quote al-Khaṭīb al-Baghdādī to the effect that the Companion ʿAbd Allāh b. ʿUmar did not like to change the order of words in a sentence even when it did not affect the meaning of the ḥadīth in the least. Mālik

b. Anas tried to be exact about each and every letter. Ibn Sīrīn did not approve of making corrections in a ḥadīth even in those cases in which there was a clear mistake by the reporter.[1] The entire corpus of *ʿulūm al-ḥadīth* was geared toward the same purpose. Elaborate methods for cross-examination, double-checking, follow-up and scrutiny of the *isnād* and text were developed and employed in order to ensure accuracy in the reception, transmission, and documentation of ḥadīth. The *ʿulamāʾ* of ḥadīth may be said to have explored and exploited every possible tool and method that could serve and facilitate the integrity and reliability of ḥadīth. Is there any further room for fresh enquiry and research into the methodology of ḥadīth? This is a question that comes to mind, and my peremptory answer to it is basically negative. There is clearly little scope for any new methodology or research that would add anything substantial and useful to the work that has already been done by people who were better positioned and qualified for what they attempted and achieved. But is there scope for new measures that the present generation of Muslims could take to enhance the reliability of ḥadīth? I believe that we do have a rich and resourceful methodology for the authentication of ḥadīth which goes a long way to achieve its desired purpose. Yet some weakness is noted with regard to its implementation especially in the early stages of the compilation of ḥadīth. The methodology of *uṣūl al-ḥadīth*, and even that of *uṣūl al-fiqh*, were developed mainly in the third century hijra, and even as late as in the days of Imām Aḥmad b. Ḥanbal (d. 241 H), questions have been raised whether he had in fact known the methodology of *uṣūl al-ḥadīth* in its final form. As indicated in the text of this work, the methodology of ḥadīth criticism originated in the work of al-Shāfiʿī but ḥadīth collection had started much earlier. By the time of al-Bukhārī, the broad outline of that methodology was admittedly in place but it was still at its early stages of development. *Uṣūl al-ḥadīth* saw its efflorescence in the works of al-Baghdādī, Ibn al-Ṣalāḥ, al-Nawawī and al-ʿAsqalānī in the course of the subsequent centuries after al-Bukhārī. It may therefore not come as a surprise to note that both *al-Bukhārī* and *Muslim* contain ḥadīth that were subsequently identified as weak (*Ḍaʿīf*) or which did not fulfil some of the prerequisites of authenticity for a *Ṣaḥīḥ* ḥadīth.[2]

One tends to notice a certain degree of imbalance in the kind of attention that ḥadīth scholars have paid to matters of transmission and *isnād* as opposed to the text or *matn* of ḥadīth. Ḥadīth experts clearly paid greater attention to the former at the expense, to some extent, of the latter. The accuracy of the ḥadīth text and its harmony or otherwise with the Qur'ān and principles of Islam that had a wider basis of support in the ḥadīth itself did not receive a commensurate level of attention from the ḥadīth scholars. In our discussion of *mukhtalif al-ḥadīth*, which is the subject of an earlier chapter, some examples are given of ḥadīth, as some are also given in the following pages, which appear in *al-Bukhārī* and *Muslim*, *Abū Dāwūd* and others. A careful reading of the text, in these examples, reveals weaknesses so much so that the ḥadīth in question could hardly be accepted as an authentic saying of the Prophet Muḥammad. One would have expected in such instances that the compiler of such controversial materials would have rejected them and refused to document them in the category of *Ṣaḥīḥ* ḥadīth, or even of any ḥadīth for that matter. Weak and even fabricated ḥadīth are found in the ḥadīth collections, and although not extensive, the presence even on a limited scale, of such controversial ḥadīth tends to undermine confidence in the veracity of the larger corpus of ḥadīth.

To say that the methodology of *uṣūl al-ḥadīth* has not been accurately observed is shown in works such as that of Abū'l-Faraj Ibn al-Jawzī (d. 597 H) entitled *Al-Mawḍuʿāt* who identified one ḥadīth in *al-Bukhārī*, two in *Muslim*, thirty-three in the *Musnad* of Imām Aḥmad b. Ḥanbal, seven in the *Sunan Abū Dāwūd,* ten in *Sunan al-Nasā'ī*, thirty in *Sunan Ibn Māja*, thirty in *Jāmiʿ al-Tirmidhī*, and sixty in *Mustadrak* of al-Hākim as forged *aḥādīth*. Musṭafā al-Sibāʿī who recorded this information added that subsequent scholars especially Ibn Ḥajar al-ʿAsqalānī (d. 852 H) and Jalāl al-Dīn al-Suyūṭī (d. 911 H) followed-up Ibn al-Jawzī's work and although they disagreed with it in some respects, they nevertheless endorsed most of Ibn al-Jawzī's conclusions on the presence of weak ḥadīth in the standard collections.[3]

Commenting on the weaknesses of al-Bukhārī, Mustafa Azami had this to say:

> Many scholars criticised Bukhārī's work. The criticism concerns about 80 narrators and some 110 *aḥādīth*. The criticism showed that though these *aḥādīth* were not mistaken or false, yet they did not measure up to the high standard which was set by Bukhārī himself.[4]

Muhammad Zubayr Siddiqi has similarly stated that "In spite of the great care of their compilers, there are still some weak or forged traditions in the standard collections, which have been discussed and criticised by their commentators".[5] Siddiqi then commented that "most of the traditions concerning the coming of Dajjāl and the Mahdī, and those concerning Khiḍr in the various collections of ḥadīth are declared by the traditionists as forged ones, and are included in the works on *Mawḍūʿāt*".[6] Siddiqi then went on to give the following examples of questionable *aḥādīth* from al-Bukhārī:

1. The ḥadīth recorded by al-Bukhārī that the Qur'ānic *āya* (al-Ḥujurāt, 49:9): "And if two parties of the believers fight one another, then make peace between them..." refers to ʿAbd Allāh b. Ubayy and that of the other Companions of the Prophet – has been criticised in that the *āya* cannot carry this explanation. This is because ʿAbd Allāh b. Ubayy had not accepted Islam even outwardly at the time when this *āya* was revealed.
2. The ḥadīth recorded with slightly different versions, one of which appears in al-Bukhārī has it that if Ibrāhīm, the Prophet's son, had lived, he would have been a Prophet. This so-called ḥadīth has been severely criticised by many and Yaḥyā Ibn ʿAlī al-Shawkānī has isolated it as a forged one.[7]
3. The ḥadīth reported by al-Bukhārī that Adam's height was sixty yards, has been criticised by Ibn Ḥajar on the basis of the measurement of the homes and dwellings of some of the ancient nations, which do not show that their inhabitants were enormously tall.[8] Siddiqi then added (p. 203):

> The *aḥādīth* reported by Ibn Māja on the excellence of Qazwīn (his own home town) have been declared by the traditionists as forged ones.

In the very last paragraph of his book, *Ḥadīth Literature*, Siddiqi wrote that there was enough material available for the "compilation of a standard collection of completely authentic traditions out of the already generally accepted compilations". This he added was "a tremendous task" but achievable by applying to each ḥadīth the principles that have been laid down and agreed by the great scholars and compilers of ḥadīth themselves.

Fahmī Huwaydī has discussed the views of Jalāl al-Dīn al-Suyūṭī (d. 911/1505) and Ibn Ḥazm (d. 994/1590) concerning the rejectors of *Sunna*, and the doubts that were expressed, in earlier times, by the heretics (Zanādiqa) and the Kharijites over the authority of ḥadīth as a source of *Sharīʿa*. Both al-Suyūṭī and Ibn Ḥazm resolutely refuted the position that the Qur'ān was the only proof of *Sharīʿa* and held that the *Sunna* itself did not support this position. They also discussed the ḥadīth in which the Prophet has been quoted to have said "whatever ḥadīth that you receive in my name, refer it to the Qur'ān – accept it if it has a basis in the Qur'ān, but reject it otherwise." Al-Suyūṭī refuted this as a fabrication of the Zanādiqa, which has, however, found support among some Muʿtazilī theologians of Baṣra, who held that the Qur'ān explained all things "*tibyānan li-kulli shay*". The Kharijites also denied the authority of a great deal of *aḥādīth* (as well as that of *ijmāʿ*) in the sphere of the *aḥkām*. They have consequently refuted stoning as a punishment for *zinā*, and wiping over boots (*masḥ ʿalā'l-khuffayn*) as these were only validated by the *Sunna* and did not occur in the Qur'ān.[9]

Huwaydī then quotes the views of Ibn Ḥazm with which he also agrees. The gist of what is said here is that the Qur'ān contains ambiguous rulings which could not be understood without the explanation of the *Sunna*. The question is thus posed: where does one find in the Qur'ān a reference that the *ẓuhr* (early afternoon) prayer is four units, and that the *maghrib* (evening) prayer is three! The Qur'ān also does not explain the manner in which certain other rituals of worship are performed. There is also no reference to the quantities of *zakāh*, or to things that must be avoided in fasting, nor does the Qur'ān expound the details of the law of sale, enforcement of punishments, and so forth. Ibn Ḥazm is then quoted to have added that it is tantamount to disbelief for a Muslim to say that he does not accept anything (i.e. any *ḥukm*) unless he finds it in the Qur'ān. Among the extremists were also those who held that there were only two obligatory prayers (morning and evening) instead of the normal five. Ibn Ḥazm declared that anyone who held such views was a denier of Islam simply because they confined themselves to the apparent text of the Qur'ān and ignored or isolated the *Sunna*.[10]

Having quoted Ibn Ḥazm, Huwaydī went on to agree with him and add that the Qur'ān itself provided ample evidence in support of the conclusion that the *Sunna* was a valid source and proof of *Sharīʿa*, and quoted Qur'ānic passages on this in 57:7; 16:44; 4:80 and so forth. Huwaydī also cited in support the renowned scholar of ḥadīth, Muḥammad Nāṣir al-Dīn al-Albānī, who wrote a treatise, entitled *Al-Ḥadīth Ḥujja bi-Nafsihi fi'l-ʿAqā'id wa'l-Aḥkām* (Ḥadīth is a proof by itself on matters of dogma and law), a title which is self-explanatory of its subject matter and purpose.[11]

Two other points Huwaydī makes may briefly be mentioned. He regretted that many unqualified people who were not knowledgeable of the methodology of ḥadīth have often lightly dismissed ḥadīth and advanced ill-considered views in the name of *ijtihād*.[12]

Huwaydī also recommended greater scrutiny in respect of research theses and dissertations that are sometimes accepted and passed by the faculties, even of al-Azhar, which are less than meticulous and on occasions ill-informed as to the correct methodology and procedure of ḥadīth.[13]

Ḥadīth critics have expressed reservations, nevertheless, over the authenticity of various *aḥādīth*. Some politically tendentious *aḥādīth* have come under criticism. One such ḥadīth that al-Bukhārī has recorded on the authority of Jābir b. Samura is as follows: "I heard the Prophet, peace be on him, saying that 'there will be twelve rulers (*amīran*),' and then the Prophet uttered words which I did not hear – but my father believed they were '... all of them will be from Quraysh'."[14]

The Shīʿī scholars have taken this ḥadīth as "decisive evidence", on the veracity of their belief in the twelve Imāms. The Sunnīs themselves have advanced different interpretations of this ḥadīth. One interpreter thus understood this to mean that the twelve *amīrs* will be simultaneous, all of whom will be laying claim to leadership, and the context is therefore one of tumult (*al-fitna*).[15] The various versions of probably this same ḥadīth that Muslim and Abū Dāwūd have recorded say something different. Briefly, Muslim recorded a ḥadīth to the effect that "this matter (i.e. the Caliphate) will not go away until twelve Caliphs have come and gone." Abū Dāwūd similarly recorded a ḥadīth to the effect that "this religion shall remain until twelve Caliphs have ruled, all of them with the agreement and support of the *umma*." The commentator of al-Bukhārī, Ibn Ḥajar al-ʿAsqalānī, has quoted these views, and reading all of them together, he thought that the reference therein was to the Caliphate. But this only added to complication in view of the common knowledge that the approved Caliphs were only four, not twelve. According to Qāḍī ʿIyāḍ al-Yaḥṣubī the ḥadīth "probably meant just leaders (*a'immat al-ʿadl*) of whom four have lived and the rest may emerge any time before the day of resurrection." This was "just the right sort of interpretation," according to Jawād Yāsīn, for its Shīʿī readers with which to vindicate their belief in occultation and the return of their twelfth Imām any time before the day of resurrection.[16]

Ibn al-Jawzī surmised on the meaning of the ḥadīth at issue and commented that the Prophet had probably meant twelve rulers excluding his Companions. It was then suggested that the ḥadīth had referred to the Umayyad Caliphs. The problem here was that the Umayyad Caliphs, starting from Muʿāwiya (d. 41 H) to Marwān al-Thānī (d. 127 H) numbered fourteen, not twelve. Ibn al-Jawzī's response to this was that Muʿāwiya may be excluded since he was a Companion. Then he added that Marwān Ibn al-Ḥakam (d. 65 H) should also be excluded as he was a usurper and took office after the people had elected ʿAbd Allāh b. al-Zubayr. This rather imaginative interpretation fitted in with the counting of the Umayyad Caliphs at twelve and the image that was consequently conveyed of them was that they were leaders who ruled with the support of the *umma*.

This interpretation was based on several questionable assumptions one of which excluded the first four Caliphs from the counting altogether; then it was assumed that Muʿāwiya was not a usurper of political power; that Marwān b. al-Ḥakam was not to be counted as a Caliph; and that ʿAbd Allāh b. al-Zubayr had been conclusively elected to be the Caliph.[17]

All of these rather weak interpretations were attempted with the pious yet questionable motive of upholding the reliability of the leading ḥadīth collections, and also to lend support perhaps to the Umayyad rule. The episode sustained itself simply because the chain of transmitters of the ḥadīth in question appeared sound. Al-Bukhārī and Muslim evidently recorded it because of its *isnād* without paying much attention to its meaning. And then the series of apologetic commentaries followed suit to justify what they had done. If the true purpose of all ḥadīth is to clarify and interpret the Qur'ān and those aspects of Islam that can properly be said to be the necessary part of its belief structure and its *Sharīʿa*, then the ḥadīth we have just reviewed is so peripheral that it hardly merits all the speculative effort that is undertaken to justify it.

This example also illustrates a situation where a certain imbalance that has remained unchecked at the outset has in turn recreated and perpetuated itself so much so that it became difficult, as time went by, to set it aside.

Another example of a questionable ḥadīth which has found its way into *Ṣaḥīḥ Muslim* is as follows:

> Sālim, the *mawlā* (freed slave) of Abū Ḥudhayfa, was with Abū Ḥudhayfa and his family at their home. Then Abū Ḥudhayfa's wife came to the Prophet, peace be on him, and said that Sālim had become an adult and in possession of his faculties, but he still enters upon us (at our home). I also think that Abū Ḥudhayfa does not like this. The Prophet then told her: "Suckle him and make him prohibited unto yourself and that would also dispel Abū Ḥudhayfa's suspicion." According to another report she said: "How can I suckle him while he is a grown up man?" The Prophet, peace be on him, smiled and said: "Have you known that he is a grown up man!" Then I went and suckled him and it helped dispel Abū Ḥudhayfa's suspicion.[18]

This is evidently a strange "ḥadīth" despite the fact that Muslim has recorded it on the merit of its chain of transmission. Ibn Qutayba al-Daynūrī has also commented that it is a "*Ṣaḥīḥ* ḥadīth",[19] with the obvious result that it is lawful for an adult male to suckle a woman's breast so as to establish a relationship of fosterage with her. This would be a wrong conclusion and the ḥadīth on which it is based also goes against the basic principles of Islam concerning interaction between members of the opposite sexes. The *Sharīʿa* proscribes even looking by a man at the body of a woman in order to avert the prospects of illicit relations between them! The correct guideline on this has been set in a ḥadīth of the Prophet where it is proclaimed that "There is no fosterage after the weaning," (*lā riḍāʿ baʿd al-fiṣāl*) which means that fosterage is confined to early childhood and it discontinues afterwards. Yet it is even more puzzling to note another incredible suggestion by Ibn Qutayba to vindicate the said ḥadīth by saying that "Sālim was perhaps a person who had no inclination toward women.[20] It has been noted in this connection that there is no ground for recourse to this type of particularisation (*takhṣīṣ*)."[21]

Muḥammad al-Ghazālī has also found certain *aḥādīth* in the standard collections which are at odds with the Qur'ān and the examples that he has given are put under the heading of *al-aḥādīth al-mardūda* (rejected ḥadīth – al-Ghazālī's labelling). Included among them are:

a. A ḥadīth narrated by Abū Hurayra and recorded by Muslim and Ibn Māja where the Prophet is quoted to have said:

> I beseeched God for permission to grant pardon to my mother, but He did not grant it; then I asked for permission to visit her grave, and He granted me this.[22]

Al-Ghazālī then wrote that "this ḥadīth is *Shādhdh* (strange) due to its disharmony with the noble Qur'ān". God Most High said "We do not punish until We send a Messenger" (al-Isrā', 17:15) as He also said in the Qur'ān: "this is because your Lord does not unjustly destroy villages while its inhabitants are unaware" (al-Anʿām, 6:131). With reference to the Arabs, God Most High said in an address to the Prophet "And We did not send to them a warner before you" (Saba', 34:44). This is confirmed further "so that you warn a people who have not been warned before you that they may be guided" (al-Sajda, 32:3).

Al-Ghazālī concluded that the Prophet's mother lived at a time when there was no revealed law for the people of Arabia, nor was the Prophet's mother warned in any way. She was therefore not liable to punishment on the basis of the clear import of these *āyāt*. This is why the ḥadīth, quoted above, which disallowed the seeking of pardon for the mother of the Prophet is in conflict with the Qur'ān. Besides a solitary (*Āḥād*) ḥadīth does not take priority over the Qur'ān. "This is a clear conclusion without any ambiguity."[23]

b. In a similar vein, al-Ghazālī has discussed the ḥadīth which Imām Aḥmad b. Ḥanbal has recorded in his *Musnad* (vol. 6, p. 269) on the authority of ʿĀ'isha in which she is quoted to have said: "the *āyāt* concerning the punishment of stoning and the ten sucklings (which establish maternity on the basis of fosterage) were (written) on a piece of paper under the bed in my house. When the Prophet became ill, we became preoccupied with him, and a domestic animal (meaning a sheep) entered and ate it up."

Al-Ghazālī here records ʿAbd Allāh al-Ṣiddīq al-Ghumārī's observation in support of his own view to say that this is odd and condemned without hesitation (*shādhdh, munkar, shadīd al-nakāra*), for the idea of abrogation of the text and ruling (*naskh al-tilāwa wa'l-ḥukm*) of which this is the only known example, is impossible. And then the message conveyed in this hardly stands to reason and tends to undermine the integrity of the Qur'ānic text, and God Most High's clear affirmation therein that "We sent down the remembrance and We shall be its preservers" (al-Ḥijr, 15:9).[24]

c. According to a clear text of the Qur'ān which does not admit any doubt or claim to the contrary, God Most High created the universe in six days, yet a ḥadīth has been recorded to the effect that the act of creation took seven days and then the detail that is provided in the said ḥadīth is way out of line with the Qur'ān. "Muslim, al-Nasā'ī and others" have thus reported from Abū Hurayra that the Prophet, peace be on him, said: "God created the dust (of the earth) on Saturday, the mountains on Sunday, the trees on Monday, the evil (*makrūh*) therein on Tuesday, the light on Wednesday, the animals on Thursday, and Adam in the evening of Friday between the *ʿaṣr* and the night fall."[25]

This is contrary to the clear text of the Qur'ān, which is why al-Bukhārī considered it defective and has questioned its accuracy.

Maḥmūd Shaltūt is critical of what he calls a "strange phenomenon that has become widespread among people," which is the attribution of *tawātur* to *aḥādīth* that do not fulfil the conditions of *tawātur* but have been included in the category of *mutawātir* because of their diffusion and frequent occurrence in the works of the *ʿulamāʾ*. This tendency has found expression in some of the Qur'ān commentaries and works on ḥadīth and history. People have been affected by this tendency so much so that "long lists of names of Companions and Followers, authors and Imāms who are frequently quoted by the ḥadīth transmitters are mentioned, despite the knowledge that the reports in question are weak and cannot stand the test of scrutiny and criticism. Some of these names which are enthusiastically put together are also found in fabricated *aḥādīth*, yet they are quoted nevertheless ... so as to mislead the general public and exploit their religious sentiment."[26] The proponents of this tendency try hard to show that the reports in question are the words of the Prophet. Since they have been quoted and requoted by many from a large number of Companions and Followers, they become *mutawātir* without any doubt. "Then anyone who criticises the ḥadīth in question or scrutinises its authenticity is misguided and has deviated from the way of the believers."[27]

Among the causes of "this phenomenon", Shaltūt explains, one may be that a particular ḥadīth became well-known in one or two of its links (*ṭabaqāt*) which is then assumed for all of its links and the ḥadīth is consequently labelled as *mutawātir* or *mashhūr* without due scrutiny and investigation. It is also possible that a ḥadīth has not become well-known at any one of the links or generations but has become the focus of attention by juristic or theological groups, and those who quoted it in support of their position labelled the ḥadīth either as *mashhūr* or *mutawātir* and their scholastic literature continued to portray it as such. The fact that the ḥadīth in question was neither of these to begin with was consequently ignored.[28]

Story-tellers and those who occupied themselves with *targhīb* and *tarhīb* (encouragement and warning) and the narrators of tumults and upheavals (*al-malāḥim wal-fitan*) also played a major role in the labelling of ḥadīth as *mutawātir* and *mashhūr*. This has happened not only with regard to doubtful *aḥādīth* but also ḥadīth that was neither sound nor acceptable in the first place. Shaltūt has in this connection quoted a brief statement of the Imām Aḥmad b. Ḥanbal who said that "there are four *aḥādīth*, which circulate among people in towns and bazaars, which have, however, no basis at all (*lā aṣla lahā*). People who took such *aḥādīth* to their hearts had no knowledge of their authenticity nor origin and simply kept repeating them until they became popular. They became careless to the extent of including "weak and even fabricated *aḥādīth*" and did not hesitate to designate solitary reports as *mutawātir*, and weak ḥadīth as sound and *Ṣaḥīḥ*. Shaltūt goes on to specify certain themes such as those of the *mahdī*, *dajjāl*, splitting of the moon (*inshiqāq al-qamar*) in which weak reports have been ascribed the attributes of *mashhūr* and *mutawātir*.[29]

Aḥmad Amīn wrote that the upsurge of scholarly activities during the early ʿAbbāsid period was particularly noted in the collection and compilation of ḥadīth. Ḥadīth scholars were distinguished for their untiring efforts to isolate the weak and doubtful from the reliable narrators of ḥadīth and as a result a careful methodology of ḥadīth criticism was developed. A certain degree of imbalance had, however, set in, as from the early days of this movement, between the external criticism (*al-naqd al-khārijī*) of the *isnād* of ḥadīth in which the ḥadīth scholars undoubtedly excelled, and its internal criticism (*al-naqd al-dākhilī*). The subject matter and content of ḥadīth were not scrutinised in the light of the prevailing socio-political realities. This would have helped ascertain the context, for example, concerning *aḥādīth* which spoke for or against the ruling dynasties or other partisan movements, and the pressure they might have generated. Had the ḥadīth scholars undertaken internal scrutiny of the text in conjunction with these realities, one would have expected that much of the alleged ḥadīth in the context of personality cult that praised or denigrated individuals, tribes, places and communities would have been verified and isolated at an early stage.[30]

One other ḥadīth that may be discussed in this connection is related to sectarian developments. The Prophet is thus reported to have said:

> My community shall be divided into seventy-three factions, one of them attains salvation and the rest will perish. Then it was asked: which is the one that attains salvation, to which the Prophet said: the *ahl al-sunna wa'l-jamāʿa* (i.e., the mainstream community). "Which one is that? it was asked again, and the Prophet said: the one for which I and my Companions stand."[31]

Najmī Zanjānī, himself a follower of Shīʿa Imāmiyya, has quoted several commentators, both Sunnī and Shīʿa, concerning this ḥadīth. He has quoted Ibn Ḥazm al-Andalusī's *Al-Fiṣal fi'l-Milal wa'l-Ahwā' wa'l-Niḥal* (*Kitāb al-Īmān wa'l-Kufr*, vol. 3, p. 138) on this and another ḥadīth in which the Prophet is reported to have said that "the Qadariyya (the predecessors of Muʿtazila) and the Murji'a are the Majūs (Magians) of this *umma*." Ibn Ḥazm has stated that in addition to being *Āḥād*, the chains of transmission of both of these two ḥadīth reports are defective.[32] Abū'l-Ḥasan al-Ashʿarī (d. 935 AD) has discussed at length the sects and factions in his *Maqālāt al-Islāmiyyīn* and put the main factions at ten but has made no reference to this ḥadīth nor to the much larger number of factions therein.[33]

Some discrepancy has also been noted in the text of the ḥadīth under review. Al-Shāṭibī's version of this ḥadīth mentions eighty-two factions (*Al-Iʿtiṣām*, vol. II, p. 164) instead of seventy-three, and Abū Isḥāq al-Isfarā'īnī (d. 406 H) (*Muqaddimat al-Tafsīr*, p. 8) has mentioned 72 instead of 73 factions, only one of which will go to Paradise and the rest to Hell. This last report also differs from the standard version in respect of its prognostication of Paradise and Hell: The standard version only mentioned that one will achieve salvation and the rest will perish (*halakū*). Another discrepancy that is noted in the various versions of the ḥadīth under review concerns the word *firqa* (faction) which appears in the standard version, and the word *milla* (nation) which occurs in al-Shāṭibī's *Al-Iʿtiṣām*, and also in al-Baghdādī's *Al-Farq bayn al-Firaq*. *Firqa* and *milla* are not the same, but even if one accepts them as synonyms, the discrepancy in the wording of ḥadīth in its various reports still remains.[34]

The question also arose as to whether the ḥadīth under review conflicts with the Qur'ān, and the point that needs to be borne in mind here is that the Qur'ān emphasises unity, not factionalism. To quote but only three of the relevant verses:

> And hold firmly to the cable of God, all of you, and avoid separation (Āl ʿImrān, 3:103).

> Be steadfast in religion and make no divisions therein. Hard is it for the associators to respond to your call (al-Shūrā, 42:13).

> You share nothing with those who divide in their religion and split off into factions (al-Anʿām, 6:159).[35]

Factionalism and division into groups and sects thus stands in conflict with the Qur'ānic emphasis on the unity of the believers.

It is further noted that the ḥadīth in question is not in consonance with historical reality, even if one tries to interpret the ḥadīth in some way. Interpretation has in fact been attempted by those who maintain that the 73 factions refer to the main divisions or sects, but not to the smaller factions and sub-divisions, simply because the smaller factions that are known to history far exceed in number as more than 700 of them have been recorded.

The assertion that there were 73 main factions has also been questioned, since the main theological groups such as the Muʿtazila, Shīʿa, Khawārij, Murji'a and Jabriyya, etc., do not exceed eight or ten in number and cannot by any means be put at 73. Even a most liberal counting cannot take the number to 20. This is what writers such as al-Baghdādī, Shahrastānī, Ibn Ḥazm and others have stated and the conclusion is that the ḥadīth under review does not correspond to historical facts.[36]

Lastly, Zanjānī has also noted the tendency among Shīʿī writers to place greater emphasis on *isnād* and the reliability or otherwise of the narrators of ḥadīth and not enough on that of the text and message of the ḥadīth. Zanjānī then discusses at length Shaykh Ṭūsī and Sharīf Murtaḍā's writings and concludes that both of these writers have actually conveyed this message and upheld the priority of text (*matn*) over the *sanad* (transmission) of ḥadīth.[37]

It may be added in passing that the Shīʿa Imāmiyya, who are the largest of the three Shīʿa groups, rely mainly on their own collections of ḥadīth. Of the four most well-known Shīʿī collections of ḥadīth, *Al-Kāfī* by Yaʿqūb al-Kulaynī (d. 329 H), is followed in order of priority by Ibn Bābwayh al-Qummī's (better known as al-Ṣadūq) (d. 381 H), *Man lā Yaḥḍuruh al-Faqīh* and *Al-Tahdhīb*, as well as *al-Istibṣār* by Shaykh Naṣīr al-Dīn al-Ṭūsī (d. 460 H). *Al-Kāfī* is the Shīʿī equivalent of *Al-Bukhārī* and contains 16,199 *aḥādīth*, whereas al-Qummī has compiled 5,963 *aḥādīth*. *Al-Tahdhīb* is the next largest of the four collections containing 13,590 *aḥādīth*, and *Al-Istibṣār* has recorded 5,511 *aḥādīth*.

The Shīʿī understanding of ḥadīth also differs somewhat to that of their Sunnī counterparts in that the Shīʿīs include the sayings of their recognised twelve Imāms in the general body of ḥadīth. Two of these Imāms who feature most prominently in this connection are the fifth and the sixth Imāms, Muḥammad al-Bāqir and Jaʿfar al-Ṣādiq.[38]

Shīʿī scholars have also expressed reservations over the existence of questionable materials in their ḥadīth collections as well as over the reliability of *Āḥād* ḥadīth in religious matters. They have on the whole maintained that all the obligatory duties of Islam and its injunctions concerning faith and *ʿibāda* need to be proven as a matter of certainty either by the authority of the Qur'ān or the authentic *Sunna* of the Prophet. The *Āḥād* ḥadīth can only establish a probability which falls below the level of certainty; it can establish a decisive ruling of the *Sharīʿa* only when it can find confirmation and support in the Qur'ān.[39]

The definition of *Āḥād* ḥadīth in Shīʿī jurisprudence is not different from its Sunnī definition. *Āḥād* is thus a ḥadīth which has not reached the level of continuous testimony or *tawātur* even if it is narrated by several narrators, say five or six, but still falls below the level of *Mutawātir*. Only the *Mutawātir* can establish positive knowledge on its own. There may be some differences of opinion among individual Shīʿī scholars on the authority of *Āḥād*, yet the majority Shīʿī opinion is that no one may take a decisive stand in matters of religion on the basis only of *Āḥād* ḥadīth unless there be supportive circumstantial evidence to confirm its authenticity and truth.[40]

Yūsuf al-Qaraḍāwī has drawn attention to weak *aḥādīth* in the category especially of encouragement and warning (*al-targhīb wa'l-tarhīb*) that do not, on the whole, contain specific rulings (*aḥkām*) but are nevertheless a cause for concern. This is because the *ʿulamā'* of ḥadīth have generally been less critical of this type of ḥadīth, which has in turn tended to undermine the reliability of ḥadīth generally. Although the *ʿulamā'* of ḥadīth have specified certain conditions for admissibility of this type of ḥadīth, even so, an uncritical acceptance of such ḥadīth can be seen in books and chapters on moral teachings, spirituality and mysticism.[41] Al-Qaraḍāwī then draws attention to the fact that works on Qur'ān exegesis (*tafsīr*) are also not free of weak ḥadīth and even forgeries on such themes as superiority and virtue of the chapters and verses of the Qur'ān. Even though much work has been done by leading scholars who have either isolated such *aḥādīth* or declared them null and void, Qur'ān commentators "such as al-Zamakhsharī, al-Thaʿālibī, al-Bayḍāwī, Ismāʿīl Ḥaqqī and others have persisted in quoting fabrications in the name of ḥadīth – *aṣarrū ʿalā ikhrāj al-ḥadīth al-makdhūb*."[42] Al-Qaraḍāwī also refers to al-Alūsī, the author of another well-known *Tafsīr* (i.e. *Rūḥ al-Bayān*) who openly comes out (at the end of his commentary on sūra al-Tawba) in defence of al-Zamakhsharī and al-Bayḍāwī, saying that the *aḥādīth* on preaching and warning are either sound, weak, or fabricated. If they are sound, there is not an issue to address, but if they are weak of *isnād* then "the *muḥaddithūn* have agreed that weak ḥadīth may be acted upon in regard to *targhīb* and *tarhīb*...". Even with reference to fabricated ḥadīth, al-Alūsī takes a surprisingly weak position and tends to vindicate those who spoke in support of the superiority and virtues of the verses of the Qur'ān; they may have resorted to lying but if their purpose was to encourage people to the path of God and adherence to His laws, then this may be said to be a permissible form of lying. This is the upshot of a long passage that al-Qaraḍāwī has quoted concerning al-Alūsī's exegesis and then followed it with the following remark: "This is very strange coming from a person who counts himself among commentators of the Book of God. Some have also described him as a *faqīh* and *uṣūlī*. What kind of *fiqh* is this where all one finds is ignorance of the very fundamentals of what is upheld by the *ʿulamā'* of distinction?"[43] Al-Qaraḍāwī then quotes a number of prominent *ʿulamā'* including al-Bukhārī and Muslim, as well as Ibn Ḥazm al-Ẓāhirī, Ibn Rajab al-Ḥanbalī and the Mālikī Ibn al-ʿArabī as well as modern experts on ḥadīth, Aḥmad Muḥammad Shākir and Muḥammad Nāṣir al-Dīn al-Albānī – all to the effect that ḥadīth of all kinds is subject to the same requirements of authenticity and standards of scrutiny, regardless as to whether its subject matter is concerned with moral teachings or the *aḥkām*, and that only the *Ṣaḥīḥ* and *Ḥasan* ḥadīth may be accepted.

In the concluding remarks in his book *Kayfa Nataʿāmal Maʿa al-Sunna al-Nabawiyya* (How should we treat the *Sunna* of the Prophet) al-Qaraḍāwī has stressed the need for compilation of no less than three encyclopaedias on ḥadīth. The first of these is to compile a comprehensive encyclopaedia on the narrators of ḥadīth (*mawsūʿa shāmila li-rijāl al-ḥadīth*) and their biographies which is inclusive and exhaustive of all of the ḥadīth narrators. Anyone who has been described and identified, whether as trustworthy or weak, including even the fabricators and liars should be included.

A second encyclopaedia is then proposed for the textual subject matter of ḥadīth, including their chains of transmission, whether one or more. The work should again be comprehensive and exhaustive of all ḥadīth that is attributed to the Prophet, everything in the *Sunna* that is available in documented materials from the beginning down to the latter third of the fifth century of the hijra.

Al-Qaraḍāwī continued to propose the third of his three-tiered proposal which brings to a conclusion and represents the basic objective of the first two projects. The third encyclopaedia that is proposed here is devoted exclusively to the *Ṣaḥīḥ* and *Ḥasan aḥādīth*, which are derived from the other two collections proposed above in accordance with the strict and scientific criteria that have been laid down for this purpose by the leading ḥadīth scholars and researchers of the past, and those among contemporary experts that enjoy the trust and confidence of the *umma*.

The three encyclopaedias that are proposed, al-Qaraḍāwī added, should be compiled with the new methods of classification and should have a comprehensive index. They should be compiled in line with the overriding objective of providing the basic tools and a source of benefit for research in all spheres of religion, social sciences and humanities, and practically all areas of knowledge that are addressed by the *Sunna*. All of this should be done with the aid of modern facilities, especially the computer, which is now a source of great benefit and enables the contemporary generation to aim at levels of accomplishment that their predecessors were not able to achieve, nor even to think of achieving.[44]

Having advanced these proposals, al-Qaraḍāwī then expresses the hope that the Centre for Research in Sunna and Sīra (CRSS) (*Markaz Buḥūth al-Sunna wa'l-Sīra*) of Qatar, of which al-Qaraḍāwī himself is the Director, will be able to cooperate with similar other institutions toward making these proposals a reality.[45] In an earlier reference to the need to isolate the *Ṣaḥīḥ* and *Ḥasan* ḥadīth from the weak ḥadīth, al-Qaraḍāwī noted that "this was what actually prompted me to compile a verified compendium (*al-Muntaqā*) of *Ṣaḥīḥ* and *Ḥasan aḥādīth* in two volumes that was published by the CRSS of Qatar." This work seems to be confined, however, to the study of a particular collection, namely that of al-Mundhirī's *Al-Targhīb wa'l-Tarhīb* and does not, as such, address the wider proposals that al-Qaraḍāwī has advanced on the compilation of encyclopaedias of ḥadīth.[46]

Al-Qaraḍāwī ends the two-page conclusion of his book with yet another suggestion which is that the *Sunna* is in need of "new commentaries (*al-Sunna fī ḥāja ilā shurūḥ jadīda*) so as to clarify the facts, elucidate the complexities, and rectify the concepts, refute the doubts and false attributions." All of this should be written in the current language of the people and address their contemporary concerns.[47] He refers in this connection to Qur'ān commentaries that have been written by some of the prominent *ʿulamā'* of the twentieth century such as Muḥammad Rashīd Riḍā, Jamāl al-Dīn al-Qāsimī, Ṭāhir b. ʿĀshūr, Abū'l Aʿlā Mawdūdī, Sayyid Quṭb and Maḥmūd Shaltūt, whose valuable endeavours advanced the knowledge of the Qur'ān to a new stage. This is also needed, al-Qaraḍāwī adds, with regard to the *Sunna*, especially with reference to al-Bukhārī and Muslim. Although some efforts have already been made by the *ʿulamā'* of India and Pakistan who wrote commentaries on the four works of *Sunna*, but "they are on the whole dominated by the imitative trend of conventional methods and do not address the concerns of contemporary minds."[48]

The present writer believes that the methodology that the *ʿulamā'* of ḥadīth have developed for the authentication of ḥadīth is basically adequate, although new methods of research, documentation and classification that are now available due to better facilities could be utilised to great advantage. If a new project along the lines suggested above were to be undertaken, the work that is proposed would be mainly in the nature of sifting through, critical evaluation, and consolidation of the existing compilations of ḥadīth. The ḥadīth critics and writers on *Mawḍūʿāt* have already carried out works which would facilitate the task to some extent. But once again since the *Mawḍūʿāt* were themselves compiled long after al-Bukhārī and Muslim, they remain unconsolidated and separate. It may therefore be worthwhile to propose that a panel of experts in ḥadīth, *tafsīr*, history, and *fiqh* should be set up, within the framework of the Organisation of Islamic Conference or such other national or international bodies as might be able and interested to undertake the proposed task. Once a project is created, along the lines of al-Qaraḍāwī's suggestions, and assigned for implementation, it would be in order to suggest that the panel of experts take into consideration the prevailing conditions and realities of the Muslim community, especially in the sphere of legal injunctions (*aḥkām*) and the need for uniformity and consensus on the basis of a comprehensive and conveniently accessible collection of ḥadīth. This might mean a separate collection of *aḥādīth al-aḥkām* that could be utilised as a reference work on *Sharīʿa*-related themes by jurists, legislators and judges. My own proposal on this, which I made at an International Conference on ḥadīth (held by the University of London's School of Oriental and African Studies in 1998) was basically focused on a critical review and consolidation of the existing collections with a view to compiling an abridged and purified version of the reliable ḥadīth from the six major collections. I had occasion to reflect on that proposal further and find that the two proposals are different only on minor points. I am now unifying my proposal with al-Qaraḍāwī's suggestions with respect to the encyclopaedic collections that he suggested on ḥadīth. This is evidently a wider proposition and would naturally require greater allocation of resources and commitment, yet I now feel that a thorough review and comprehensive approach along the lines al-Qaraḍāwī has suggested is preferable and would naturally command greater credibility. This is truly a challenging task but it is necessary if one is to hope for setting aside, hopefully once and for all, the incessant controversy that has persisted over the authenticity of ḥadīth and accuracy of its text, message and purpose. If I were to suggest an adjustment in the conventional methodology of ḥadīth criticism, it would be to pay balanced attention to the verification of both the *isnād* and *matn*, and not to the one at the expense of the other. Greater attention would thus have to be paid to the question of internal harmony between the *Sunna* itself and then of the *Sunna* with the Qur'ān, and also the broad and general principles of *Sharīʿa* that are derived from the overall reading of these sources.

As for the reference al-Qaraḍāwī has made to the need for commentaries and hermeneutics on ḥadīth that seek to advance the understanding of ḥadīth from the viewpoint of contemporary conditions, this should be taken into consideration as a step beyond the compilation of the suggested encyclopaedic works, in conjunction perhaps with the specialised collection I proposed on legal *aḥādīth*. But the actual writing of such commentaries should, for practical reasons of not diluting the focus of the main project, not be made a part of the basic project on ḥadīth compilation. This second proposal may be the kind of work that expert institutions of higher learning and individual scholars can take up over a longer period, or even be made the subject of a new project after the proposed encyclopaedic works have been accomplished. The wider project that is undertaken as a result should naturally draw on the best expertise and resources as are available at the dawn of the 21st century so that it becomes a source of inspiration and invigorated learning for the generations of Muslims to come. It would, in my opinion, be an act of outstanding academic and spiritual merit and a most valuable service that Islamic scholarship can give to the *umma* of the 21st century. What is proposed to be undertaken in this way would bear credible resemblance to the third Caliph ʿUthmān's initiative so long ago for the authentication of the text of the Qur'ān and the decision which he consequently took to validate only the authentic text to the exclusion of all the variant versions of the Holy Book. For the purpose solely of uniformity, the Caliph actually issued orders that all the variant versions of the Qur'ān be burnt and destroyed. Depending on the nature of the result, participation and support that is realised for this project, one may even be able, in due course, to invoke the support of general consensus (*ijmāʿ*) for it provided that the explicit approval of the learned councils, academies, and individuals in the Muslim world is duly solicited and obtained.

Bibliography

Abū Dāwūd, Sulaymān b. Ashʿath al-Sijistānī, *Mukhtaṣar Sunan Abī Dāwūd*. Ed. Muṣṭafā Dīb al-Bughā, Damascus: Dār al-ʿUlūm al-Insāniyya, 1416/1995.

______________. Eng. Trans. Aḥmad Hasan. Lahore: Ashraf Press, 1984.

Abū Shahba, Muḥammad Ibn Muḥammad. *Al-Wasīṭ fī ʿUlūm wa Muṣṭalaḥ al-Ḥadīth*. Jedda: ʿĀlam al-Maʿrifa, 1403/1983.

Abū Zahra, Muḥammad. *Ibn Ḥanbal, Ḥayātuhu Wa ʿAṣruhu, Ārā'uhu wa Fiqhuh*. Cairo: Dar al-Fikr al-ʿArabī, 1367/1947.

Amīn, Aḥmad. *Fajr al-Islām*. 14th edn. Cairo: Maktaba al-Nahḍa al-Miṣriyya, 1986.

________________. *Ḍuḥā al-Islām*. 5th edn. Cairo: Maktaba al-Nahḍa, 1956.

Amīn, Bakrī Shaykh. *Adab al-Ḥadīth al-Nabawī*. 4th edn. Beirut: Dār al-Shurūq, 1399/1979.

ʿAsqalānī, Ḥāfiẓ Shihāb al-Dīn Aḥmad b. ʿAlī b. Ḥajar al-. *Taqrīb al-Tahdhīb*. Delhi: Maṭbaʿa Ḥajar, 1320 H.

________________. *Fatḥ al-Bārī Sharḥ Ṣaḥīḥ al-Bukhārī*. Cairo: Bulaq, 1301 H.

Azami, Muhammad Mustafa. *Studies in Ḥadīth Methodology and Literature*. Indianapolis (Indiana): American Trust Publications, 1977.

Badrān, Abū'l-ʿAynayn. *Uṣūl al-Fiqh al-Islāmī*. Alexandria: Mu'assasa Shabāb al-Jāmiʿa, 1402/1982.

Baghdādī, Aḥmad b. ʿAlī al-Khaṭīb al-. *Al-Kifāya fī Maʿrifat Uṣūl ʿIlm al-Riwāya*. 2nd edn. Ed. Aḥmad ʿUmar Hāshim. Beirut: Dār al-Kitāb al-ʿArabī, 1406/1986.

______________. *Taqyīd al-ʿIlm*. Ed. Yūsuf al-ʿIshsh. Damascus: 1949.

Bahnasāwī, Sālim ʿAlī. *Al-Sunna al-Muftarā ʿAlayhā* al-. 3rd edn. Kuwait: Dār al-Buḥūth al-ʿIlmiyya, 1401/1981.

Bakar, Osman. *Tawhid and Science: Essays on the History and Philosophy of Islamic Sciences*. Kuala Lumpur: Secretariat for Islamic Philosophy and Science, 1991.

Barr, Abū ʿUmar Yūsuf Ibn ʿAbd al-. *Jāmiʿ Bayān al-ʿIlm Wa Faḍlih*. Cairo: Idāra al-Ṭibāʿa al-Munīriyya, n.d.

Bughā, Muṣṭafā Dīb Al-. *Buḥūth fī ʿUlūm al-Ḥadīth wa Nuṣūṣih*. Damascus: Maṭbaʿa al-Ittiḥād, 1411/1990.

Bukhārī, Muḥammad b. Ismāʿīl al-. *Ṣaḥīḥ al-Bukhārī*. Istanbul: Cagri Yayinlari, 1981.

______________. *The Translation of the Meaning of Ṣaḥīḥ al-Bukhārī*. Eng. Trans. Muḥammad Muhsin Khan. Lahore (Pakistan): Kazi Publications, 6th printing, 1986.

Dhahabī, Shams al-Dīn Muḥammad b. Aḥmad al-. *Mīzān al-Iʿtidāl fī Naqd al-Rijāl*. Cairo: Maṭbaʿa al-Khānjī, 1325 H.

Dihlawī, Shāh Walīullāh al-. *Ḥujjat Allah al-Bāligha*. Cairo: al-Maṭbaʿa al-Khayriyya, 1322 H.

Ghazālī, Muḥammad al-. *Turāthunā al-Fikrī fī Mīzān al-Sharʿ wa'l-ʿAql.* Herndon, Va., 4th edn. Al-Maʿhad al-ʿĀlamī li'l-Fikr al-Islāmī, 1417/1996.

Hāshim, Aḥmad ʿUmar. *Al-Sunna al-Nabawiyya wa ʿUlūmuhā.* Cairo: Maktaba Gharīb, n.d.

Haythamī, Nūr al-Dīn ʿAlī b. Abī Bakr Ibn Ḥajar al-. *Majmaʿ al-Zawā'id wa Manbaʿ al-Fawā'id.* Cairo: Maktabat al-Quds, 1352 H.

Ibn Ḥazm, Muḥammad ʿAlī b. Aḥmad b. Saʿīd al-Ẓāhirī. *Al-Muḥallā.* Cairo: Idārat at al-Ṭibāʿa al-Munīriyya, 1351/1932.

Hītū, Muḥammad Ḥasan. *Al-Wajīz fī Uṣūl al-Tashrīʿ al-Islāmī.* 2nd edn. Beirut: Mu'assasa al-Risāla, 1405/1984.

Huwaydī, Fahmī. *Ḥattā lā Takūna Fitna.* Cairo: Dār al-Shurūq, 1410/1989.

Ibn Taymiyya, Shaykh al-Islām Taqī al-Dīn. *Minhāj al-Sunna al-Nabawiyya fī Naqḍ Kalām al-Shīʿa wa'l-Qadariyya.* Egypt (Bulaq): al-Maṭbaʿa al-Amīriyya, 1352 H.

_______________. *Muqaddima fī Uṣūl al-Tafsīr.* Cairo: al-Maṭbaʿa al-Salafiyya, 1370/1950.

ʿIrāqī, al-Ḥāfiẓ Ibn Ḥusayn al-. *Al-Mughnī ʿan Ḥaml al-Asfār fi'l-Asfār fī Takhrīj mā fi'l-Iḥyā' min al-Akhbār.*

Al-Jaʿfar, Musāʿid Muslim. *Al-Mūjaz fī ʿUlūm al-Ḥadīth.* Baghdad: Dār al-Risāla, 1978.

Jammāz, ʿAlī Muḥammad. *Muhāḍarāt fī ʿUlūm al-Ḥadīth.* Kuwait: Dār al-Qalam, 1402/1982.

Kamali, Mohammad Hashim. *Principles of Islamic Jurisprudence.* Cambridge: The Islamic Texts Society, 1991. Reprint by Ilmiah Publishers of Kuala Lumpur, 1998. Third enlarged ed., Cambridge, 2003.

Ibn Kathīr, Abū'l-Fidā' Ismāʿīl. *Ikhtiṣār ʿUlūm al-Ḥadīth*. 2nd edn. Cairo: 1370/1951. Beirut: Dār al-Kitāb, 1983.

Khaṭīb, Muḥammad ʿAjjāj al-. *Uṣul al-Ḥadīth ʿUlūmuh wa Muṣṭalaḥuh*. Beirut and Damascus: Dār al-Fikr li'l-Ṭibāʿa wa'l-Nashr, 1409/1989.

Khuḍarī, Shaykh Muḥammad al-. *Uṣūl al-Fiqh*. 7th edn. Cairo: Dār al-Fikr, 1401/1981.

Al-Khusht, Muḥammad ʿUthmān. *Mafātīḥ ʿUlūm al-Ḥadīth wa Ṭuruq Takhrījih*. Cairo: Maktabat al-Qur'ān, n.d.

Muslim, Abū'l-Ḥusayn Ibn Hajjāj al-Nīsābūrī. *Mukhtaṣar Ṣaḥīḥ Muslim*. Ed. Muḥammad Nāṣir al-Dīn al-Albānī, 4th edn. Beirut: al-Maktab al-Islāmī, 1402/1982.

Mutahharī, Morteza. *Jurisprudence and Its Principles*. Trans. Mohammad Salman Tawheed. New York (Elmhurst): Tarikhe Tarsile Qur'ān Inc., c. 1982.

Nīsābūrī, al-Ḥākim Abū ʿAbd Allāh Muḥammad b. ʿAbd Allāh al-. *Maʿrifat ʿUlūm al-Ḥadīth*. 4th edn. Ed. Syed Muʿazzam Husayn. Beirut: Dār al-Afāq al-Jadīda, 1400/1980.

Qaraḍāwī, Yūsuf al-. *Kayfa Nataʿāmal maʿa al-Sunna al-Nabawiyya*. 2nd edn. Herndon, Va.: al-Maʿhad al-ʿĀlami li'l-Fikr al-Islami, 1411/1990.

Qāsimī, Jamāl al-Dīn al-. *Qawāʿid al-Taḥdīth*. Damascus: Maṭbaʿa Ibn Zaydān, 1353/1925.

Qaṭṭān, Mannāʿ Khalīl al-. *Mabāḥith fī ʿUlūm al-Ḥadīth*. Cairo: Maktaba Wahba, 1412/1992.

Qurṭubī, Abū ʿAbd Allāh Muhammad al-. *Jāmiʿ li-Aḥkām al-Qur'ān* (known as *Tafsīr al-Qurṭubī*). Cairo: Maṭbaʿa Dār al-Kutub, 1387/1967.

Rahman, Fazlur. *Islam*, 2nd ed., Chicago & London: University of Chicago Press, 1979.

______________. *Islamic Methodology in History*. Karachi: Central Institute of Islamic Research, 1965.

Rauf, Muḥammad ʿAbdul. "Ḥadīth, Its Authority and Authenticity." *IIUM Law Journal*, Vol. 1 (1989), pp. 1-51.

Rāzī, ʿAbd al-Raḥmān Ibn Abī Ḥātim al-. *ʿIlal al-Ḥadīth*. Ed. Muḥibb al-Dīn al-Khaṭīb. Cairo: al-Maṭbaʿa al-Salafiyya, 1343 H.

Ibn Saʿd, Muḥammad b. Manīʿ. *Al-Ṭabaqāt al-Kubrā*, Beirut: Dār Ṣādir, 1398/1978.

Ibn al-Ṣalāḥ, Abū ʿAmr ʿUthmān b. ʿAbd al-Raḥmān al-Shahrazūrī. *ʿUlūm al-Ḥadīth*. Ed. Nūr al-Dīn ʿĪṭr. 3rd edn. Damascus: Dār al-Fikr, 1404/1984.

Ṣāliḥ, Ṣubḥī al-. *ʿUlūm al-Ḥadīth wa Muṣṭalaḥuh*. 20th edn. Beirut: Dār al-ʿIlm li'l-Malāyīn, 1406/1996.

Shākir, Aḥmad Muḥammad. *Al-Bāʿith al-Ḥathīth Ikhtiṣār ʿUlūm al-Ḥadīth*. Beirut: Dār al-Kitāb, 1983.

Sharfī, ʿAbd al-Majīd al-. *Al-Islām wa'l-Ḥadātha*. Tunis: al-Dār al-Tūnisiyya li'l-Nashr, 1990.

Shawkānī, Yaḥyā Ibn ʿAlī al-. *Irshād al-Fuḥūl min Taḥqīq al-Ḥaqq ilā ʿIlm al-Uṣūl*. Cairo: Dār al-Fikr, n.d.

Sibāʿī, Muṣṭafā Ḥusnī al-. *Al-Sunna wa Makānatuhā fī'l-Tashrīʿ al-Islāmī*. 3rd edn. Beirut: 1302/1982; also Lahore: Dār Nashr al-Kutub al-Islāmiyya, n.d.

Siddiqi, Muhammad Zubayr. *Ḥadīth Literature: Its Origin, Development, Special Features and Criticism*. Calcutta: Calcutta University Press, 1961.

Suyūṭī, Jalāl al-Dīn ʿAbd al-Raḥmān al-. *Tadrīb al-Rāwī Sharḥ Taqrīb al-Nawawī*. Ed. ʿAbd al-Wahhāb ʿAbd al-Laṭīf: Cairo: Maktaba al-Qāhira, 1379/1959.

______________. *Al-La'āli' al-Maṣnūʿa fi'l-Aḥādīth al-Mawḍūʿa*. Cairo: al-Maṭbaʿa al-Ḥusayniyya, 1352 H.

______________. *Al-Durr al-Manthūr fi'l-Tafsīr bi'l-Ma'thūr*.

______________. *Ṣaḥīḥ al-Jāmiʿ al-Ṣaghīr*. Ed. Muḥammad Nāṣir al-Dīn al-Albānī. 4th edn. Cairo: Muṣṭafā al-Bābī al-Ḥalabī, 1954.

Tabrīzī, ʿAbd Allāh al-Khaṭīb al-. *Mishkāt al-Maṣābīḥ*. Ed. Muḥammad Nāṣir al-Dīn al-Albānī. 2nd edn. Beirut: al-Maktab al-Islāmī, 1399/1979.

Tirmidhī, Abū ʿĪsā Muḥammad al-. *Sunan al-Tirmidhī*. Beirut: Dār al-Fikr, 1400/1980.

Walīullāh, Shāh, *Ḥujjatullāh al-Bāligha*. Cairo: Dār al-Kutub al-Ḥadītha, n.d.

Zanjānī, Muḥammad Najmī. *Tārīkh-e Firaq-e Islāmī*. Tehran: Tehran University Press, 1340 H.

______________. *Uṣūl al-Fiqh*. Cairo: Dār al-Fikr al-ʿArabī, 1377/1958.

Zaylaʿī, Jamāl al-Dīn al-. *Naṣb al-Rāya fī Takhrīj Aḥādīth al-Hidāya*. 2nd edn. Beirut: al-Maktab al-Islāmī, 1393 H.

Glossary

ʿadāla:	probity and uprightness of character.
ʿadl:	upright and just.
āhād:	a solitary report or ḥadīth.
ʿāmmī:	a commoner or unqualified person.
ʿāmm:	general as opposed to specific.
ʿal-ashara mubashara:	the ten Companions to whom the Prophet gave the tidings of admission to Paradise.
ʿazīz:	strong – ḥadīth with at least two chains of transmission.
bidʿa:	pernicious innovation that stands contrary to valid precedent.
ḍaʿīf:	weak, as opposed to strong and reliable.
dirāya:	the meaning and purport of ḥadīth as opposed to its transmission or *riwāya*.
fard:	lit. single – ḥadīth that only one Companion has reported from the Prophet.
fiʿlī:	actual, as opposed to verbal.
fitna:	turmoil, tumult.

gharīb: lit. strange – ḥadīth which is reported by only one narrator at any level of its *isnād*.

gharīb al-ḥadīth: strange and unfamiliar word or words in a ḥadīth text.

ghaybiyyāt: metaphysical, not detected by the senses.

ghība: backbiting.

ḥāfiẓ: retentive of memory, a competent scholar of ḥadīth.

ḥalāl: lawful, permissible.

ḥarām: forbidden.

ḥasan: lit. good, fair, a reliable ḥadīth whose narrator might have been suspected of poor retention.

ḥujja: proof, a highly competent scholar of ḥadīth.

ḥukm (pl. *aḥkām*): law, value or ruling of *Sharīʿa*.

ʿibāda (pl. *ʿibādāt*): worship, rituals of worship.

ibāḥa: permissibility.

ijmāʿ: general consensus of scholars and jurists over a juridical ruling.

ijtihād: original thinking, independent interpretation by a qualified scholar who obtains a legal ruling from the sources of *Sharīʿa*.

ʿilla (pl. *ʿilal*): a hidden defect in a ḥadīth. It also means effective cause or rationale of a particular ruling.

isnād: lit. support, with reference to ḥadīth, it is the chain of transmission which supports the ḥadīth.

khāṣṣ: particular, as opposed to general, in purport and meaning.

jamʿ: bringing together, reconciliation of two apparently conflicting ḥadīths.

jarḥ: lit. wounding, or impugnment, as opposed to validation, of a ḥadīth.

kāfir: an unbeliever or denier of Islam.

kufr: lit. hiding, disbelief, rejection of the dogma of Islam.

majāzī: metaphorical, as opposed to the literal, meaning.

majhūl: unknown, obscure, in reference particularly to a transmitter of ḥadīth.

maʿlūl: afflicted – ḥadīth that contains a hidden defect or *ʿilla*.

mansūkh: abrogated, overruled and repealed.

marfūʿ: elevated – ḥadīth that is elevated and attributed to the Prophet Muḥammad himself.

mashhūr: well-known, famous – a ḥadīth which has become well-known during the first three generations of Islam.

mastūr: hidden, undetected.

matn: text or contents of a ḥadīth as opposed to its chain of transmission.

mawḍūʿ: a fabricated ḥadīth.

mudallas: concealed – a distorted ḥadīth with hidden defects.

mufassar: explained, clarified.

mujmal: ambiguous, in need of clarification.

mukhtalif al-ḥadīth: conflict in ḥadīth.

mursal: ḥadīth which a Follower (*tābiʿī*) has reported directly from the Prophet without mentioning the upper link, or the Companion, from whom it is received.

musnad: supported – ḥadīth supported by a chain of transmission.

mutawātir: recurrent, proven by recurrent testimony.

nāsikh: abrogator.

naskh: abrogation, repeal by a stronger ruling or evidence.

naṣṣ: a clear and unequivocal text.

ṣaḥīḥ: sound, authentic, ḥadīth which fulfils all the requirements of authenticity.

al-ṣiḥāḥ al-sitta: the six renowned collections of ḥadīth, including *Ṣaḥīḥ al-Bukhārī*, *Ṣaḥīḥ Muslim*, etc.

shādhdh: outlandish – ḥadīth that disagrees with a more reliable ḥadīth text.

sunna taqrīriyya: tacitly approved *Sunna*.

taʿāruḍ: conflict of evidence.

ṭabaqa (pl. *ṭabaqāt*): generation – such as that of the Companions, Followers, Successors, etc.

tābiʿī: a Follower, that is, one who belongs to the generation following the Companions.

tābiʿ al-tābiʿī: successor, one who lived in the generation after the Companions and Followers.

taʿdīl: validation as opposed to impugnment.

tadlīs: concealment of defects as opposed to outright forgery.

tafsīr: interpretation that is confined to the words of the text, as opposed to allegorical interpretation, which is not confined to the words.

takhṣīṣ: particularisation of the general.

tarjīḥ: preference of one of the two conflicting pieces of evidence over the other.

tawaqquf: suspension – to do nothing and leave things as they are due to intractable conflict of evidence.

ta'wīl: allegorical interpretation which is not confined to the words of the text.

tayammum: dry ablution by sand as opposed to ablution by water (*wuḍū'*).

thiqa: reliable, trustworthy.

umma: the Muslim community worldwide.

waḍ' al-ḥadīth: ḥadīth forgery.

wahm: suspicion.

wahmī: imaginary and unreal.

Notes

[01] Introduction

1. Osman Bakar, *Tawhid and Science*, p. 9.
2. Ibid., p. 10.
3. Ibid.
4. Al-Khaṭīb, *ʿUlūm al-Ḥadīth*, p. 451; Abū Shahba, *Al-Wasīṭ*, p. 28 f.
5. See for details on these branches of ḥadīth Ibn al-Ṣalāḥ, *ʿUlūm al-Ḥadīth*, p. 324 ff.
6. Cf. Ibn al-Ṣalāḥ, *ʿUlūm al-Ḥadīth*, p. 344.
7. Ibid., p. 375 ff.
8. Ibid., p. 373 ff.
9. Cf. al-Suyūṭī, *Tadrīb al-Rāwī*, p. 5 ff, and ʿUmar Hāshim, *Al-Sunna al-Nabawiyya wa ʿUlūmuhā*, pp. 363-365.

[02] Reception (*Taḥammul*) and Delivery (*Adā'*) of Ḥadīth

1. Al-Bukhārī, *Ṣaḥīḥ al-Bukhārī, Kitāb al-Manāqib, bāb. Ṣifāt al-Nabī s.a.w.*
2. Ibid., *Kit. al-ʿIlm, bāb. man Samiʿa Shay'an fa-Rajaʿa.*
3. Al-Bughā, *Buḥūth*, p. 24; Shaykh Amīn, *Adab al-Ḥadīth*, p. 96.
4. Ibid., Shaykh Amīn, *Adab al-Ḥadīth*, p. 96.
5. Al-Bukhārī, *Ṣaḥīḥ al-Bukhārī, Kitāb al-ʿIlm, bāb. al-Tanāwub fi'l-ʿIlm.*
6. Al-Bughā, *Buḥūth fī ʿUlūm al-Ḥadīth*, pp. 32-33; Shaykh Amīn, *Adab al-Ḥadīth*, p. 74.
7. Al-Bukhārī, *Ṣaḥīḥ al-Bukhārī, Kitāb al-ʿIlm, bāb matā yaṣiḥḥu samaʿ al-ṣaghīr.*
8. Al-Bughā, *Buḥūth fī ʿUlūm al-Ḥadīth*, p. 34.
9. Ibn al-Ṣalāḥ, *ʿUlūm al-Ḥadīth*, p. 132 ff; Shaykh Amīn, *Adab al-Ḥadīth*, p. 76; al-Bughā, *Buḥūth*, p. 35.
10. Ibid., pp. 135-136.

11. Al-Suyūṭī, *Tadrīb al-Rāwī*, p. 131; Shaykh Amīn, *Adab al-Ḥadīth*, p. 76.
12. Ibn al-Ṣalāḥ, *ʿUlūm al-Ḥadīth*, p. 138.
13. Ibid., p. 147.
14. Ibid., p. 150 ff.
15. Cf. Shaykh Amīn, *Adab al-Ḥadīth*, p. 77; al-Bughā, *Buḥūth*, p. 36.
16. Cf. Ibn al-Ṣalāḥ, *ʿUlūm al-Ḥadīth*, pp. 152-153.
17. Ibid., p. 151.
18. Ibid., p. 164.
19. Cf. al-Bukhārī, *Ṣaḥīḥ al-Bukhārī*, *Kitāb al-ʿIlm*, *bāb mā Yudhkar fi'l-Munāwala*; Ibn al-Ṣalāḥ, *ʿUlūm al-Ḥadīth*, pp. 165–166.
20. Ibn al-Ṣalāḥ, *ʿUlūm al-Ḥadīth*, p. 168.
21. Ibid., p. 174.
22. Ibid., p. 176.
23. Ibid., p. 176; al-Bughā, *Buḥūth*, p. 38; Shaykh Amīn, *Adab al-Ḥadīth*, pp. 79–80.
24. Ibn al-Ṣalāḥ, *ʿUlūm al-Ḥadīth*, p. 178.
25. Al-Bughā, *Buḥūth*, pp. 80-91; Shaykh Amīn, *Adab al-Ḥadīth*, p. 39.
26. Cf. al-Bughā, *Buḥūth*, p. 40.

[03] Documentation of Ḥadīth – Early Developments

1. Muslim, *Mukhtaṣar Ṣaḥīḥ Muslim*, p. 429, ḥadīth 1861.
2. Ibn al-Ṣalāḥ, *ʿUlūm al-Ḥadīth*, p. 183; Ṣubḥī al-Ṣāliḥ, *ʿUlūm al-Ḥadīth*, p. 21; Shaykh Amīn, *Adab al-Ḥadīth*, p. 30.
3. Al- Suyūṭī, *Tadrīb al-Rāwī*, p. 287; ʿUmar Hāshim, *Al-Sunna al-Nabawiyya*, p. 58.
4. Cf. ʿUmar Hāshim, *Al-Sunna*, p. 58; Ṣubḥī al-Ṣāliḥ, *ʿUlūm al-Ḥadīth*, p. 22; Shaykh Amīn, *Adab al-Ḥadīth*, p. 33.
5. Ibn al-Ṣalāḥ, *ʿUlūm al-Ḥadīth*, p. 181 f; Shaykh Amīn, *Adab al-Ḥadīth*, p. 33.
6. Ibid., Shaykh Amīn, *Adab al-Ḥadīth*, p. 33.
7. Al-Tirmidhī, *Sunan al-Tirmidhī*, *Kitāb al-Aḥkām*, *bāb. al-yamīn maʿ a'l-shāhid.*
8. Al-Bukhārī, *Ṣaḥīḥ al-Bukhārī*, *Kitāb al-Jihād*, *bāb. al-Ṣabr ʿala'l-Qitāl*. There are references in a number of places in *al-Bukhārī* to ḥadīth that so and so reported from so and so that "ʿAbd Allāh b. Abī Awfā read from what he had written ...".
9. Cf. Ṣubḥī al-Ṣāliḥ, *ʿUlūm al-Ḥadīth*, p. 25.
10. Al-Bukhārī, *al-Tārīkh al-Kabīr*, Vol. IV, p. 182; Shaykh Amīn, *Adab al-Ḥadīth*, p. 35. Al-Baqara which contains 286 verses is the longest sūra of the Qur'ān.
11. Cf. Ṣubḥī al-Ṣāliḥ, *ʿUlūm al-Ḥadīth*, p. 26. Jābir's disciples included Muḥammad b. al-Ḥanafiyya (d. 80 H), Abū Jaʿfar al-Bāqir (d. 114) and ʿAbd Allāh b. Muḥammad b. ʿAqīl.

12. The name was used by ʿAbd Allāh b. ʿAmr b. al-ʿĀṣ himself who said "al-Ṣādiqa is a collection that I wrote from the Messenger of God, peace be on him ...." See al-Khaṭīb al-Baghdādī, *Taqyīd al-ʿIlm*, p. 84.
13. A section of the *Musnad* bears the title "Musnad ʿAbd Allāh b. ʿAmr b. al-ʿĀṣ".
14. Ṣubḥī al-Ṣāliḥ, *ʿUlūm al-Ḥadīth*, p. 27.
15. Ibn ʿAbd al-Barr, *Jāmiʿ Bayān al-ʿIlm*, Vol. I, p. 71; Ṣubḥī al-Ṣāliḥ, *ʿUlūm al-Ḥadīth*, p. 28; Shaykh Amīn, *Adab al-Ḥadīth*, p. 33.
16. Shaykh Amīn, *Adab al-Ḥadīth*, p. 33.
17. Ibn Saʿd, *Ṭabaqāt*, Vol. II, p. 123; Ṣubḥī al-Ṣāliḥ, *ʿUlūm al-Ḥadīth*, p. 30; Shaykh Amīn, *Adab al-Ḥadīth*, p. 36.
18. ʿUmar Hāshim, *Al-Sunna al-Nabawiyya*, p. 55.
19. Ṣubḥī al-Ṣāliḥ, *ʿUlūm al-Ḥadīth*, p. 32. Details of this *Ṣaḥīfa* can be found also in Ibn Saʿd, *Ṭabāqat*, Vol. V, p. 396.
20. ʿUmar Hāshim, *Al-Sunna al-Nabawiyya*, p. 56, also referring to al-Nadwī's *Rijāl al-Fikr wa'l-Daʿwa*, p. 82.
21. Al-Suyūṭī, *Tadrīb al-Rāwī*, p. 287; Ṣubḥī al-Ṣāliḥ, *ʿUlūm al-Ḥadīth*, p. 40.
22. ʿAmrah bt. ʿAbd al-Raḥmān was a leading woman and a learned figure among the *tābiʿūn* who had kept the company of ʿĀ'isha al-Ṣiddīqa and had taken ḥadīth from her. See Ṣubḥī al-Ṣāliḥ, *ʿUlūm al-Ḥadīth*, p. 45; Shaykh Amīn, *Adab al-Ḥadīth*, p. 39; al-Sibāʿī, *Al-Sunna wa-Makānatuhā*, p. 104.
23. Cf. al-Sibāʿī, *Al-Sunna wa-Makānatuhā*, p. 105; ʿUmar Hāshim, *Al-Sunna al-Nabawiyya*, p. 117; Shaykh Amīn, *Adab al-Ḥadīth*, p. 40.
24. Cf. Shaykh Amīn, *Adab al-Ḥadīth*, p. 41.

[04] Ḥadīth Literature – The Major Collections

1. Al-Sibāʿī, *Al-Sunna wa Makānatuhā*, p. 105 f; ʿAbdul Rauf, "Ḥadīth, Its Authority and Authenticity," p. 16.
2. Abū Zahra, *Ibn Ḥanbal*, p. 170; ʿUmar Hāshim, *Al-Sunna*, p. 130; Shaykh Amīn, *Adab al-Ḥadīth*, p. 26; Azami, *Studies in Ḥadīth Methodology*, p. 86.
3. Cf. Shākir, *Al-Bāʿith al-Ḥathīth*, p. 25; ʿUmar Hāshim, *Al-Sunna al-Nabawiyya*, p. 171.
4. ʿUmar Hāshim, *Al-Sunna al-Nabawiyya*, p. 161; Abū Shahba, *al-Wasīṭ*, p. 22.
5. Ibid., pp. 154-155.
6. Cf. ʿUmar Hāshim, *Al-Sunna al-Nabawiyya*, p. 164.
7. Ibid., p. 168.
8. Ibid., pp. 162-163; Rauf, "Ḥadīth", p. 17.
9. Ibid., p. 161.
10. According to Muḥammad Fu'ād ʿAbd al-Bāqī's computation, *Ṣaḥīḥ Muslim* contains 3,033 *aḥādīth* without repetition. ʿAbd al-Bāqī's calculation is not based

on the number of *isnāds* but on subject matter. Usually the *ʿulamā'* of ḥadīth base their computation on the number of *isnād*. Cf. Azami, *Studies in Ḥadīth Methodology*, p. 96.

11. Cf. ʿUmar Hāshim, *Al-Sunna al-Nabawiyya*, pp. 198–199; al-Bughā, *Buḥuth fī ʿUlūm al-Ḥadīth*, p. 54.
12. Muslim, *Ṣaḥīḥ Muslim*, Introduction at p. 37; see also ʿUmar Hāshim, *Al-Sunna al-Nabawiyya*, p. 172.
13. ʿUmar Hāshim, *Al-Sunna al-Nabawiyya*, p. 205.
14. Ṣubḥī al-Ṣāliḥ, *ʿUlūm al-Ḥadīth*, p. 120; Shaykh Amīn, *Adab al-Ḥadīth*, p. 44.
15. Shaykh Amīn, *Adab al-Ḥadīth*, p. 44; al-Qaṭṭān, *Mabāḥith*, p. 105; ʿUmar Hāshim, *Al-Sunna al-Nabawiyya*, pp. 225-226.
16. Abū Dāwūd, *Sunan*, Vol. I, p. 5; see also ʿUmar Hāshim, *Al-Sunna*, p. 249.
17. This is attributed to Abū Ḥāmid al-Ghazālī.
18. Al-Sūyūṭī, *Tadrīb al-Rāwī*, p. 97.
19. Al-Bughā, *Buḥūth fī ʿUlūm al-Ḥadīth*, p. 54.
20. Cf. al-Bughā, *Buḥūth fī ʿUlūm al-Ḥadīth*, pp. 59-60; Shaykh Amīn, *Adab al-Ḥadīth*, p. 48; Siddiqi, *Ḥadīth Literature*, p. 116.
21. Ibid., p. 58; Azami, *Studies in Ḥadīth Methodology*, p. 101; Ṣubḥī al-Ṣāliḥ, *ʿUlūm al-Ḥadīth*, p. 119.
22. Cf. ʿUmar Hāshim, *Al-Sunna al-Nabawiyya*, p. 259.
23. Ibid.
24. Shāh Waliullāh Dihlawī, *Ḥujjat*, Vol. I, p. 107.
25. Cf. Ṣubḥī al-Ṣāliḥ, *ʿUlūm al-Ḥadīth*, p. 119.
26. Al-Suyūṭī, *Tadrīb al-Rāwī*, Vol. I, p. 12; Abū Zahra, *Ibn Ḥanbal*, p. 170; Ṣubḥī al-Ṣāliḥ, *ʿUlūm al-Ḥadīth*, p. 124; Shaykh Amīn, *Adab al-Ḥadīth*, p. 26.
27. Ibid., p. 100.
28. Shaykh Amīn, *Adab al-Ḥadīth*, p. 27; Ṣubḥī al-Ṣāliḥ, *ʿUlūm al-Ḥadīth*, p. 125; ʿUmar Hāshim, *Al-Sunna*, p. 380.
29. Siddiqi, *Ḥadīth Literature*, pp. 123-124.
30. Ibid., p. 125.

[05] Biographies of Ḥadīth Transmitters (*ʿIlm Tārīkh al-Ruwāt*)

1. Ibn al-Ṣalāḥ, *ʿUlūm al-Ḥadīth*, p. 399; al-Jaʿfar, *al-Mūjaz fī ʿUlūm al-Ḥadīth*, pp. 167–168.
2. Cf. Shaykh Amīn, *Adab al-Ḥadīth al-Nabawī*, p. 60 ff.
3. Ibn al-Ṣalāḥ, *ʿUlūm al-Ḥadīth*, p. 380; Shaykh Amīn, *Adab al-Ḥadīth*, p. 62.
4. Ibid., Shaykh Amīn, *Adab al-Ḥadīth*, p. 62.
5. Ibid., p. 382; Shaykh Amīn, *Adab al-Ḥadīth*, p. 63.
6. Cf. Ṣubḥī al-Ṣāliḥ, *ʿUlūm al-Ḥadīth*, p. 111.
7. Ibn al-Ṣalāḥ, *ʿUlūm al-Ḥadīth*, p. 398.

8. Cf. Ṣubḥī al-Ṣāliḥ, *ʿUlūm al-Ḥadīth*, p. 344; Siddiqi, *Ḥadīth Literature*, p. 173.
9. Ibid., p. 346.
10. Siddiqi, *Ḥadīth Literature*, p. 177.
11. Cf. al-Bughā, *Buḥūth fī ʿUlūm al-Ḥadīth*; Siddiqi, *Ḥadīth Literature*, p. 170 ff.
12. Cf. Ṣubḥī al-Ṣāliḥ, *ʿUlūm al-Ḥadīth*, pp. 349-351; Siddiqi, *Ḥadīth Literature*, pp. 179-183.
13. Al-Suyūṭī, *Tadrīb al-Rāwī*, Vol. II, p. 216 ff; Ṣubḥī al-Ṣāliḥ, *ʿUlūm al-Ḥadīth*, p. 353 f.
14. Ibid., pp. 217-218.

[06] Ḥadīth Terminology (*Muṣṭalaḥ al-Ḥadīth*)

1. Abū Dāwūd, *Sunan* (Ḥasan's trans.), Vol. III, p. 1294, ḥadīth 4590.
2. Cf. Kamali, *Principles of Islamic Jurisprudence*, p. 48 ff.
3. Shaykh Amīn, *Adab al-Ḥadīth*, pp. 10-11; Ṣubḥī al-Ṣāliḥ, *ʿUlūm al-Ḥadīth*, p. 3 ff.
4. Cf. ʿUmar Hāshim, *Al-Sunna al-Nabawiyya*, p. 17 ff; Shaykh Amīn, *Adab al-Ḥadīth*, p. 12; al-Jaʿfar, *Al-Mūjaz fī ʿUlūm al-Ḥadīth*, pp. 41-42.
5. Ṣubḥī al-Ṣāliḥ, *ʿUlūm al-Ḥadīth*, p. 11; Abū Shahba, *Al-Wasīṭ*, p. 214 f; ʿUmar Hāshim, *Al-Sunna*, p. 22; Shaykh Amīn, *Adab al-Ḥadīth*, p. 11; al-Jaʿfar, *al-Mūjaz*, p. 20.
6. Ḥākim al-Nīsābūrī, *Maʿrifat ʿUlūm al-Ḥadīth*, p. 18; Ṣubḥī al-Ṣāliḥ, *ʿUlūm al-Ḥadīth*, p. 218; al-Bughā, *Buḥūth*, p. 149.
7. Al-Suyūṭī, *Tadrīb*, Vol. I, p. 43; Shaykh Amīn, *Adab al-Ḥadīth*, p. 27; Ṣubḥī al-Ṣāliḥ, *ʿUlūm al-Ḥadīth*, p. 75; Abū Shahba, *Al-Wasīṭ*, p. 19.
8. Shaykh Amīn, *Adab al-Ḥadīth al-Nabawī*, p. 28; Ṣubḥī al-Ṣaliḥ, *ʿUlūm al-Ḥadīth*, p. 78; al-Jaʿfar, *Al-Mūjaz fī ʿUlūm al-Ḥadīth*, p. 45.

[07] Ḥadīth Forgery (*Waḍʿ al-Ḥadīth*)

1. Al-Sibāʿī, *Al-Sunna wa Makānatuhā*, p. 385; Ṣubḥī al-Ṣāliḥ, *ʿUlūm al-Ḥadīth*, p. 63. Much of the information in this section is also drawn from Kamali, *Principles of Islamic Jurisprudence*, chapter on *Sunna*.
2. Aḥmad Amīn, *Fajr al-Islām*, p. 211.
3. Ibid., p. 75; Azami, *Studies*, p. 69; Hītū, *Wajīz*, p. 999.
4. Azami, *Studies*, pp. 68-70; Hītū, *Wajīz*, p. 292.
5. Al-Sibāʿī, *Al-Sunna*, pp. 76-80; Azami, *Studies*, pp. 68-73; Aḥmad Amīn, *Fajr al-Islām*, p. 212.
6. Shaykh Amīn, *Adab al-Ḥadīth*, p. 50.
7. Al-Sibāʿī, *Al-Sunna*, p. 84.

8. Ibid., p. 82.
9. Al-Suyūṭī, *Al-La'āli' al-Māṣnū'a*, Vol. I, p. 238; Azami, *Studies*, p. 68; Hītū, *Wajīz*, p. 290.
10. Ibid., p. 85 ff; Aḥmad Amīn, *Fajr al-Islam*, p. 213.
11. Abū Shahba, *Al-Wasīṭ*, p. 331; Shaykh Amīn, *Adab al-Ḥadīth*, p. 50; ʿUmar Hāshim, *Al-Sunna al-Nabawiyya*, p. 82.
12. Al-Sibāʿī, *Al-Sunna*, pp. 86-87; Azami, *Studies*, p. 69; Hītū, *Wajīz*, p. 290.
13. Shaykh Amīn, *Adab al-Ḥadīth*, p. 54.
14. See for further details al-Sibāʿī, *Al-Sunna*, p. 122; Abū Shahba, *Al-Wasīṭ*, p. 362.
15. Al-Ṣubḥī al-Ṣāliḥ, *ʿUlūm al-Ḥadīth*, p. 272.
16. Zaylaʿī, *Naṣb al-Rāya*, Vol. I, p. 41; Abū Shahba, *Al-Wasīṭ*, p. 353.
17. This may be a corrupted version of an accepted ḥadīth which al-Nasā'ī has recorded wherein the Prophet said when taking homage from women "My words given to one woman apply also to a hundred of them".
18. Abū Shahba, *Al-Wasīṭ*, p. 354.
19. Ibid., p. 345.
20. Cf. Abū Shahba, *Al-Wasīṭ*, p. 346.
21. Ibn Taymiyya, *Uṣūl al-Tafsīr*, p. 32; Abū Shahba, *Al-Wasīṭ*, p. 346.
22. Cf. Abū Shahba, *Al-Wasīṭ*, pp. 347-348.
23. Abū Shahba, *Al-Wasīṭ*, p. 354. The author has also noted two works of al-Samarqandī, namely *Tanbīh al-Ghāfilīn*, and *Bustān al-ʿArifīn* that are afflicted with *mawḍūʿāt* and *Isrā'iliyāt*, and so is al-Suhrawardī's (d. 632) book *ʿAwārif al-Maʿārif.*
24. See for details Abū Shahba, *al-Wasīṭ*, pp. 344-358.
25. Shākir, *al-Bāʿith al-Ḥathīth*, p. 81; ʿUmar Hāshim, *Buḥūth*, p. 95.
26. Ibid., p. 82.
27. Ibid., p. 180.
28. Al-Sibāʿī, *Al-Sunna wa Makānatuhā*, p. 117.
29. Ṣubḥī al-Ṣāliḥ, *ʿUlūm al-Ḥadīth*, pp. 265-266.
30. Ibn Taymiyya, *Minhāj al-Sunna*, Vol. III, p. 31.
31. Shaykh Amīn, *Adab al-Ḥadīth*, p. 57.

[08] Impugnment and Validation (*al-Jarḥ wa'l-Taʿdīl*)

1. Muslim, *Mukhtaṣar Ṣaḥīḥ Muslim*, ḥadīth 1861.
2. Ibid., ḥadīth 1863.
3. Al-Suyūṭī, *Tadrīb al-Rāwī*, p. 22; al-Khaṭīb, *Uṣūl al-Ḥadīth*, p. 274.
4. See for details al-Sibāʿī, *Al-Sunna*, p. 109 ff; Azami, *Studies in Ḥadīth*, p. 46 ff; al-Khaṭīb, *Uṣūl al-Ḥadīth*, p. 260 ff; Siddiqi, *Ḥadīth Literature*, p. 189 ff.

5. Al-Nīsābūrī, *Maʿrifat ʿUlūm al-Ḥadīth*, p. 52; ʿUmar Hāshim, *Al-Sunna al-Nabawiyya*, p. 364; Mannāʿ al-Qaṭṭān, *Mabāḥith*, pp. 75-76; al-Bughā, *Buḥūth fī ʿUlūm al-Ḥadīth*, p. 87.
6. Al-Sibāʿī, *Al-Sunna wa Makānatuhā*, pp. 111-112; Siddiqi, *Ḥadīth Literature*, p. 169.
7. Muḥammad Ibn Ḥibbān al-Bustī, "*Majruḥīn Min al-Muḥaddithīn*", Aya Sofya Ms. No. 496, Istanbul, quoted in Azami, *Studies in Ḥadīth*, pp. 52-53.
8. Muslim b. Ḥajjāj al-Nīsābūrī, *al-Tamyīz*, ed. M.M. Azami, Riyad: University of Riyad Press, 1395, pp. 136-138; see also Azami, *Studies in Ḥadīth*, p. 55.
9. Ibn al-Ṣalāḥ, *ʿUlūm al-Ḥadīth*, pp. 122-124.
10. Al-Suyūṭī, *Tadrīb al-Rāwī*, p. 111.
11. Al-Baghdādī, *al-Kifāya*, p. 109 ff; Ibn al-Ṣalāḥ, *ʿUlūm al-Ḥadīth*, p. 106.
12. Ibid., p. 156.
13. Ṣubḥī al-Ṣāliḥ, *ʿUlūm al-Ḥadīth*, p. 136.
14. Al-Baghdādī, *Al-Kifāya*, p. 127.
15. Ibid., p. 129.
16. Ibid., p. 130.
17. Ibid., p. 131.
18. Ibid., p. 132.
19. Ibid., p. 145.
20. Ibn al-Ṣalāḥ, *ʿUlūm al-Ḥadīth*, p. 116.
21. Ibid.
22. Ibid., p. 118.
23. Ibid., p. 119.
24. Al-Suyūṭī, *Tadrīb*, Vol. I, pp. 344-345.
25. Abū Shahba, *al-Wasīṭ*, p. 391.
26. Al-Suyūṭī, *Tadrīb*, Vol. I, p. 346.
27. Al-ʿAsqalānī, *Taqrīb al-Tahdhib*, p. 5 ff; al-Shawkānī, *Irshād*, p. 69; Shākir, *Al-Bāʿith al-Ḥathīth*, pp. 118-119; Azami, *Studies in Ḥadīth*, pp. 58-59; al-Khaṭīb, *Uṣūl al-Ḥadīth*, p. 274 ff; al-Qaṭṭān, *ʿUlūm al-Ḥadīth*, pp. 71-75; Ṣubḥī al-Ṣāliḥ, *ʿUlūm al-Ḥadīth*, pp. 137-138.
28. Ibn al-Ṣalāḥ, *ʿUlūm al-Ḥadīth*, p. 109; al-Baghdādī, *al-Kifāya*, p. 132; al-Jaʿfar, *al-Mūjaz fī ʿUlūm al-Ḥadīth*, p. 161.
29. Ibid., p. 116.
30. Al-Baghdādī, *Al-Kifāya*, p. 136; Ibn al-Ṣalāḥ, *ʿUlūm al-Ḥadīth*, p. 106; Abū Shahba, *Al-Wasīṭ*, p. 393.
31. Abū Shahba, *Al-Wasīṭ*, p. 393.
32. Ibn al-Ṣalāḥ, *ʿUlūm al-Ḥadīth*, p. 110; Abū Shahba, *Al-Wasīṭ*, p. 398.
33. Al-Suyūṭī, *Tadrīb*, p. 208; Ibn al-Ṣalāḥ, *ʿUlūm al-Ḥadīth*, p. 110.
34. Ibn al-Ṣalāḥ, *ʿUlūm al-Ḥadīth*, p. 109.
35. Ibid., p. 111.

36. Abū Shahba, *al-Wasīṭ*, pp. 393-394.
37. Ibid., p. 386.
38. Al-Baghdādī, *Al-Kifāya*, p. 135; Abū Shahba, *Al-Wasīṭ*, p. 387.
39. Al-Dhahabī, *Mizān al-Iʿtidāl fī Naqd al-Rijāl*, Vol. I, pp. 26, 40-42, 53.
40. Ibid., pp. 116, 210; ʿUmar Hāshim, *Al-Sunna al-Nabawiyya*, pp. 100-102.

[09] Hidden Defects I (*ʿIlal al-Ḥadīth*)

1. Ibn al-Ṣalāḥ, *ʿUlūm al-Ḥadīth*, p. 90.
2. Al-Khaṭīb, *Uṣūl al-Ḥadīth*, p. 291 ff; al-Qaṭṭān, *Mabāḥith*, p. 82 ff; Azami, *Studies in Ḥadīth*, p. 67; Ṣubḥī al-Ṣāliḥ, *ʿUlūm al-Ḥadīth*, p. 183.
3. Al-Nīsābūrī, *Maʿrifat ʿUlūm al-Ḥadīth*, pp. 112-113.
4. Cf. Ṣubḥī al-Ṣāliḥ, *ʿUlūm al-Ḥadīth*, p. 180; Mannāʿ al-Qaṭṭān, *Mabāḥith fī ʿUlūm al-Ḥadīth*, p. 82.
5. See for details al-Khaṭīb, *Usūl al-Ḥadīth*, *ʿUlūmuh wa Muṣṭalaḥuh*, p. 296.
6. Al-Rāzī, *ʿIlal al-Ḥadīth*, Vol. I, p. 172; al-Khaṭīb, *Usūl al-Ḥadīth*, p. 295.
7. Al-Nīsābūrī, *Maʿrifat ʿUlūm al-Ḥadīth*, p. 115.
8. Ibid., pp. 113-119; al-Qaṭṭān, *Mabāḥith*, p.118; al-Bahnasāwi, *Al-Sunna al-Muftari ʿAlayhā*, p. 75; al-Khusht, *Mafātih ʿUlūm al-Ḥadīth,* p. 95.
9. Al-Bukhārī, *Ṣaḥīḥ al-Bukhārī*, Vol. VII, pp. 172-173.
10. ʿAbdul Rauf, "Ḥadīth, Its Authority and Authenticity", p. 6.
11. Al-Suyūṭī, *Tadrīb al-Rāwī*, Vol. I, p. 254.
12. Al-Nīsābūrī, *Maʿrifat ʿUlūm al-Ḥadīth*, pp. 113-114.
13. Ibid., pp. 114-115.
14. Ibid., p. 116; see also al-Suyūṭṭ, *Tadrīb*, Vol. I, p. 260.
15. Ibid., p. 117; see also al-Suyūṭī, *Tadrīb*, Vol. I, p. 261.
16. Ibid., pp. 117-118; see also al-Suyūṭī, *Tadrīb*, Vol. I, p. 261.
17. Ibid., pp. 118-119; see also al-Suyūṭi, *Tadrīb*, Vol. I, p. 261.
18. Ibid., p. 164; Ibn as-Ṣalāḥ, *ʿUlūm al-Ḥadīth*, pp. 92-129.

[10] Hidden Defects II (*Tadlīs al-Ḥadīth*)

1. Al-Nīsābūrī, *Maʿrifat ʿUlūm al-Ḥadīth*, p. 103; al-Khusht, *Mafātīḥ ʿUlūm al-Ḥadīth,* p. 106.
2. Cf. Ṣubḥī al-Ṣāliḥ, *ʿUlūm al-Ḥadīth*, p. 174.
3. Ibn al-Ṣalāḥ, *ʿUlūm al-Ḥadīth,* p. 74; Ṣubḥī al-Ṣāliḥ, *ʿUlūm al-Ḥadīth,* p. 177; Azami, *Studies in Ḥadīth*, p. 65; al-Sibāʿī, *Al-Sunna*, p. 232.
4. Al-Baghdādī, *Al-Kifāya*, p. 357; Ṣubḥī al-Ṣāliḥ, *ʿUlūm al-Ḥadīth*, p. 179; al-Khusht, *Mafātīḥ,* p. 112.
5. Cf. al-Khusht, *Mafātīḥ ʿUlūm al-Ḥadīth,* p. 104.

6. Cf. Azami, *Studies in Ḥadīth,* pp. 65-66; al-Sibāʿī, *Al-Sunna,* p. 232; al-Khaṭīb, *Uṣūl al-Ḥadīth,* p. 342.
7. See for details al-Suyūṭī, *Tadrīb al-Rāwī,* Vol. II, p. 268 ff.

[11] Conflict in Ḥadīth (*Mukhtalif al-Ḥadīth*)

1. Other similar expressions that have been used are *ta'wīl al-ḥadīth*, and *talfīq al-ḥadīth*, both implying the attempt to reconcile apparent conflicts in ḥadīth. See for details Abū Shahba, *Al-Wasīṭ*, pp. 442-444.
2. Ibn Māja, *Sunan Ibn Māja*, Vol. I, p. 72, ḥadīth 518.
3. Abū Shahba, *Al-Wasīṭ*, p. 444; al-Qaṭṭān, *Mābāḥith*, p. 92.
4. Al-Suyūṭī, *Tadrīb*, p. 388 f; Abū Shahba, *Al-Wasīt*, p. 444 f.
5. Ibid., p. 197; see also al-Bughā, *Buḥūth fī ʿUlūm al-Ḥadīth*, p. 91.
6. Al-Suyūṭī, *Ṣaḥiḥ al-Jāmiʿ al-Ṣagḥīr*, ed. al-Albānī, ḥadīth 1261.
7. Ibid., ḥadīth 1288.
8. Muslim, *Mukhtaṣar Ṣaḥīḥ Muslim*, p. 555, ḥadīth 2088.
9. Al-Suyūṭī, *Ṣaḥīḥ al-Jāmiʿ al-Ṣagḥīr*, ed. al-Albānī, ḥadīth 1285; al-Qaraḍāwī, *Kayfa Nataʿāmal maʿa al-Sunna*, pp. 40-41.
10. Abū Dāwūd, *Mukhtaṣar Sunan Abī Dāwūd*, ed. al-Mundhirī, ḥadīth 4112.
11. Cf. al-Qaraḍāwī, *Kayfa Nataʿāmal*, p. 114.
12. Muslim, *Ṣaḥīḥ Muslim, Kitāb al-Ṭalāq, bāb fī khurūj al-mutallaqa min baytihā.*
13. Al-Bukhārī, *Ṣaḥīḥ al-Bukhārī, Kitāb al-Ṣalāt, bāb aṣḥāb al-ḥirāb fīʿl-masjid*; Muslim, *Ṣaḥīḥ Muslim, Kitāb Ṣalāt al-ʿĪdayn, bāb al-rukhsa fī'l-laʿib al-ladhī lā maʿṣiya fīhi.*
14. Al-ʿAsqalānī, *Fatḥ al-Bārī*, Vol. II, p. 445.
15. Al-Qaraḍāwī, *Kayfa Nataʿāmal*, p. 114.
16. See for illustrations of metaphors in the Qur'ān, al-Qaraḍāwī, *Kayfa Nataʿāmal maʿa al-Sunna*, pp. 156-157.
17. Al-Haythamī, *Majmaʿ al-Zawā'id*, Vol. 10, p. 190. As for the actual ḥadīth concerning the cat, both al-Bukhārī and Muslim have recorded it from Abū Hurayra as reviewed below.
18. Al-Qaraḍāwī, *Kayfa Nataʿāmal maʿa al-Sunna*, pp. 46-47.
19. Al-Tabrīzī, *Mishkāt al-Maṣābīḥ*, Vol. I, ḥadīth 1903.
20. Ibid., Vol. III, ḥadīth 5591.
21. Muslim, *Mukhtaṣar Ṣaḥīḥ Muslim*, p. 570, ḥadīth 2149.
22. Al-Qaraḍāwī, *Kayfa Nataʿāmal maʿa al-Sunna*, p. 161.
23. Quoted by al-Qaraḍāwī without reference to source. Ibid., p. 161.
24. Muslim, *Mukhtaṣar Ṣaḥīḥ*, p. 471, ḥadīth 1764.
25. Al-Qaraḍāwī, *Kayfa Nataʿāmal maʿa al-Sunna*, pp. 161, 170.
26. Ibn Ḥazm, *Al-Muḥallā*, Vol. VII, pp. 230-231. See also al-Qaraḍāwī, *Kayfa Nataʿāmal maʿa al-Sunna*, p. 167.

27. Muslim, *Mukhtaṣar Ṣaḥīḥ Muslim,* p. 157, ḥadīth 580.
28. Al-Qaraḍāwī, *Kayfa Nataʿāmal maʿa al-Sunna,* p. 169.
29. A *wasq* (pl. *awsuq*) is equivalent to a camel load. See for details Kamali, *Jurisprudence,* p. 112; Shaykh Amīn, *Adab al-Ḥadīth,* p. 70; al-Bughā, *Buḥūth fī ʿUlūm al-Ḥadīth,* pp. 91-93.
30. Al-Tirmidhī, *Sunan al-Tirmidhī, Kitāb al-Zakāh, bāb ma jāʾa fiʾl-khuḍrāwāt.*
31. Al-Qaraḍāwī, *Kayfa Nataʿāmal maʿa al-Sunna,* p. 69.
32. Abū Dāwūd, *Sunan Abī Dāwūd,* ed. al-Mundhirī, p. 678, ḥadīth 4717.
33. Ibid., ḥadīth 4718; Muslim, *Mukhtaṣar Ṣaḥīḥ Muslim,* p. 423, ḥadīth 1600.
34. Cf. al-Qaraḍāwī, *Kayfa Nataʿāmal maʿa al-Sunna,* p. 97.
35. Al-Bukhārī, *Ṣaḥīḥ al-Bukhārī,* (tr. Muhsin Khan), Vol. VIII, ḥadīth 666.
36. Ṣubḥī al-Ṣāliḥ, *ʿUlūm al-Ḥadīth,* p. 111; Mannāʿ al-Qaṭṭān, *Mabāḥith,* p. 112; Shaykh Amīn, *Adab al-Ḥadīth,* p. 7.

[12] Unfamiliar Expressions in Ḥadīth (*Gharīb al-Ḥadīth*)

1. Abū Shahba, *Al-Wasīṭ,* p. 434.
2. Al-Bukhārī, *Ṣaḥīḥ al-Bukhārī, Kitāb al-Shufʿa, bāb. ʿarḍ al-Shufʿa ʿalā Sāḥibihā qabl al-bayʿ waʾl-saqab.*
3. Mannāʿ al-Qaṭṭān has listed about 15 works on *gharīb al-ḥadīth* in his *Mabāḥith fī ʿUlūm al-Ḥadīth,* pp. 78-99. See also Shaykh Amīn, *Adab al-Ḥadīth,* p. 69.
4. See for details al-Ḥākim al-Nīsābūrī, *Maʿrifat ʿUlūm al-Ḥadīth,* p. 89; Ibn al-Ṣalāḥ, *ʿUlūm al-Ḥadīth,* p. 274; Mannāʿ al-Qaṭṭān, *Mābaḥith fī ʿUlūm al-Ḥadīth,* pp. 80-81; ʿUmar Hāshim, *Al-Sunna,* p. 373.
5. Cf. ʿUthmān al-Khusht, *Mafātīḥ ʿUlūm al-Ḥadīth,* p. 125.
6. Al-Ḥākim al-Nīsābūrī, *Maʿrifat ʿUlūm al-Ḥadīth,* p. 88.
7. Ibid., pp. 89-92.

[13] The Abrogator and Abrogated in Ḥadīth (*al-Nāsikh waʾl-Mansūkh fiʾl-Ḥadīth*)

1. Ibn al-Ṣalāḥ, *ʿUlūm al-Ḥadīth,* p. 277.
2. Cf. Shaykh Amīn, *Adab al-Ḥadīth,* p. 73; Muṣṭafā al-Bughā, *Buḥūth fī ʿUlūm al-Ḥadīth,* p. 95.
3. Cf. Kamali, *Principles of Islamic Jurisprudence,* Ch. 7 on abrogation.
4. Muslim, *Mukhtaṣar Ṣaḥīḥ Muslim,* p. 133, ḥadīth 496.
5. Both of these ḥadīths are recorded in al-Ḥakīm al-Nīsābūrī, *Maʿrifat ʿUlūm al-Ḥadīth,* pp. 86-87.
6. Abū Dāwūd, *Mukhtaṣar Sunan Abī Dāwūd,* p. 22, ḥadīth 192. Ibn al-Ṣalāḥ has recorded the relevant phrase as "*massat al-nār*" instead of "*ghayyarat al-nār*";

ʿUlūm al-Ḥadīth, p. 278. Details of both of these ḥadīths can be found in al-Ḥākim al-Nīsābūrī, *Maʿrifat ʿUlūm al-Ḥadīth*, p. 85 f.

7. Al-Nīsābūrī, *Maʿrifat*, pp. 87-88.
8. Al-Tabrīzī, *Mishkāt*, Vol. I, ḥadīth 2012; al-Bukhārī, *Ṣaḥīḥ al-Bukhārī*, *Kitāb al-Ḥajj, bāb. al-hijāma li'l-muḥrim.*
9. Ibn al-Ṣalāḥ, *ʿUlūm al-Ḥadīth*, p. 278; Shaykh Amīn, *Adab al-Ḥadīth*, p. 72; al-Qaṭṭān, *Mabāḥith*, p. 115.
10. Al-Suyūṭī, *Tadrīb al-Rāwī*, Vol. II, p. 192.
11. Ibid., al-Qaṭṭān, *Mabāḥith*, p. 114.
12. Cf. al-Bughā, *Buḥūth fī ʿUlūm al-Ḥadīth*, p. 95; Abū Shahba, *Al-Wasīṭ*, p. 463.

[14] Additional Segments to Ḥadīth by Reliable Narrators (*Ziyādāt al-Thiqāt*)

1. Cf. Abū Shahba, *Al-Wasīṭ*, p. 376 ff; Kamali, *Principles of Islamic Jurisprudence*, p. 78 f.
2. Al-Baghdādī, *Al-Kifāya*, pp. 226-228.
3. Ibid., p. 464.
4. Al-Suyūṭī, *Tadrīb al-Rāwī*, Vol. I, p. 246; Abū Shahba, *Al-Wasīṭ*, p. 376; al-Qaṭṭān, *Mabāḥith fī ʿUlūm al-Ḥadīth*, p. 160; al-Jaʿfar, *Al-Mūjaz fī ʿUlūm al-Ḥadīth*, p. 94 ff.
5. Al-Ḥākim al-Nīsābūrī, *Maʿrifat ʿUlūm al-Ḥadīth*, pp. 130-131; al-Suyūṭī, *Tadrīb*, Vol. I, p. 248; al-Baghdādī, *al-Kifāya*, p. 469.
6. Al-Nīsābūrī, *Maʿrifat*, p. 134.
7. Ibn al-Ṣalāḥ, *ʿUlūm al-Ḥadīth*, pp. 286-287.
8. Ibid.
9. Ibid., p. 287.
10. Al-Baghdādī, *al-Kifāya*, pp. 223-224.
11. Ibid., pp. 223-227.
12. Ibid., p. 465.
13. Ibid., pp. 367-369.

[15] Ḥadīth Classification I (*Ṣaḥīḥ, Ḥasan* and *Ḍaʿīf*)

1. Al-Shawkānī, *Irshād al-Fuḥūl*, p. 64; al-Sibāʿī, *Al-Sunna*, p. 94; al-Khaṭīb, *Uṣūl al-Ḥadīth*, p. 34; Azami, *Studies in Ḥadīth*, p. 61 ff.
2. Cf. Ṣubḥī al-Ṣāliḥ, *ʿUlūm al-Ḥadīth*, p. 161 and p. 153.
3. Ibn al-Ṣalāḥ, *ʿUlūm al-Ḥadīth*, p. 18; Ṣubḥī al-Ṣāliḥ, *ʿUlūm al-Ḥadīth*, p. 152.
4. Al-Qāsimī, *Qawāʿid al-Taḥdīth*, p. 59; Ṣubḥī al-Ṣāliḥ, *ʿUlūm al-Ḥadīth*, pp. 153-154.

5. Ibn al-Ṣalāḥ, *ʿUlūm al-Ḥadīth*, p. 35; al-Bughā, *Buḥūth*, p. 101; Jammāz, *Muhāḍārāt fi ʿUlūm al-Ḥadīth*, p. 72 ff.
6. Al-Nīsābūrī, *Maʿrifat ʿUlūm al-Ḥadīth*, pp. 54-55; Ibn al-Ṣalāh, *ʿUlūm al-Ḥadīth*, pp. 14-15.
7. Al-Suyūṭī, *Tadrīb al-Rāwī*, Vol. I, p. 78.
8. Al-Sibāʿī, *Al-Sunna*, p. 94; al-Khaṭīb, *Uṣūl al-Ḥadīth*, p. 331; Shaykh Amīn, *Adab al-Ḥadīth*, p. 85.
9. Ibn al-Ṣalāḥ, *ʿUlūm al-Ḥadīth*, p. 40; al-Jaʿfar, *Al-Mūjaz*, p. 92.
10. Al-Suyūṭī, *Tadrīb*, p. 195; al-Khaṭīb, *Uṣūl al-Ḥadīth*, p. 313; Ṣubḥī al-Ṣalīḥ, *ʿUlūm al-Ḥadīth*, p. 167; al-Kamali, *Principles of Islamic Jurisprudence*, p. 79.
11. Ibn al-Ṣalāḥ, *ʿUlūm al-Ḥadīth*, p. 56; Ṣubḥī al-Ṣāliḥ, *ʿUlūm al-Ḥadīth*, p. 167; al-Suyūṭī, *Tadrīb*, Vol. I, p. 239.
12. Cf. Ṣubḥī al-Ṣāliḥ, *ʿUlūm al-Ḥadīth*, p. 166; al-Khusht, *Mafātīḥ ʿUlūm al-Ḥadīth*, p. 108 ff.
13. Al-Suyūṭī, *Tadrīb*, p. 119.
14. Al-Ḥākim al-Nīsābūrī, *Maʿrifat ʿUlūm al-Ḥadīth*, p. 39.
15. Ibn al-Ṣalāḥ, *ʿUlūm al-Ḥadīth*, p. 93; al-Sibāʿī, *Sunna*, p. 96; al-Khaṭīb, *Uṣūl al-Ḥadīth*, p. 344; Jammāz, *Muḥāḍārāt*, p. 78; al-Khusht, *Mafātīḥ*, p. 81; Siddiqi, *Ḥadīth Literature*, p. 192.
16. Ṣubḥī al-Ṣalīḥ, *ʿUlūm al-Ḥadīth*, p. 157; ʿUmar Hāshim, *Al-Sunna al-Nabawiyya*, p. 143.
17. Cf. al-Jaʿfar, *Al-Mūjaz*, p. 125.
18. Ibn al-Ṣalāḥ, *ʿUlūm al-Ḥadīth*, p. 103; Yūsuf al-Qaraḍāwī, *Kayfa Nataʿāmal maʿa al-Sunna al-Nabawiyya*, p. 75; al-Qaṭṭān, *Mabāḥith*, p. 118; ʿUmar Hāshim, *Al-Sunna al-Nabawiyya*, pp. 143-144.
19. Ibid., pp. 102-103.
20. Ibid., pp. 13-14.
21. Cf. al-Bughā, *Buḥūth fi ʿUlūm al-Ḥadīth*, pp. 104-105; al-Jaʿfar, *Al-Mūjaz*, p. 82.
22. Cf. ʿUthmān al-Khusht, *Mafātīḥ ʿUlūm al-Ḥadīth*, pp. 66-67; al-Qaṭṭān, *Mabāḥith*, p. 108.
23. Cf. Ṣubḥī al-Ṣāliḥ, *ʿUlūm al-Ḥadīth*, p. 158; al-Khusht, *Mafātīḥ*, p. 71.
24. Cf. al-Nīsābūrī, *Maʿrifat ʿUlūm al-Ḥadīth*, p. 54; al-Qaṭṭān, *Mabāḥith fi ʿUlūm al-Ḥadīth*, pp. 116-117; al-Bughā, *Buḥūth fi ʿUlūm al-Ḥadīth*, p. 104.
25. Al-Khaṭīb, *Uṣūl al-Ḥadīth*, pp. 352-353; al-Qaṭṭān, *Mabāḥith*, p. 118; Azami, *Studies in Ḥadīth*, p. 64; al-Qaraḍāwī, *Kayfa Nataʿāmal maʿa al-Sunna*, p. 34.
26. Ṣubḥī al-Ṣāliḥ, *ʿUlūm al-Ḥadīth*, p. 146; Kamali, *Jurisprudence*, p. 81. Ibn al-Ṣalāḥ, *ʿUlūm al-Ḥadīth*, pp. 102-103.
27. Al-Shawkānī, *Irshād al-Fuḥūl*, p. 68; al-Khaṭīb, *Uṣūl al-Ḥadīth*, pp. 267-268; Ṣubḥī al-Ṣālih, *ʿUlūm al-Ḥadīth*, p. 133.

[16] Ḥadīth Classification II (*Marfūʿ*, *Mawqūf*, *Muttaṣil*, *Maqṭūʿ*, *Muʿanʿin*, *Muʿannan* and *Muʿallaq*)

1. Al-Suyūṭī, *Tadrīb al-Rāwī*, Vol. I, p. 184; al-Bughā, *Buḥūth fī ʿUlūm al-Ḥadīth*, p. 147.
2. Ibn al-Ṣalāḥ, *Ulūm al-Ḥadīth*, p. 45.
3. Al-Suyūṭī, *Tadrīb*, Vol. I, p. 187; Abū Shahba, *Al-Wasīṭ*, p. 49.
4. Ibid., p. 185.
5. Cf. Ibn al-Ṣalāḥ, *ʿUlūm al-Ḥadīth*, p. 50.
6. An example of disconnected *Mawqūf* that consists of a saying of a Companion is this: Mālik reported from Nāfiʿ that ʿUmar wrote to his officials that "the most important of your affairs in my view is the *ṣalāh* ...". This is disconnected because Nāfiʿ did not meet with ʿUmar, and it is *Mawqūf* because it stops at the level of a Companion. Cf. Ibn al-Ṣalāḥ, *ʿUlūm al-Ḥadīth*, p. 46. An example of action (*fiʿl*) would be a report for example that ʿĀlī b. Abī Ṭālib did such and such, and of tacit approval would be to say that "so and so did such and such in the presence of Abū Bakr and he did not object to it".
7. Ibn al-Ṣalāḥ, *ʿUlūm al-Ḥadīth*, p. 50; al-Baghdādī, *Al-Kifāya*, p. 463; Abū Shahba, *Al-Wasīṭ*, pp. 210-211.
8. Cf. Ṣubḥī al-Ṣāliḥ, *ʿUlūm al-Ḥadīth*, p. 208.
9. Ṣubḥī al-Ṣāliḥ, *ʿUlūm al-Ḥadīth*, p. 220.
10. Ibn al-Ṣālaḥ, *ʿUlūm al-Ḥadīth*, p. 44.
11. Ibid., p. 47.
12. Al-Suyūṭī, *Tadrīb*, Vol. I, p. 194.
13. Ibn al-Ṣalāḥ, *ʿUlūm al-Ḥadīth*, p. 61; Ṣubḥī al-Ṣāliḥ, *ʿUlūm al-Ḥadīth*, p. 222; al-Suyūṭī, *Tadrīb*, Vol. I, pp. 214-215.
14. *Ṣaḥīḥ Muslim*, Introduction, p. 23; Ṣubḥī al-Ṣāliḥ, *ʿUlūm al-Ḥadīth*, p. 222.
15. Ibn al-Ṣalāḥ, *ʿUlūm al-Ḥadīth*, p. 66.
16. Ibid., p. 65; al-Suyūṭī, *Tadrīb*, Vol. I, p. 214.
17. Cf. Ṣubḥī al-Ṣāliḥ, *ʿUlūm al-Ḥadīth*, p. 224.
18. See for further details, Ibn al-Ṣalāḥ, *ʿUlūm al-Ḥadīth*, p. 62 ff; al-Suyūṭī, *Tadrīb*, Vol. I, p. 215 ff; Ṣubḥī al-Ṣāliḥ, *ʿUlūm al-Ḥadīth*, p. 224; al-Jaʿfar, *Al-Mūjaz*, p. 57.
19. Ibn al-Ṣalāḥ, *ʿUlūm al-Ḥadīth*, pp. 67-70; al-Suyūṭī, *Tadrīb*, Vol. I, pp. 219-221; al-Jaʿfar, *Al-Mūjaz*, p. 58; Ṣubḥī al-Ṣāliḥ, *ʿUlūm al-Ḥadīth*, pp. 224-225.

[17] Ḥadīth Classification III (*Fard*, *Gharīb*, *ʿAzīz*, *Mashhūr*, *Mutawātir* and *Āḥād*)

1. Ibn al-Ṣalāḥ, *ʿUlūm al-Ḥadīth*, p. 76; al-Bughā, *Buḥūth*, p. 152.
2. Ibid., al-Bughā, *Buḥūth*, p. 152.

3. Al-Nīsābūrī, *Ma*ʿ*rifat* ʿ*Ulūm al-Ḥadīth*, p. 100; Ṣubḥī al-Ṣāliḥ, ʿ*Ulūm al-Ḥadīth*, p. 228.
4. Ibid., al-Bughā, *Buḥūth*, p. 152.
5. Ibn al-Ṣalāḥ, ʿ*Ulūm al-Ḥadīth*, p. 78.
6. Ibid.
7. Al-Bukhārī, *Ṣaḥīḥ al-Bukhārī, Kitāb al-Īmān, bāb Ḥubb al-Raṣūl s.a.w. min al-Īmān.*
8. Ibid., *Kitāb al-Īmān, bāb al-Muslim man salima'l-Muslimūn...*
9. Al-Nīsābūrī, *Ma*ʿ*rifat* ʿ*Ulūm al-Ḥadīth*, p. 92.
10. Ibid.
11. Ibid.
12. See for these and other examples Ṣubḥī al-Ṣāliḥ, ʿ*Ulūm al-Ḥadīth*, pp. 232-233; Abū Shahba, *Al-Wasīṭ*, p. 199.
13. Al-Bukhārī, *Ṣaḥīḥ al-Bukhārī, Kitāb al-*ʿ*Ilm, bāb Ithm man kadhaba* ʿ*alā al-Nabī.*
14. Al-Suyūṭī, *Tadrīb al-Rāwī*, Vol. I, p. 191.
15. Al-Bukhārī, *Ṣaḥīḥ al-Bukhārī, Kitāb al-Ṭahāra, bāb. al-Masḥ* ʿ*alā'l-Khuffayn.*
16. See for details Kamali, *Jurisprudence*, p. 72 ff.
17. Cf. Kamali, *Jurisprudence*, p. 76.
18. Ibid.
19. Al-Tabrīzī, *Mishkāt al-Maṣābīḥ*, Vol. I, p. 104, ḥadīth 319.

[18] Confirmation and Follow-up (*al-Mutābi*ʿ *wa'l-Shāhid*)

1. Al-Bukhārī, *Ṣaḥīḥ al-Bukhārī, Kitāb al-Ṣiyām, bāb. Idhā ra'aytum al-hilāla fa-ṣūmū.*
2. Ibn al-Ṣalāḥ, ʿ*Ulūm al-Ḥadīth*, p. 85. The various versions of this ḥadīth also appear in *Ṣaḥīḥ Muslim* in the chapter on *al-Ṭahara*.
3. Ibn al-Ṣalāḥ, ʿ*Ulūm al-Ḥadīth*, p. 80 f; Abū Shahba, *al-Wasīt*, p. 364 f; Ṣubḥī al-Ṣāliḥ, ʿ*Ulūm al-Ḥadīth*, p. 241 f.

[19] Prerequisites of Authenticity

1. ʿAbdul Rauf, "Ḥadīth, Its Authority and Authenticity", p. 10; ʿAjājj al-Khaṭīb, *Uṣūl al-Ḥadīth*, p. 313.
2. Al-Shawkānī, *Irshād*, p. 65; Azami, *Studies in Ḥadīth Methodology*, p. 33.
3. Al-Nīsābūrī, *Ma*ʿ*rifat* ʿ*Ulūm al-Ḥadīth*, pp. 53-54; Ibn al-Ṣalāḥ, ʿ*Ulūm al-Ḥadīth*, p. 256; al-Qaṭṭān, *Mabāḥith fī* ʿ*Ulūm al-Ḥadīth*, pp. 179-180.
4. Ibn al-Ṣalāḥ, ʿ*Ulūm al-Ḥadīth*, p. 257; Abū Shahba, *Al-Wasīṭ*, p. 119 f.
5. Ibid., p. 262; al-Jaʿfar, *Al-Mūjaz*, p. 148.

6. ʿAbdul Rauf, "Ḥadīth, Its Authority and Authenticity", p. 23; ʿAjājj al-Khaṭīb, *Uṣūl al-Ḥadīth*, p. 306; Ṣubḥī al-Ṣāliḥ, *ʿUlūm al-Ḥadīth wa Muṣṭalaḥuh*, 1996, pp. 134-135.

7. Ibn al-Ṣalāḥ, *ʿUlūm al-Ḥadīth*, p. 52; al-Shawkānī, *Irshād al-Fuḥūl*, p. 64; Abū Zahra, *Uṣūl al-Fiqh*, p. 87.

8. Muslim, *Ṣaḥīḥ Muslim, Muqaddima, bāb. Ṣiḥḥat al-Iḥtijāj bi'l-Ḥadīth al-muʿanʿan*; see also Ibn al-Ṣalāḥ, *ʿUlūm al-Ḥadīth*, p. 55.

9. Al-Bughā, *Buḥūth*, p. 118.

10. Al-Nīsābūrī, *Maʿrifat ʿUlūm al-Ḥadīth*, p. 25.

11. Al-Khaṭīb al-Baghdādī, *Al-Kifāya fī ʿIlm al-Riwāya*, pp. 100-106.

12. Cf. Jammāz, *Muḥāḍarāt*, p. 68; Abū Shahba, *Al-Wasīṭ*, p. 85.

13. Ibn al-Ṣalāḥ, *ʿUlūm al-Ḥadīth*, p. 112.

14. Al-Baghdādī, *Al-Kifāya*, p. 100.

15. Ibid., p. 111.

16. Being the verbal noun of *ʿadāla* (to be just, or do justice) *taʿdīl* is a variant of compurgation *tazkiya*, the latter being employed for similar purposes in reference to witnesses in a court of justice.

17. Al-Khudārī, *Uṣūl al-Fiqh*, pp. 218-219; ʿAbdul Rauf, "Ḥadīth, Its Authority and Authenticity", p. 19; al-Khaṭīb, *Uṣūl al-Ḥadīth*, p. 271; Ṣubḥī al-Ṣāliḥ, *ʿUlūm al-Ḥadīth*, pp. 129-130.

18. Note for instance the chapter on the virtues of the Companions (Faḍāʾil Aṣḥāb al-Nabī) in many a well-known collection of Ḥadīth including *Ṣaḥīḥ Muslim*.

19. Ibn al-Ṣalāḥ, *ʿUlūm al-Ḥadīth*, p. 105; Abū Shahba, *Al-Wasīṭ*, p. 89; al-Shawkānī, *Irshād al-Fuḥūl*, p. 67; Badrān, *Uṣūl al-Fiqh al-Islāmī*, p. 92; al-Khudārī, *Uṣūl al-Fiqh*, p. 217; al-Khaṭīb, *Uṣūl al-Ḥadīth*, pp. 268-269.

20. Azami, *Studies in Ḥadīth Methodology and Literature*, p. 60; ʿAbdul Rauf, "Ḥadīth, Its Authority and Authenticity", p. 19.

21. Cf. Abū Shahba, *Al-Wasīṭ*, p. 86.

22. Ibid., p. 88.

23. Ibid., p. 226.

24. Abū Shahba, *Al-Wasīṭ*, p. 394.

25. Ibn al-Ṣalāḥ, *ʿUlūm al-Ḥadīth*, p. 115.

26. Al-Baghdādī, *Al-Kifāya*, pp. 148-154; Abū Shahba, *Al-Wasīṭ*, p. 396.

27. Al-Shawkānī, *Irshād al-Fuḥūl*, pp. 68-69; al-Khaṭīb, *Uṣūl al-Ḥadīth*, p. 273; al-Sibāʿī, *Al-Sunna wa Makānatuhā fī'l-Tashrīʿ al-Islāmī*, Lahore: Dār Nashr al-Kutub al-Islāmiyya, n.d., p. 113.

28. Ibn al-Ṣalāḥ, *ʿUlūm al-Ḥadīth*, p. 116; al-Jaʿfar, *Al-Mūjaz fī ʿUlūm al-Ḥadīth*, p. 158.

29. Shākir, *Al-Bāʿith al-Ḥathīth*, p. 19; al-Sibāʿī, *Al-Sunna Wa Makānatuhā fī'l-Tashrīʿ al-Islāmī*, p. 100; Kamali, *Jurisprudence*, p. 67.

30. Ibid., p. 19; Abū Zahra, *Uṣūl*, p. 85; ʿAbdul Rauf, "Ḥadīth, Its Authority and Authenticity", p. 20; al-Sibāʿī, *Al-Sunna*, p. 97; al-Jaʿfar, *Al-Mūjaz*, p. 70.
31. Al-Shawkānī, *Irshād al-Fuḥūl*, p. 52; Abū Zahra, *Uṣūl al-Fiqh*, p. 86; Shākir, *Al-Bāʿith al-Ḥathīth*, p. 33; Ṣubḥī al-Ṣāliḥ, *ʿUlūm al-Ḥadīth*, p. 128.
32. Ibn al-Ṣalāḥ, *ʿUlūm al-Ḥadīth*, p. 117.
33. Ibid., p. 118.
34. Ibid., p. 186 f; Abū Shahba, *Al-Wasīṭ*, p. 92.
35. Ibid., pp. 119-120; Abū Shahba, *Al-Wasīṭ*, p. 93.
36. Al-Suyūṭī, *Tadrīb*, Vol. I, p. 276; al-Sibāʿī, *Al-Sunna*, p. 98; Azami, *Studies in Ḥadīth*, p. 72; Ṣubḥī al-Ṣāliḥ, *ʿUlūm al-Ḥadīth*, p. 264.
37. Cf. al-Sibāʿī, *Al-Sunna*; Shākir, *Al-Bāʿith al-Ḥathīth*, p. 19; Azami, *Studies in Ḥadīth*, p. 72; ʿUmar Hāshim, *Al-Sunna*, p. 109; al-Qaṭṭān, *Mabāḥith fī ʿUlūm al-Ḥadīth*, p. 112 ff.
38. Ibid., p. 100; Azami, *Studies in Ḥadīth*, p. 72.
39. Suyūṭī, *Tadrīb*, Vol. I, p. 278; al-Sibāʿī, *Al-Sunna*, p. 98; Ṣubḥī al-Ṣāliḥ, *ʿUlūm al-Ḥadīth*, p. 265; al-Qaraḍāwī, *Kayfa Nataʿāmal maʿa al-Sunna al-Nabawiyya*, p. 68; Siddiqi, *Ḥadīth Literature*, p. 201.
40. Al-Sibāʿī, *Al-Sunna*, p. 102; Ṣubḥī al-Ṣāliḥ, *ʿUlūm al-Ḥadīth*, p. 265; Siddiqi, *Ḥadīth Literature*, p. 281.
41. Ibn al-Ṣalāḥ, *ʿUlūm al-Ḥadīth*; al-Jaʿfar, *Al-Mūjaz*, p. 68.
42. Ibid., p. 112; Abū Shahba, *Al-Wasīṭ*, p. 404.
43. Ibid., Abū Shahba, *Al-Wasīṭ*, p. 404.
44. Al-Suyūṭī, *Tadrīb*, Vol. I, p. 43; al-Jaʿfar, *Al-Mūjaz*, pp. 71-74.
45. Shākir, *Al-Bāʿith al-Ḥathīth*, p. 60; Azami, *Studies in Ḥadīth*, p. 67.

[20] Conclusion and Reform Proposals

1. Siddiqi, *Ḥadīth Literature*, pp. 156-157. Siddiqi also refers to al-Baghdādī's *Kitāb al-Kifāya* (without, however, giving the page number).
2. Critics have identified about 210 *aḥādīth* in the weak category in *al-Bukhārī* and *Muslim*. Out of this 32 appear in both, another 75 appear in *Al-Bukhārī*, and the rest, that is, about 100 appear in *Muslim*. Cf. Abū Shahba, *Al-Wasīṭ*, p. 257.
3. Al-Sibāʿī, *Al-Sunna wa Makānatuhā fī'l-Tashrīʿ*, p. 121; Abū Shahba, *Al-Wasīṭ*, p. 237.
4. Azami, *Studies in Ḥadīth Methodology and Literature*, p. 92.
5. Siddiqi, *Ḥadīth Literature*, p. 202.
6. Ibid., p. 203.
7. Ibid., p. 202.
8. Ibid.
9. Fahmī Huwaydī, *Ḥattā lā Takūna Fitna*, p. 132.

10. Ibid., p. 133 (refers to Ibn Ḥazm, *Al-Iḥkām fī Uṣūl al-Aḥkām*, Vol. II, p. 79).
11. Ibid., p. 136.
12. In this connection Huwaydī cited by way of illustration, one Aḥmad Ṣubḥī, a matriculation student of al-Azhar, whose views Huwaydī has criticized, and then he posed the question: Could he not wait at least until he graduated his degree course?
13. Ibid., p. 138.
14. Al-Bukhārī, *Ṣaḥīḥ al-Bukhārī, Kitāb al-Aḥkām, bāb al-Istikhlāf*. See also Jawād Yāsīn, *Al-Sulṭa fī'l-Islām*, p. 250.
15. Cf. Jawād Yāsīn, *Al-Sulṭa fī'l-Islām*, p. 250.
16. Ibid., p. 252.
17. Ibid., p. 254.
18. Muslim, *Mukhtaṣar Ṣaḥīḥ Muslim*, *Kitāb al-Riḍāʿ*, *bāb fī Riḍāʿat al-Kabīr*, ḥadīth 880.
19. Quoted by Jawād Yāsīn, *Al-Sulṭa*, p. 280.
20. Ibn Qutayba, *Ta'wīl Mukhtalif al-Ḥadīth*, p. 306; also quoted in Yāsīn, *Al-Sulṭa fī'l-Islām*, p. 281.
21. Jawād Yāsīn, *Al-Sulṭa*, p. 281.
22. Muslim, *Ṣaḥīḥ Muslim, Kitāb al-Janā'iz, bāb fī ziyārat al-qubūr wa'l-istighfār lahum*.
23. Muḥammad al-Ghazālī, *Turāthunā al-Fikrī fī Mīzān al-Sharʿ wa'l-ʿAql*, pp. 146-147.
24. Ibid., p. 147.
25. Muslim, *Mukhtaṣar Ṣaḥīḥ Muslim, Kitāb Dhikr al-Anbiyā' Wa Faḍluhum, bāb. Fī Ibtidā' Khalq Adam*.
26. Shaltūt, *Al-Islām ʿAqīda wa Sharīʿa*, pp. 62-63.
27. Ibid., p. 63.
28. Ibid.
29. Ibid., p. 64.
30. Aḥmad Amīn, *Ḍuḥā al-Islām*, Vol. 2, pp. 106-137. See for a discussion also al-Sharfī, *Al-Islām wa'l-Hadātha*, pp. 98-99.
31. This version of the ḥadīth appears in ʿAbd al-Karim Shahrastānī, *Al-Milal wa'l-Niḥal*, Vol. II, p. 31; Zanjānī, *Tārīkh*, p. 287. ʿAbd al-Qāhir al-Baghdādī's *Al-Farq Bayn al-Firaq*, p. 10, also records this version albeit with a major variation in one word which is explained below.
32. Zanjānī, *Tārīkh*, pp. 289-290.
33. Ibid., p. 286.
34. Ibid., pp. 291-292.
35. See also al-Rūm, 30:31-32; al-Baqara, 2:176; al-Jāthiya, 17.
36. Zanjānī, *Tārīkh*, pp. 293-300.
37. Ibid., pp. 258-261.

38. Cf. Jawād Yāsīn, *Al-Sulṭa fī'l-Islām*, p. 213.
39. Cf. Najmī Zanjānī, *Tārīkh-e Firaq-e Islāmī*, p. 176.
40. Ibid., p. 171.
41. Many prominent *ʿulamāʾ* have allowed themselves to quote quite liberally this type of ḥadīth. Al-Ghazālī's renowned *Iḥyāʾ Ulūm al-Dīn* is often cited in example. Ḥāfiẓ Zayn al-Dīn al-ʿIrāqī's book, *Al-Mughnī ʿan Ḥaml al-Asfār fī'l-Asfār fī Takhrīj mā fī'l-Iḥyāʾ min al-Akhbār*, which he wrote on the margin of *Iḥyāʾ* was written with the purpose of identifying the weak ḥadīth in the *Iḥyāʾ*. ʿIrāqī has identified a large number of *aḥādīth* in the *Iḥyāʾ* as being obscure, without foundation, weak and even forgeries. At times he noted that he had not seen this or that ḥadīth and that it was unreliable and so forth. Others have noted a certain weakness in al-Ghazālī's knowledge of ḥadīth in that his work bore the influence of some early books on mysticism and *fiqh*.
42. Al-Qaraḍāwī, *Kayfa Nataʿāmal maʿa al-Sunna al-Nabawiyya*, p. 35.
43. Ibid., p. 36.
44. Ibid., pp. 183-184.
45. Ibid.
46. Ibid., p. 69. In the list of al-Qaraḍāwī's publications that appears on pp. 193-194, the full title of this work is given as *Al-Muntaqā min al-Targhīb wa'l-Tarhīb li'l-Mundhirī*.
47. Ibid., p. 184.
48. Ibid.

Index